Decolonizing solidarity

About the author

CLARE LAND is a long-time supporter of Indigenous struggles. She works on research at Victoria University's Moondani Balluk Indigenous Academic Unit, supports social change projects at the Reichstein Foundation, and consults to community organizations on race relations.

Clare has been engaged since 1998 with the history and present of settler colonialism. An Anglo-identified non-Aboriginal person living and working in south-east Australia, inspired by Aboriginal struggles, she has undertaken community-based organizing in solid support of a range of Aboriginal-led campaigns. Since 2004 Clare has collaborated with Krauatungu-lung (Gunai)/Djapwurrung (Gunditjmara) man Robbie Thorpe on campaigns, projects and a long-running radio programme on 3CR in Fitzroy, Melbourne, which focuses on colonialism and resistance.

Decolonizing solidarity

*Dilemmas and directions
for supporters of Indigenous struggles*

CLARE LAND

BLOOMSBURY ACADEMIC
LONDON • NEW YORK • OXFORD • NEW DELHI • SYDNEY

BLOOMSBURY ACADEMIC
Bloomsbury Publishing Plc
50 Bedford Square, London, WC1B 3DP, UK
1385 Broadway, New York, NY 10018, USA
29 Earlsfort Terrace, Dublin 2, Ireland

BLOOMSBURY, BLOOMSBURY ACADEMIC and the Diana logo
are trademarks of Bloomsbury Publishing Plc

First published in 2015 by Zed Books Ltd.
This edition published in 2022 by Bloomsbury Academic

Cover design: www.burgessandbeech.co.uk

A catalogue record for this book is available from the British Library.

ISBN: HB: 978-1-7836-0173-8
PB: 978-1-3503-5235-3
ePDF: 978-1-7836-0174-5
ePub: 978-1-7836-0175-2

Designed and typeset in Monotype Bembo Book
by illuminati, Grosmont
Index: John Barker

To find out more about our authors and books visit
www.bloomsbury.com and sign up for our newsletters.

Contents

Acknowledgements

I have lived, worked and met principally on Wurundjeri (Woi-wurrung) and Wathaurong land during the research for and writing of this book.

The book is an attempt to understand, synthesize and honour the political guidance that people like Gary Foley, Robbie Thorpe, Wayne Atkinson, Marjorie Thorpe, Tony Birch, Lillian Holt, Joy Murphy Wandin and the late Lisa Bellear have offered to people like me. Their influence on me personally and politically has been formative, as should be evident.

All those I interviewed shaped my thinking and some went further, alerting me to sources and reading draft chapters or papers. I am very grateful for the investment that many people made in this project. Very special thanks to the families of the late Chicka Dixon (1928–2010), the late Bill Roberts (1928–2009) and the late Targan (1955–2014).

Conversations with the following people were important: Eve Vincent; Daniel Bendix and Thomas Viola Rieske in Berlin; Jen Margaret, Christine Herzog and the Auckland Workers' Educational Association and all those who contributed to the workshop in Auckland in March 2010; and everyone who supported and attended the forum at MAYSAR in Fitzroy in August 2010. Thanks to those past and present members of and organizers at RISE (Refugees, Survivors and Ex-Detainees) who discussed allyship and solidarity politics with me.

I thank Bob Pease, supervisor of the research I conducted as a Ph.D. student, which is the basis for this book. His grounded and theorized insight into a pro-feminism, with its parallel set of politics, both supported the development of the ideas in this book and smoothed the pathway for me and my work within Deakin University. Thanks also to those among my family, friends and colleagues who read draft chapters, and to those key friends and activist colleagues who read segments of the conclusion, including Nida Alahmad, Mera Sivanesan and Sally Goldner.

As a Ph.D. student, I had much-needed financial support in the form of an Australian Postgraduate Award and I was lucky to get significant support from Deakin University in relation to maternity leave, as well as in the form of small research support grants. I also enjoyed the in-kind support of the Brotherhood of St Laurence Research and Policy Centre and the extensive material and personal support of my parents Penny Collings, Julian Land and Sylvia Geddes, and of Mary and Peter Nicholson. Special thanks to Frank Hytten. Thanks to Tom, Luci, Jean and Joseph for being so forgiving of the time it took to create this book.

I relied heavily on the support and encouragement of family and friends during this project, especially in the final months. Thank you.

Foreword

This is a book about a difficult topic that is rarely discussed in contemporary Australia. It addresses situations and ideas that few non-Aboriginal Australians who say they are supporters of Aboriginal peoples' quest for justice ever really consider. And yet these issues are major problems for those who seek a role as empathetic and constructive allies for the Aboriginal cause. Within the pages of the book there are also valuable insights for the broader range of non-Aboriginal people who are employed in the range of bureaucracies and private philanthropic bodies that loosely comprise what I define as the 'Aboriginal industry'. Thus, I would strongly recommend this as a book that assists in developing a better understanding among all who might work in association with Indigenous peoples.

In my work over the past four and a half decades, many of the most difficult conversations I have had have been with people who insisted that they were supporters of the Aboriginal struggle rather than with those who were opposed to our cause. In the fifteen years that Clare Land has been an associate of mine she has been an astute observer of this contradiction whereby historically, it seems to me, sometimes our best friends are our worst enemies. She has observed and been party to many situations where I have had to try to enlighten and educate non-Aboriginal activist supporters whose enthusiasm sometimes obfuscates their ability to comprehend notions of Aboriginal agency and self-determination. As a consequence of having observed first-hand these stressful and distressing situations, which can too often lead to heated argument, Clare Land was in the perfect position to write a book such as this.

The situation whereby non-Aboriginal supporters can sometimes become part of the problem is not a new one. From the 1950s through to the early 1970s many nominally Aboriginal organizations were in fact run and controlled by non-Aboriginal people. In fact, the executive of the first national Aboriginal political organization, the Federal Council for the Advancement of Aborigines and Torres Strait Islanders (FCAATSI), was controlled by well-intentioned non-Aboriginal supporters. So, too, was the board of the historically significant Victorian Aborigines Advancement League (AAL) until the late 1960s. It was within the AAL in 1969 that Aboriginal people under the leadership of Bruce McGuinness and Bob Maza mounted the first significant challenge to white control.

The era of 'Black Power' had begun. The assertion of Aboriginal self-determination at the AAL in Melbourne had national repercussions when the move inspired an identical push for Aboriginal control of FCAATSI a year or so later. But a rarely examined consequence of these moves by Aboriginal activists to take control of their own organizations was the deep hurt and recriminations that developed in the ranks of white supporters of these organizations, who felt that somehow the Aboriginal people were being 'ungrateful' for the decades of fund-raising and other support activities that they had undertaken. This was an extremely unfortunate side effect of the positive moves by Aboriginal people towards self-determination, because financial and community support for the AAL and FCAATSI diminished dramatically.

It is therefore a great pity that this book was not around during that era, because it might have made a significant difference to the ideas and attitudes of the well-meaning white supporters of that time. As Clare Land has correctly observed, the underlying problems in the relationship between Aboriginal groups and their white supporters continue in many instances into recent times. The difficulties experienced by the famous Jabiluka anti-mining campaign by Mirrar people of Arnhem Land with their white support groups in southern Australia are a classic example of the ongoing problem, a situation that Clare Land was able to observe first-hand.

So I believe that the contribution that this book will make towards creating a greater depth of understanding among non-Aboriginal supporters of the Aboriginal cause is its most important aspect. If in any way it can help to eliminate many of the unfortunate misunderstandings that invariably develop between Aboriginal groups and their white supporters then it will have served an admirable purpose. Furthermore, as Clare Land states, it hopefully will assist a new generation to 'reflect on the practice of solidarity in their own particular context and situation', and in doing so should help create better understanding in the next generation of committed and passionate advocates of social and political change in Australia.

Dr Gary Foley
Victoria University

This book is dedicated to Gary Foley and Robbie Thorpe

Introduction

Something is not quite right.

The Aboriginal partner in a supposedly co-organized event doesn't show up on the day.

A highly committed and active white person, a key ally in a campaign, arrives for a meeting, but her heightened busyness and urgency seem not to leave room for those more directly affected by the issue to talk or be noticed in the space.

An Aboriginal-activist-type white person says after an event, 'Wasn't that great? It worked really well.' Yet Aboriginal people on the panel had seemed really uneasy and they even said 'I feel really uncomfortable doing this.' But the organizers and white people in the audience don't notice it and gloss over questions about it.[1]

There are many Aboriginal and non-Aboriginal people involved in addressing Aboriginal community needs and agendas in Australia. This activity includes people working in state and federal government departments, schools and universities, in self-organized groups at the local suburban level, as social justice activists, as local council workers, via philanthropy, towards legal and constitutional reform, in land councils and in

---

1. The third observation is one made by Helen (interview).

Aboriginal community-controlled or other health and welfare organizations.

However, there is a discernible pattern in non-Aboriginal peoples' journeys of involvement in the field. For those who become concerned about gross inequality there may be initial passion to do something towards positive change. For some people, the passion fades relative to other concerns; others try to join with like-minded people, volunteer or search around for a way to make a difference. For those who make the effort, many seem sooner or later to hit a minor or a major sticking point. A project or initiative hasn't worked and they don't know why; they are flummoxed, even bruised, and have no idea how to channel their concern effectively. On having initial attempts to establish rapport rebuffed (Aveling, 2004a), or on having their practice challenged further along the track, some get hurt, angry or confused. Some retreat to look in the mirror, adopt a questioning attitude and reaffirm their determination to stay involved. Some walk away thinking 'It's too hard.' Some stalk away thinking Aboriginal people are ungrateful or unreliable.

From an Aboriginal perspective, there can sometimes seem to be a revolving door of non-Aboriginal people. Many of them will rapidly reveal themselves as a missionary, a mercenary or a misfit (Nicoll, 2000: 376). Is there anything to guide non-Indigenous people, a way of being beyond the limited repertoire of available subjectivities – guilty liberals, conservative nationalists or honorary blacks – that could be more appropriate for cultivating a collective, political project (Aveling, 2004a: 69; Maddison, 2011)?

This book provides an urgently needed new framework for action by non-Indigenous people in support of Indigenous struggles.[2] It sheds light on the dilemmas facing non-Aboriginal people seeking to play a role in addressing the situation in which Aboriginal people find themselves in Australia today, exploring ways Aboriginal community leaders and non-Aboriginal activists have negotiated relationships of solidarity.

The book synthesizes and presents the politics of this particular solidarity project, and its complexities and challenges. Tensions inherent in such relationships of solidarity play out in the postcolonial setting of Australia, where, despite strident challenge, the vestiges of British law, cultural power and the tainted sovereignty of the Crown restrain the nation's emergence out of colonizing dynamics.

The lingering injustices of colonization and the need for a fresh approach to righting them are nowhere better reflected than in the Fourth World conditions, morbidity and mortality of Indigenous people in settler nations. The Indigenous experience within wealthy settler colonial nations such as Australia, the USA, Aotearoa/New Zealand and Canada is one of continuing colonization in which a particular process of genocide is proceeding, and against which Indigenous peoples' struggle is one for survival as peoples.[3]

This book was written and is situated historically and politically in a settler-colonial context in which Britain declared

---

2. The terms 'Aboriginal' and 'Indigenous' are used in particular but also overlapping ways in this book. The term 'Aboriginal' is used to refer to those nations, clans and language groups who are the original peoples of south-east Australia and whose contemporary political struggle is the anchor point of this book. The term 'Indigenous' is also used, usually to enable the argument of the book to be read in reference to settler-colonial settings worldwide. In Australia the term 'Indigenous' may be used as a convenient way to refer to both Aboriginal and Torres Strait Islander people.

3. Settler colonies are the colonies in which the colonizers came to stay, containing and/or eliminating Indigenous peoples through various means in order to replace them on the land (Wolfe, 1994).

sovereignty illegally and against the interests of Indigenous polities on the continent now known as Australia. Following an initial invasion of coastal sites in the south-east, the various colonies and then the federated Australian state set about invading the vast territories of Australia, securing their claim of sovereignty bit by bit, and either killing or containing Indigenous people as a means and a consequence. This process of colonization is entrenched and continuing. Cognizant of these colonizing conditions, this book is concerned with interactions between Indigenous people and non-Indigenous people who are at once struggling against two things: these overarching structural conditions, and their interpersonal expression. This book sets out what kind of politics could frame this two-part struggle. Solidarity should be directed to decolonization; and the way solidarity is undertaken needs to be decolonized.

As in Canada (Simpson, 2010: 19), Aboriginal peoples in the south-east of Australia maintain the longest running political movement in postcolonial Australia. At heart this has been a struggle against colonial invaders' murderous possessiveness in relation to land, and, crucially, for survival as distinct peoples. As part of this struggle, Indigenous peoples have created and nurtured relationships with supporters (see Simpson, 2010).

I am one such supporter. My approach to this support or solidarity work is strongly formed by four years of guidance from Gary Foley, of the Gumbaynggirr Nation; and nuanced through my overlapping and subsequent work with Krauatungulung/Djapwurrung man Robbie Thorpe. Foley and Robbie are Aboriginal community members and activist leaders in south-east Australia and key theorists of the politics of solidarity.

I have always been struck by the profound optimism that Foley's work expresses. He displays a high degree of faith in people's ability to learn and understand, believing that if provoked in the right way, and encouraged, they will find out for themselves what is wrong with the world and with their practices and work out what to do. In 1999 he invited members of a student collective I was involved in (Students for Land Justice and Reconciliation, SLJR) to witness the operations of another collective, the Melbourne Jabiluka Action Group (JAG). I went along to a number of JAG meetings. In that context I witnessed Foley challenge people's racism within a meeting, and instruct them to meet up at the pub after the meeting to talk with him about it. I observed him spend more time with people whose practices were problematic, explaining and educating, than with those whose practices were helpful.

The conversation about solidarity politics, of which this book is a part, is directed towards eventual solidarity. The conversation is not about being accused of being good or bad, right or wrong. In this, the generosity of people like Foley who invest so much in those who locate themselves as supporters or potential allies, but who inadvertently display their privilege and power, should inspire others engaged in the conversation to be similarly generous with each other, or at least to think about what the end goal is. One of the tactics for achieving the end goal is to build and nurture the support base, to get more people onside and get them to understand the issues and in turn become good, strong, well-informed, effective organizers. The work of educating those who are giving you headaches is debilitating – non-Aboriginal people should be helping Aboriginal people out by educating each other, taking responsibility for each other.

I can remember deciding to believe what Foley said about how I should work even though I didn't know the political importance of that 'how' in 1998–99. The political importance of Foley's instructions is something that I have come to understand over a long period, including during the research for this book. The book is an exploration of how to work and a discussion of why it is important to work like that.

I first met Foley in 1998. I worked with him particularly intensely in 1998–2002 while I was an editor of the student paper at the University of Melbourne and then as a member of SLJR. I also worked closely with him in 2005–06, during the Black GST/Stolenwealth Games campaign. Foley has written the Foreword to this book, and I refer to his published work often in what follows. Along with writer and historian Tony Birch and community practitioner Marjorie Thorpe, Foley provided guidance and feedback on the book's development as part of a critical reference group (CRG) established to review the research plan (who to interview and what to ask) and to safeguard the interests of the political community of which they are a part.

Robbie Thorpe's voice is presented in this book in implicit conversation with, and often challenging, mine. This presentation is based both on a recorded discussion between Robbie and me about our work together, and on the sense I have made of the weekly conversations I've had with Robbie across the panel at 3CR, a left-wing community radio station, since 2004. The conversation takes place both live-to-air and while the mics are off as we co-present a radio programme, a collaboration Robbie instigated.

Despite my sensitivity to the voices, guidance and challenges of members of the political community this book supports, I remain the author of this text: the power over the text remains mine (Richardson, 1995: 200). At points throughout the book I show how I have been influenced by Robbie and by members of the critical reference group, but others' voices never approach authorship over the text, for which I accept responsibility.

As a prominent member and intellectual of the Aboriginal land rights movement, Foley gets asked a lot by fellow Kooris,[4] 'Why does it often seem that some of our best white friends behave like some of our worst enemies?' He argues that 'One of the greatest causes of underlying tension and dispute between Kooris and their non-Koori supporters is how these support groups and their members relate to Koori people' (Foley, 1999: 1). He identifies 'patronizing and paternalistic' treatment as a common experience, and suggests that supporters fail to understand 'the importance of "Aboriginal control of Aboriginal affairs" to indigenous people'. Elsewhere, Marjorie Thorpe (of the Gunai and Gunditjmara nations) has invoked Aboriginal sovereignty as an ideal in the activist context (Black GST, 2006), making it clear that the paternalism and tension in relationships between non-Indigenous and Indigenous activists are, at heart, generated by colonial conditions.

The work of dealing with such issues is debilitating and over the long term a cause of frustration for Aboriginal people (Foley, 2000: 86). Foley provides a case study from the campaign against the Jabiluka uranium mine proposed for a site within the World Heritage-listed Kakadu National Park – during which the Gundjehmi Aboriginal Corporation and the Mirrar people

---

4. 'Koori' is a word that 'means "man" or "people" in numerous languages of south-eastern Australia'; its variations are found in the north coast and Riverina districts of New South Wales, south-western Victoria and Lower Murray in South Australia (Horton, 1994, vol. 1: 559).

'sought a greater say' over the operations and actions of their 'support groups', arguing:

> So, without even realising it, members of JAG [Jabiluka Action Group] in 1999 are in the course of a struggle identical to that which occurred among their counterparts at the Aborigines Advancement League thirty years before, in 1969. Is it any wonder that long term Koori activists get frustrated at having to re-invent the wheel for each new generation of non-Koori supporters? (Foley, 1999; 2000: 86)

Sharing the hope that the problems Foley outlines could be 'eliminated for future generations of Australians', I was driven to find out more about the problem, more about the context, and more about the politics of the endeavour of working together. The particular impetus for this book arises from my own observations of non-Indigenous people attempting to engage with south-east Indigenous peoples through activism, community development, and the philanthropic and social-service sectors.

Experiences and reflections: towards a new framework

This book is the result of interviews with long-serving activist leaders and supporters in south-east Australia. Specifically, I interviewed Aboriginal people who engage politically with and work to educate non-Aboriginal people, and non-Aboriginal people who are regarded by the Aboriginal people in my critical reference group, or whom I interviewed, as reflective about the issues at stake. They are members of a particular political community – Aboriginal people from south-east Australia who have pursued land rights, community control and sovereignty – and their supporters. The contradictions inherent in relationships between Indigenous and non-Indigenous people in the context of struggles for land rights, sovereignty and community control are particularly stark because people are positioned in opposition: as colonized and colonizer; as dispossessed and beneficiary; as community members or not. My focus on this particular context enables a consideration of the impact of colonizing societal conditions on interpersonal relationships in a context in which these conditions are explicitly the focus of critical attention. The site-specific nature of this book is necessary to its decolonizing ethic. Its grounded specificity to a particular place, struggle and practice provides a credible basis from which to theorize. It also gives the book the ability to be read from and be applicable to other contexts, as the local specificities of readers' situations will be evident to each in their contrasts with the south-east Australian situation.

Most of the Aboriginal people I interviewed were aged 50 years and over, whereas there was more of a spread in the ages of non-Aboriginal people involved. Among everyone I interviewed, one man identified as gay and one woman as lesbian. Among the non-Indigenous people were participants who understood their family backgrounds as Anglo-Irish Australian; British Raj-Indian; Maori, Samoan and Tongan; Welsh; Iranian-Scottish; Greek and Polish-Jewish; and Polish-German. All the Aboriginal participants elected to be named in the research, and to have documentation of their interviews (transcripts and recordings) archived. Most of the non-Indigenous people did the same.[5] Where this was not the case, I provided

---

5. There was an interesting dynamic around anonymity, Indigeneity and privilege in the research process. Five non-Indigenous people wished to remain anonymous. In one case this was couched as a concern about being harassed as a result of observations made about other white people. Arguably, in some of the other cases, requesting anonymity was a strategy for avoiding criticism for the views expressed.

a changed first name and omitted the last name in an attempt to maintain these participants' anonymity. Where interviewees named third parties in their interview, I either made up names for those third parties or asked their permission to be included by name in the transcripts.

The interviews enabled me to gather together reflections on collaborations, alliances and support relationships from those best placed to comment thoughtfully on this. I was attentive to accounts of the effort it took to work across differences in social location. The collective reflections of these experienced activists, read alongside relevant academic theorizing, are the grounding for the politics and theory that I suggest can more consciously, and therefore productively, inform activist practice. The use of interviews and small group conversations was intended as an intervention into activist spaces; these were an experience of and a model for future reflective conversations that support conscious and critical practice (Denzin, 2003; Margaret, 2009).

The book also draws on my own experiences and reflections before and during the research; on discussions within community forums on the topic, with the CRG, Robbie and my research supervisor and with activist and academic peers in Melbourne, Auckland and Berlin; and feedback from the examiners of the Ph.D. thesis that is the basis of the book.

This book will be of interest to both experienced and newer activists wanting to reflect on the practice of solidarity in their own particular context and situation. There is no protocol or rule book to follow; the work is context-specific with a number of inherent dilemmas, as befits an imperfect, because colonizing, scene. The core of the activist aptitude and practice of the people I interviewed was their ability to decide which among a range of possibly competing priorities needed to be upheld in particular situations. The importance of historical, political and geographic context for the politics of solidarity is demonstrated by the ways in which the specific history of non-Indigenous support action has played out in south-east Australia. The detail in which the historical context is recounted in the opening chapters of this book is necessary for two reasons. First, it is necessary to show how the politics of solidarity outlined in later chapters are inflected by their context. Second, it indicates what sort of contextual knowledge is needed for those wishing to come to grips with the politics of solidarity in different contexts.

The politics presented in this book were discerned in conversation with people who have maintained a long-term political involvement outside of paid work and independent of institutional structures, even if they have at times also worked in government bureaucracies or social-service-sector organizations.[6] This was to allow me to unpack the tensions and dilemmas specific to those who were involved through dedication, not because it was their job.

Of course, many people working in Aboriginal Affairs settings are highly committed and feel that is where they can best make an impact on the injustice that drives them. The politics set out in this book will be very familiar and applicable to such settings. Institutional and employment obligations

6. Where an organization was activist-based (as the Victorian Aboriginal Health Service was during its early years), or where a staff member did significant unpaid activist work beyond the paid hours, they were included. I also included two non-Aboriginal former student activists who were at the time of the interviews employed in Aboriginal-related jobs.

generate particularly acute tensions and dilemmas for people working across Indigenous–non-Indigenous difference. This is because there is usually some tension between the policies and urgencies of the institution or employer and the ideals held by the worker and the community about how work should be done. Almost always the burden of this tension is shifted onto the community, and the worker is stuck in the middle. Tess Lea (2008: 158–9), in her ethnography of bureaucratic culture, has demonstrated how the dictates of 'central office' target conflict with the 'community development' maxims dearly held by health professionals in Aboriginal community settings in the Northern Territory. The need to establish partnerships or conduct consultation with Aboriginal people in order to give credibility to or generate community ownership of a programme that government has dictated has to happen obviously conflicts with the conditions for genuine community control and is a common source of angst.

The book speaks to both Indigenous and non-Indigenous people, but places an emphasis on exploring the kinds of self-questioning that non-Indigenous people are asked to perform. In this way the book is particularly useful in suggesting ways for more recently involved non-Indigenous activists to come to grips with the politics of solidarity.

Now more than ever, Aboriginal people in south-east Australia are aware of the need to garner critically informed support. The Aboriginal Embassy established on the lawns of the Federal Parliament in 1972, the 1991 Report of the Royal Commission into Aboriginal Deaths in Custody, and the sixty-day occupation of King's Domain in Melbourne which hit international headlines during the 2006 Commonwealth Games with the slogan 'Stolenweath Games' have perforated Australia's image as a lucky country. The response of the state has been to orchestrate a reconciliation process and issue an apology. These have worked to restore a sense of comfort to settler Australians but are empty of structural or material redress for Indigenous people. Working against this complacency, and striving for substantive change, a key strategy in Aboriginal struggles for land rights, self-determination and economic independence in south-east Australia is to nurture a critical and committed support base among settler Australians.

Indeed, this book is envisaged as being supportive of this Indigenous strategy as it is expressed in the social justice activist community in south-east Australia. It is intended as a resource to support the efforts of Indigenous people who have had to contest with each new generation of non-Indigenous supporters the mode of their solidarity. Knowledge of genuinely productive and transformative modes has until now been discerned by individual actors largely through a process of repeating the mistakes of the past. The book clearly explains the modes of solidarity that Indigenous people have identified as problematic, and explains the alternative frameworks they offer. This includes a critique of romantic, sometimes ignorant, conceptions of Indigenous people that are expressed in the national settler pastime of worrying about Indigenous people and that underlie the impulse to 'help them'.

The dynamics and dilemmas negotiated by Indigenous people and non-Indigenous people in the social justice activist world play out against state and national government manoeuvres in Aboriginal Affairs. Debates about how Australian federal and state governments go about engaging with Indigenous people were reignited in 2007 by the controversial 'Northern Territory Emergency Response'. That non-consultative programme, instigated by the Liberal–National coalition federal government, relied on the suspension of the Racial Discrimination Act 1975. It involved military personnel, compulsory health checks and the delivery of welfare payments on a Basics Card whose value is redeemable only at major supermarket chain stores. In 2012 it was extended for another ten years by the Australian Labor Party (ALP).

However, these debates were smothered by a related government move: the apology delivered by then-prime minister Kevin Rudd (ALP) on behalf of the Federal Parliament to the Stolen Generations in February 2008. While on a rhetorical level this belated apology concluded a long period of overt government hostility to reconciliation, an apology and native title – which had inspired the establishment of many white support groups in the preceding decade (Burgmann, 2003b: 85) – it did not mark a significant change in government policies or practices (Foley and McKinnon, 2008; Fredericks, 2010; Hinkson, 2008: 3–4; Maddison, 2011).

The dynamics between Indigenous people and non-Indigenous people in the social justice activist world also play out in relation to the recent history of that world itself. The recent political history of this community has generated a legacy with which non-Indigenous activists may not be familiar but which nevertheless shapes the contemporary politics of solidarity. A key political antecedent to the contemporary situation is 'Aboriginalization', a process through which Aboriginal people wrested control of organizations from non-Aboriginal members (Victorian Aborigines Advancement League, 1985:

91). While the importance of Aboriginal control of Aboriginal affairs gained wide acceptance from the 1970s onwards, in some cases the appearance of Indigenous people being up front belies a more complex reality of interdependence, or lack of Indigenous decision-making power (Batty, 2005; Melbourne Kungkas, group interview; Gary Murray, interview).

This book is relevant to parallel situations overseas, where there is growing interest in yet still not a large scholarly literature on solidarity relationships. Activist and researcher Jennifer Margaret has found that certain characteristics of ally relationships in North America resonate with those in Aotearoa/New Zealand and North America, namely:

- *Coalition as a microcosm of colonial relationships* – Issues of power and control which are manifest in the broader context of colonial relationships are present and manifest within alliances.
- *Coalition as a site of learning and transformation* – Being part of alliances generates significant learning for those involved, particularly for non-indigenous people.
- *Coalition as a site of pain* – Working to address the impacts of colonization can be a hurtful and difficult process for both indigenous and non-indigenous people. (Margaret, 2010: 9–10)

Margaret has recently extended her analysis to Australia, again affirming that similarities exist in settler–Indigenous ally relationships in these parallel settings (Margaret, 2013). Recent contributions from the closely related settler-colonial contexts of Canada, the USA and Aotearoa/New Zealand offer much to understandings of the Australian context (Land, 2011a).

Yet works primarily concerned with the attempts by white people to come to terms with the fact of living and working in a 'disputed Black sovereign space' remain uncommon (Kessaris, 2006: 348). Lynne Davis writes of the Canadian situation that there has been much written on Indigenous–non-Indigenous relationships in general, both contemporary and historical in focus. However, she points out that 'one of the under-explored areas of research remains relationships between Indigenous peoples and social movement organizations such as social justice groups, the women's movement, environmental organizations, and organized labour' (Davis, 2010: 4).

By contrast with Davis's assessment of the Canadian litera-ture, in Australia there has been some important writing on relationships between Indigenous peoples and other political actors – such as feminists, trade unionists and the nationally influential Federal Council for the Advancement of Aborigines and Torres Strait Islanders (FCAATSI) (Burgmann and Burg-mann, 1998; Paisley, 2000; Taffe, 2005). However, the writing is mainly historical and, with the exception of work by Foley (2012), Howell (2013) and Paasonen (2007), is not explicitly self-reflective. In anthropology it is harder now to pretend that the 'field' contains 'only Aborigines' (Cowlishaw, 2000: 112). In some cases this has led, productively, to studies of the cultures of those who are interacting with Aboriginal people, such as bureaucrats and health workers (Kowal, 2006; Lea, 2008).

Davis's observation in Canada is that it is the people who are engaged in Indigenous–non-Indigenous political alliances who are contributing the most to understandings of it. This seems to hold in Australia: activists themselves continue to be the key theorists of their own practice. This theorizing happens in solo private reflections and conversations with other activists; it is synthesized and presented in this book.

Doing and writing about solidarity

It is my activist involvement, my interactions and discussions with and consideration of the challenges made by Aboriginal community leaders, that generated questions and led to the writing of this book. My involvement has been focused on supporting Aboriginal-led campaigns and has comprised collectively organized work towards self- and community education about Aboriginal struggles and colonial history in south-east Australia.

Without this background of involvement, I would not actually have been able to write this book – no one would have talked to me. One Indigenous participant commented that she would normally hold research and researchers in general or specific suspicion. However, because she knew about my activist background and commitments, she was happy to do the interview. Another Indigenous participant questioned me for half an hour on the phone when I rang her to discuss the prospect of an interview, before deciding that she was willing to do it. She then went on to promote my project to other people she thought I should interview. I was very moved by her full support for my project – beyond just involving herself, she was prepared to back me with other people close to her. One non-Indigenous person turned down my interview request because her experiences of the issues under study felt too raw. Another non-Indigenous person with whom I had no connection prior to requesting an interview exchanged emails with me about her hesitation to be interviewed (because of the emotional toll she expected it to take). She attended a public workshop I gave on my topic, following which she emailed to say that although she had some issues with the way I presented she was happy to go ahead. It was clear to me that in cases where I knew or had been introduced to a potential interviewee by mutual acquaintances this greatly facilitated my research. If I was a relatively unknown quantity, my involvement in activism and my approach to the topic at hand were investigated with some rigour before people agreed to be interviewed.

At the time I conducted the interviews I was twenty-eight weeks pregnant, expecting my second baby, which was duly born at term. One interview I was attempting to schedule during that time did not go ahead because our dates kept falling through and I ran out of time before the birth. The fact of my pregnancy impacted on the research in this practical way. Further, being obviously pregnant during the period of conducting the majority of the interviews impacted on the way the people I interviewed saw me, and the generosity they showed me. People felt they could ask me things about being pregnant. This was beneficial for me as an interviewer because of the methodology I chose. The method was predicated on the values of reciprocity, and I emphasized that conversation, not a one-way interrogation, was encouraged. If I had chosen a more 'alienated' methodology, my pregnant embodiedness would not have had the same impact on the research. Being pregnant was a visual way of telling people something about my life, and provided an opening for people to ask me about my pregnancy, any other children, and my family, and likewise to tell me about their families, or their hopes for having children, or their own pregnancies and births. This is not to suggest that experiences of pregnancy and mothering are 'cultural universals' or politically neutral, as Lisa Maher points out (2000: 222–3). In the context of a slightly awkward social interaction before turning on the recorder and starting the formal interview proceedings, I believe my embodied pregnant state served as an ice-breaker, and broke down barriers.

In one instance, the fact of being pregnant and also parenting a twelve-month-old infant led to one of my participants, Wayne Atkinson, relinquishing his principle of agreeing to interviews only if they are conducted on his Yorta Yorta homelands. While I respected Dr Atkinson's stance, and his right, and was willing to do the interview on Yorta Yorta country, I had to admit that being pregnant and having a child already would indeed have increased the difficulty of organizing the interview at this location. It would have involved travelling three hours each way, and organizing my partner to come with me in order to look after our child (who was still breastfeeding), so that I could be freed up to conduct the interview once there. Although I agreed to do it, and said I would look into a time it would be possible, Wayne Atkinson came back to me and offered to undertake the interview at his office at the University of Melbourne. This was a situation in which I suspect his knowledge of my personal situation, and his consideration of the degree of organization that travelling would entail, and perhaps a protective concern for me as a new mother, a former student, a personal friend, all worked to make him decide to compromise on his homelands principle. This was an offer I felt was given with no resentment. I accepted the offer, but with some ambivalence politically.

There are many instances – both historically and in contemporary settings – in which Indigenous activists have claimed the right to direct or shape in some way (or in major ways) the nature of the involvement of non-Indigenous people in their struggles or their business more broadly. Responding to arguments put by Gary Foley (1999) and Lillian Holt (1999), among others, the book attends to the history of non-Indigenous support, and to the activist project of interrogating and critically reconstructing white and non-Indigenous selves.

The book is envisaged as a kind of reply to Indigenous people's assertions about the nature of non-Indigenous support or engagement with their struggles; part of an ongoing conversation directed towards understanding the challenges, dilemmas and even the impossibilities of this work and how these can be shifted, worked through or lived with.

I set out to see how Indigenous activists might talk about these dynamics, what non-Indigenous people knew about these dynamics, how they reflected on these things and what kept them involved despite the challenges and difficulties. Through an early conversation with a member of my critical reference group, I came quickly to recognize that Indigenous people 'put up' with a lot from non-Indigenous people. I have come to think of the forbearance of Indigenous people in dealing with their supporters as under-recognized *work*. I had at first seen Indigenous people as doing the 'easier' job of challenging, and non-Indigenous people the 'harder' job of interpreting, these challenges and 'sticking around' despite the criticism. The need to challenge – usually done in a studiously encouraging way – is borne, of course, from the pain of dealing with supporters' 'whitely' ways, ways of relating that are dominated by white stereotypes of Indigenous peoples. To be whitely is to embrace 'habits and dispositions that reproduce racial hierarchy and white privilege'; not all white people are whitely and not all whitely people are white (Pease, 2010b: 121, citing Frye; S.

Sullivan, 2006). Instead of reading the times when conflict is absent as the absence of a problem, I now read the periods of interaction between the moments of conflict, or challenge, as often being enabled by Indigenous forbearance. In this reading, challenges are made when the whitely ways of non-Indigenous activists become too much to put up with. This picture is complicated by the potential for Indigenous people to behave in whitely or exploitative ways too. It is also complicated by friendship, such that Aboriginal people may put up with more from people they like, even if they are racist.

My own participation in political work in support of Indigenous struggles provides a participatory research character to this book. The period of researching and writing the book was in turn an elongated moment of reflection and learning in an ongoing commitment to collectivist political action. It was necessary for me to conduct the research reflexively and to include auto-ethnographic text in the book in acknowledgement of my own involvement in the phenomena I am writing about (Ellis, 2004; Etherington, 2004). My project would lack integrity if I did not ask the same questions of myself as I did of those I interviewed. I do not attempt or pretend to objectivity; rather, I attempt to interrogate the form of my own partiality. To leave my own social locatedness unnamed would be to imply the universality and objectivity of my argument. Further, I weave through the book a 'learning-story' which attempts to make visible my understanding of how the research changed me. This strategy takes as its cue Richardson's (1995) idea of a 'writing-story'. I also accepted the proposal from Robbie that I become a participant in the research by joining him as part of a paired interview for the research. These might be considered as strategies for other researchers developing methodologies for the sociological and ethnographic study of whiteness and people positioned as colonizers in the Australian context.

A key preoccupation for me in this research was to consider the implications of attempting it as a white, non-Indigenous person. The project of being a white critic of whiteness throws up many questions (Probyn, 2004). For instance, is it possible to be a white critic of whiteness? Is it possible to gain sufficient critical distance from whiteness to contribute usefully to its critique? Is the earnest attempt useful, for whatever reason (for example, for its failures as much as any possible insights yielded)?

The challenges issued by non-white people, activists and scholars about the way whiteness impacts on non-whites, as well as how white lives are racialized, demand a response. White people, including scholars, are exhorted to work to understand, critique and confront the workings of white privilege. Yet such projects are taken up less often in favour of research or projects which focus on subordinate groups (Hesse-Biber and Leavy, 2006: xiv; Moreton-Robinson, 2006: 231; Pease, 2010b: 32).

My engagement with the workings of my own whiteness and my own colonial complicities in both my research and my attempts to contribute to Indigenous struggles is an informed and crucial element of my critique of whiteness. It recognizes that I am 'very much part of the problem that [I am] trying to articulate' and that 'doing critical whiteness studies as a white necessitates that we place ourselves in it, otherwise we've missed the whole point' (Probyn, 2004: para. 17).

However, there are many potential pitfalls of including a personal voice in my white critique of privilege. To write about a struggle with privilege risks becoming confessional, redemptive, self-serving (Roman, 1997). It is necessary to find an auto-ethnographic voice that does progressive political work.

I have struggled with questions such as, how can I include (the right amount of) my own story without this reading as confessional or redemptive? Will an account of my learning about racism in activism and research 'amount to' or 'do any' anti-racist work? (See Ahmed, 2004.) Like queer- and critical-whiteness scholar Thomas Viola Rieske (2008: 108), 'I wanted to produce a text of a kind that I like the most in the field of critical whiteness studies: one that interests me, ashames me, unsettles me.' Yet works in critical whiteness studies and 'anti-racist' projects can so easily, though not inevitably, function to *reinscribe* white privilege (Ahmed, 2004; Moreton-Robinson, 2006; Pease, 2010a; Probyn, 2004).

That privilege could be discursive and material; there are obvious ironies in being/becoming a white academic comfortably advancing one's career through the critique of the workings of privilege. Further, if one does 'succeed' as a personal narrative writer, one's very ability to be reflexive and self-critical and to write in this way can attract more prestige to oneself (Pease, 2010a).

In attempting to avoid the various pitfalls, my approach was to ensure that auto-ethnographic content in the book should never become its major preoccupation. It was important to work against a personal account that was self-serving; it is very tempting to construct a narrative that is redemptive. The personal narrative should be 'a form of confession not of sins but of the experience of power and the resistance to it' (Rieske, 2008: 109). This is a way through the problem whereby 'The white critic of whiteness consumes the Indigenous critique of whiteness by attempting to become a good disciplinary subject who is sometimes "bad"' (Probyn, 2004: para. 30).[7] That would be confession gone wrong, confession framed around who is 'good' and who is 'bad', rather than being about successes or failures at resisting complicity and the exercise of power.

I came to better know, feel and understand the relative importance or unimportance of my project alongside the intellectual and political concerns of other activists through an interaction with Robbie Thorpe. I showed Robbie a draft case study I had written of Camp Sovereignty, the focal point for the Black GST protest that we had both been heavily involved in just prior to my embarking on this research. The case study – being prepared at the time for publication – set out to analyse some of the Indigenous–non-Indigenous interactions around a particular happening at Camp Sovereignty, which I saw as encapsulating many of the central concerns of my research. I was really nervous about Robbie's feedback, (a) because he is very incisive and I really value his opinion; and (b) because when he read the piece he smiled and handed back the pages without a word. When Robbie finally spoke he did not comment directly on my draft. Instead he told me what he had been concerned about at the time of the protest. His concerns had nothing to do with interactions between Indigenous and non-Indigenous activists. This is an excerpt of what I wrote after that conversation:

---

7. This metaphor of eating and consuming echoes Irene Watson's (2005) deployment of cannibalization: Watson sees white people in various ways consuming things Indigenous in the attempt to become Indigenous. This attempt to legitimize our flawed sovereignty always fails, but its appropriative approach to Indigenous people is a continuation of white approaches to Indigenous land, culture, knowledge and everything else (Watson, 2005).

When Robbie spoke like that, I realized that the focus of my
research, while of some value as a subject to analyse, was just
my own preoccupation. *His* preoccupation was on sovereignty.
For one thing, this exchange gave me insight into the different
concerns we had during the action. Secondly, it pointed to an
intellectual and real project about the assertion of sovereignty
that Robbie undertakes. And finally, it was a case of a quiet and
powerful message delivered in an indirect way.

So, while I mount an argument for the rationale and importance of my research project for academic and activist
audiences, I maintain a sense of perspective on the relativity
of this valuing. This experience with Robbie was a significant
moment in coming to know, feel and understand my research as
contingent (see also Tedlock, 2000: 466–7). While my approach
to research accepts contingency as a premiss, I find it necessary – as part of a struggle to undo the privilege I accrue most
particularly as a middle-class white woman and a colonizer – to
critique the limitations that my partiality and situatedness place
on my research, to uncover the oppressive work of my partial
vision; that is, the creation of yet *more* stories from a colonizer
perspective which remains unnamed.

I acknowledge that I am changed by the research: in particular, the workings of my own privileges have become more
apparent (although not fully transparent) to me throughout
the research project. It will be apparent to the reader how the
project and the text reflect those ways in which the workings
of my own privileges remain opaque to me. I understood the
interrogation of my own position as activist and researcher
as part of my response to the ethical issues thrown up by a
project of this kind.

Progressive non-Indigenous research

The politics around research related to Indigenous peoples has significant implications for the way I thought about and went about my research. As Smith (1999: 1) demonstrated in her influential book *Decolonizing methodologies*, research itself is inextricably linked to European imperialism and colonialism: 'The word itself, "research", is probably one of the dirtiest words in the indigenous world's vocabulary.'

Given the implication of research in the colonization of Indigenous peoples and the appropriation of Indigenous knowledges, the prospect of undertaking research in connection with Indigenous peoples is problematic. I needed to ask myself, why do I want to interview Indigenous people? Is this appropriate? Would it be appropriate to do this project without interviewing Indigenous people? What safeguards are in place?

In seeking to avoid recolonizing Indigenous participants via my own research, I designed the research to correspond with principles, where they have been articulated, for culturally appropriate research by non-Indigenous researchers.[8] In a formal sense, I gained approval to undertake the research included in this book by the Deakin University Human Research Ethics Committee (Project EC 330–2006) while I was a Ph.D. student

---

8. I gave local protocols, chiefly the report *We Don't Like Research... But in Koori Hands It Could Make a Difference* (VicHealth Koori Health Research and Community Development Unit, 2000), the most weight, while critical Indigenous methodologies were also informative (in particular Smith, 1999: 177, which heeds Maori concerns). *We Don't Like Research...* lays out key principles, which are found to be echoed, along with more detail, by guidelines issued by the Australian Institute of Aboriginal and Torres Strait Islander Studies, *Guidelines for Ethical Research in Indigenous Studies* (2000), and the National Health and Medical Research Council (NHMRC), *National Statement on Ethical Conduct in Research Involving Humans* (1999: Part 8, Research Involving Collectivities). More recent local contributions by Aunty Joan Vickery et al. (2010) and the work of Noonuccal scholar Karen Martin (2008) significantly develop ideas of remuneration for community investment in research and researcher protocols and accountability (see also Denzin et al., 2008). On recolonizing, see Villenas as cited in Ladson-Billings, 2000.

there. The ethics plan for the project covered a broad range of issues, including consent to participate, strategic and political considerations of the research, and returning research to communities. One of the key strategies in line with the relevant guidelines was to establish the critical reference group.

I also drew on my own sense of ethics (partly learned through harmful transgressions) to establish additional boundaries. Specifically, I sought to interview and be guided in the research by Aboriginal community members who had engaged politically with and worked to educate non-Indigenous people. This criterion would ensure that those with whom I was trying to engage were at some level willing to engage with non-Aboriginal people as a strategic political project serving their own interests. Further, there was a basis for a shared understanding of the research process (see Fontana and Frey, 2000: 664). Aboriginal people have used various forms of research in their repertoire of social change strategies. This includes collecting oral histories, documenting police harassment, assessing community health needs, producing radio, film and theatre, and conducting Indigenist academic research in what have been politically informed, community-controlled strategies (Atkinson, 1989; Foley, 2012; Howell, 2013; Nathan, 1980).

Second, I sought to be appraised of, cognizant of, informed by and working to promote, or at least not undermine, an Indigenous research agenda (Smith, 1999) in developing my research questions and priorities. That said, I don't imagine that my work could necessarily advance that agenda. If non-Indigenous activist work supporting Indigenous rights is ideally located in parallel with, and informed by, the Indigenous decolonization agenda, then I see it as necessary, in a moral and intellectual sense, to have the same orientation to Indigenous research agendas in proceeding with my research. Martin's (2008) work on Burungu, Kuku-Yalanji regulation of outsiders and researchers demonstrates how the two are related.

In *Decolonizing Methodologies*, Smith goes beyond explaining techniques for harm-minimization in research to explore, from an Indigenous point of view, how research might be decolonized, and how Indigenous peoples may use research to further their political interests. Given that Smith identifies a strategic research agenda as part of the global Indigenous movement, it is necessary for researchers like me to understand this agenda and examine my research in relation to it. This involves considering a further issue: how my work might contribute towards understanding how white researchers may be able to serve the interests of Indigenous people through research.

The global Indigenous movement can be seen to be pursuing a number of projects within a strategic research agenda (Smith, 1999: 116). In the Australian context, an Indigenous, decolonizing research paradigm both tells marginalized Indigenous stories and encourages 'Mununga [white people's] stories that interrogate whiteness and its accompanying privilege' to be told too (Kessaris, 2006). In certain contexts and under certain conditions, research by progressive non-Indigenous people can support Indigenous research agendas towards decolonization (Martin, 2008; Rigney, 1999).

This book contains the stories of privilege-cognizant white and non-Indigenous peoples and is, overall, offered up in support of Indigenous agendas, albeit indirectly. It is probably best understood as making a contribution to an imagined progressive non-Indigenous research agenda. I would conceive of such an agenda as supportive of Indigenous agendas, and as contributing to these indirectly. To seriously develop such progressive non-Indigenous research agendas would require accountability constructs to be established so that non-Indigenous researchers were located as challengeable by Indigenist researchers.

This book can be considered as a response to Indigenous agendas across the projects of *indigenizing, intervening, reading, reframing* and *restoring* identified by Smith (1999). In terms of the *indigenizing* project, which works to disconnect 'many of the cultural ties between the settler society and its metropolitan homeland', and to re-centre the 'landscapes, images, languages, themes, metaphors and stories' in the Indigenous world (Smith, 1999: 146), I highlight the importance of non-Indigenous people examining our complicity in colonialism, including by interrogating who we are in terms of identity, culture and history, and the shape of our lives. This is part of a practice of critical self-reflection and of dealing honestly with the impact of dominant culture on Aboriginal people. This is a non-Indigenous effort in parallel with the Indigenous project of *indigenizing*.

Projects concerning *intervention* 'are usually designed around making structural and cultural changes' (Smith, 1999: 147). This research is supportive of the Indigenous project of *intervention* through its clear structural concerns and its attention to strategic questions about what will engage and maintain the contribution to meaningful social change by members of dominant groups. Further, the research for the book generated reflection among participants, and, parallel with the research, Robbie and I co-convened a forum which aimed to widen the conversation within the broader activist community (Land, 2011a). It was clearly directed at questions of non-Indigenous people's responsibility to change ourselves and our institutions, rather than 'changing indigenous peoples to fit the structures' (Smith, 1999: 147).

The project of *reading*, connected to postcolonial and cultural studies, involves a 'critical rereading of Western history', and an attempt to understand what has informed both colonialism and neocolonialism – a genealogy of ideas and practices. In relation to this, my research has engaged with key debates about colonialist identity thought and the colonialist binary distinction between 'Indigenous' and 'non-Indigenous', demonstrating a particular sensitivity to Indigenous-authored theoretical insights. This includes looking for Indigenous ways of addressing difference that innovate against imperialist ways of addressing difference. This could be seen to engage with the Indigenous project of *reading*, as well as that of *reframing*. For Smith (1999: 153) one part of the project of reframing occurs 'where indigenous people resist being boxed and labelled according to categories which do not fit'. Some Aboriginal people – notably Robbie Thorpe – challenged the way I framed the research according to the binary distinction just mentioned. Part of the journey of the research became to develop a more ambivalent address of this binary. In this way I promoted a recognition of Indigenous efforts at *reframing*.

Finally, my research in a broad sense acknowledges the Indigenous project to *restore* Indigenous well-being. Specifically, the research challenges the lack of understanding by non-Indigenous people of their/our collective and individual impact on Indigenous well-being, and their/our inherent privilege.[9]

---

9. Although I write as a non-Indigenous person, I use 'their/our' (and related sets of

Progressive white racial projects and their dangers

To understand white privilege should also be to consider ways to undo it. There is some debate over the proper aims and methods of the progressive white racial project – that is, the endeavour to challenge systems which create white privilege and maintain white supremacy, including anti-racist white activism as well as activism which supports Indigenous struggles in settler nations. There are some dangers among the variety of forms for the progressive white racial project that others have articulated and pursued. These need to be considered in order for a more nuanced practice to be developed.

Out of the extensive literature on how whiteness shapes white people's lives and how to challenge systems which create white privilege and maintain white supremacy, some of the progressive white racial projects that appeal to me include:

> Trying to unlearn whiteliness. (Sullivan, 2006)

> Cultivating a character that predisposes a person to animate privilege-cognizant instead of privilege-evasive white scripts. Developing such a character is like cultivating a virtue: through habit, not nature; and it includes the experience of travelling between 'worlds'. (Bailey, 1998: 38)

> Practising a playful 'world'-travelling. (Lugones, 1987)

> Hyper- but pessimistic activism (pessimistic because of danger of ontological expansiveness). (Sullivan, 2006)

> Acting politically with self-understanding. (Frankenberg, 1993)

What unites these projects is that their proponents are all sure that at this moment in history it is not possible, and it is

---

pronouns) in this and other instances so that both Indigenous and non-Indigenous readers might feel addressed by this text.

harmful, to attempt to 'abolish whiteness', or to 'move beyond race categories'. In supporting these projects I suggest going beyond a polarized debate that opposes the two main strategies for critical white people – those which seek to 'abolish whiteness' and those which suggest 'moving beyond race categories'. I'm constructing an alternative to these positions, which are both problematic. I talk about reconstructing whiteness rather than abolishing it.

As Alcoff (1998: 18) argues, 'Racism appears to be deeply sedimented into white psyches in a process that is newly reenforced [sic] each day.' This means one can see white racism as at once very difficult to transform, yet possible to transform (by working to slow down, halt or even reverse that daily reinforcement of racism). Alcoff (1998: 24) asks, 'Should we not move beyond race categories? I doubt that this can be done anytime soon. The weight of too much history is sedimented in these marked bodies with inscriptions that are very deep.'

In the project of reconstructing whiteness, attentiveness to the dynamics of gentrification is important. To transform whitely subjectivities some scholars suggest the practice of excursions out of white/Anglo 'worlds', into an engagement with non-white spaces. Such relocation can be a powerful way of 'disrupting and transforming unconscious habits of white privilege', but it can also work to reinforce them, for example by increasing that person's ontological expansiveness (tendency to take over) (Sullivan, 2006: 10). The many dangers are cause for pessimism, but despite this the urgency of challenging white privilege animates hyper-activism.

My approach to the question, 'what should white people do?', the question posed by Alcoff, is one that springs from the conviction that race, while socially constructed and without basis in biology, is nevertheless real, a social fact. I keep returning to the disposition Jane Belfrage – a middle-class, tertiary educated Australian of Anglo-Irish descent who is a musician and a single parent – brings to her identity, revealed in our interview: 'I'm gonna be stuck with that. I'm going to move, you know, from one space to another within it … But I accept it. Cos that is, you know, who I am in this time and place, in this lifetime.' This excerpt from the interview with Jane indicates a profound internalization of an Indigenous view of whiteness, a recognition of the historical and political specificities of the moment in which it is salient (likely to be a long moment), and the struggle to overcome the self-hate that can flow from that. Indebted to Jane, I consider the progressive project of reconstructing white subjectivities in the Australian context as 'moving from one space to another within colonizer identity'.

Overview of the book

The first chapter sets out who and what the land rights, Black Power and avowedly sovereign political community in south-east Australia is, its inspiring history and its significant though unfinished successes in confronting the legacy of British colonization. It explains why the way the history of these struggles has been written and taught is a political issue with real consequences. It also explains the political moment in which the book was written: the era of bureaucratization in Aboriginal Affairs, and in the wake of the long-awaited – yet ultimately disappointing – government apology. It shows that this political community has long nurtured its non-Indigenous support base and regards this as a strategic necessity.

Chapter 2 sets out a genealogy of non-Indigenous people's support action for the struggles already introduced, providing the historical and political context for the work of the non-Indigenous people interviewed for the book. At the outset it reminds readers of Indigenous people's solidarity with each other's struggles within Australia and internationally. The history of non-Indigenous solidarity in south-east Australia includes the work of the Communist Party of Australia, church-related groups, unionists, civil rights organizations, university students, feminists, 'white' support and 'reconciliation' groups, environmentalists and emerging areas of support such as anti-corporate globalization and anarchist groups. It discusses instances in which Indigenous people contested the nature of non-Indigenous support. Often without newly involved activists being aware of it, this history impacts on the terms for solidarity relationships today.

Chapter 3 shows how binary identity categories (colonizer/ colonized, Indigenous/non-Indigenous) are invoked within the social world of people pursuing social justice against the workings of settler colonialism in south-east Australia. These categories are at different times used, refused and critiqued, and, crucially, innovated against: not so much blurred as departed from. Their use reflects 'social facts': that is, their social and material consequences. However, their refusal does important work against colonialist discourses and is part of bringing into being a world in which decolonization would be realized structurally, materially and culturally.

Chapter 4 throws into doubt the positive connotations of 'collaboration' and 'dialogue' as ways of dealing with structural difference in community sector and activist settings.

The discussion is sensitive to strategic tensions negotiated by Aboriginal people and includes: consideration of parties' readiness to enter dialogue or partnership; questions about the desire for collaboration and whose interests it serves; exploration of ways to manage a working relationship in the context of lack of trust – such as protocols, partnership agreements and accountability constructs. It also cautions against the common desire among prospective allies for friendship as an outcome of solidarity work. Throughout, awareness of the political necessity of optimism about prospects for collaboration is maintained, while limits to and/or the impossibilities within the project of dialogue are held in view.

Chapters 5, 6 and 7 present the three key elements of the practice of solidarity with Indigenous struggles. Chapter 5 explains why it is necessary for non-Indigenous supporters to act politically with self-understanding and how to get to that point. Questions for reflection and forms that political action can take are presented by bringing together interview and secondary material – this grounds the chapter in activists' experiences and in relevant theory. This chapter is a serious engagement with the kinds of challenges Indigenous people have articulated about the nature and form of non-Indigenous support for their struggles, and articulates the political significance of these challenges. It also explores some of the dilemmas and challenges negotiated by solidarity activists. These include the dynamic of humility – how much is too much?; knowing enough but not too much about politics internal to Aboriginal communities; and the importance of being a long-term ally for this long-term struggle.

Chapter 6 presents a moral and political framework for non-Indigenous people's solidarity, which hinges on the political necessity of reconstructing non-Indigenous people's interests. This involves non-Indigenous people interrogating our/their sense of our/their interests and understanding them as served by support for Indigenous struggles, and social justice struggles more broadly. The chapter shows why it is important for non-Indigenous people to develop their understanding of Indigenous struggles before they rush in, on an impulse, to fulfil their desires to 'help' Indigenous people. Indigenous people, scholars and activists are clearly working to shift would-be allies' understandings of what the 'problem' is and of the broader context of social change. This underscores the importance of non-Indigenous people developing a moral and political framework through which to be supportive of Indigenous people. Strategically, reconstruction of interests is seen to create a healthier (less paternalistic) basis on which to build solidarity. It is also seen to lead to a greater determination by non-Indigenous people to fight for social justice.

Chapter 7 shows that non-Indigenous people are challenged to confront complicity – to confront the ways in which we/they are 'wedded to the system' both culturally and economically. It argues that this is what produces a fundamental reluctance among non-Indigenous people to change the system, and sets implicit limits on what would be done or given up in the name of solidarity. The challenge in reckoning with complicity is to admit it, to resist it, to undo it, yet also to see how it provides opportunities to resist the workings of colonialism. The hard work of reckoning with complicity springs from the recognition by non-Indigenous people that the place where one lives and works is Aboriginal land. For non-Indigenous people, this recognition should not only inform our public political action (particularly attention to local, not only far-away, issues), but should also be reflected in the shape of our lives. Non-Indigenous people might ask, how does the shape of my life keep the system intact? How does the shape of my life reflect the acknowledgement of sovereignty and/or the dismantling of privilege? The chapter considers strategic and political debates around the contradiction of living comfortably in the system, yet being an agent for changing it.

As is evident in the elements of personal narrative that I have included at points in the text to follow, the experience of undertaking this project – the research and the writing of this book – has changed me as much as it has generated the ideas set out. I now undertake to return these ideas to fellow activists and those who have challenged, worked with and educated me.

ONE

Land rights, sovereignty and Black Power in south-east Australia

In the late 1960s, Aboriginal people in the south-eastern cities of Australia began to press for changes in state policies and practices much more stridently than ever before. This movement had its roots in the struggle of previous generations, but its young intellectuals noted that the strategies and even the achievements of the past decade in particular had not resulted in substantive change. The much-celebrated 1967 referendum, which empowered the federal government to take responsibility for Aboriginal policy, did not result in the immediate dismantling of discriminatory state regimes, which was the expectation of Aboriginal supporters of that campaign.

In addition to these immediate local antecedents were the decolonization struggles occurring across Africa. The ejection of colonial rulers energized and inspired other struggles: the anti-apartheid movement in South Africa and the civil rights, Black Power and native movements in North America (Hemingway, 2012). Liberation movements were arising worldwide. This context and the concurrent mass migration of Aboriginal people off reserves into major Australian cities produced both new needs and the urgency and confidence to address them.

Those who were teenagers and young adults in the late 1960s; those who, backed by older leaders, seized the political initiative and reshaped modes of resistance; had a long-standing influence on the political landscape. They put Aboriginal affairs on the national political agenda, where they have remained ever since. They re-centred land rights as the core of the Aboriginal political agenda, and succeeded in overturning the long-standing policy of assimilation (Foley, 2012). From 1972 onwards, Australia's liberal democracy had to consider how to respond to Aboriginal people's determination to survive as distinct peoples (Hemingway, 2012). The question is salient in all relationships between Aboriginal and non-Aboriginal polities, organizations and individuals that intersect with the public sphere.

The Aboriginal people who have pursued the politics of land rights, sovereignty and Black Power in the south-east of Australia have also been the ones to set out most clearly the role of non-Aboriginal people in their struggle. This political community has an inspiring history and has had significant, though unfinished, successes in confronting the legacy of British colonization. Members of this community have also recognized the politics of the way Aboriginal struggles have been represented by historians, and have been active in telling and interpreting the history of the Aboriginal movement.

Struggles in the south-east

Members of this community that I interviewed are people who were active in, and/or identify as core to their more recent political roots, the modern national land rights movement, the movement for Aboriginal control of Aboriginal affairs (with which Black Power and the community-controlled health movement are connected) and the famous Aboriginal Embassy, with its emphasis on sovereignty and material deprivation. For Foley (2011) these core ideas are interconnected in his view of the 'Koori struggle'. Three key agendas are subtitled by their practical implications: 'Land Rights (*Land as an economic base*), Self Determination (*Aboriginal control of Aboriginal affairs*) and Economic Independence (*Aboriginal sovereignty*).'

To characterize this political community here is to sketch out a genealogy and a politics in relation to which non-Aboriginal supporters and the nature of their support and roles can be understood.

Foley (2001) attributes a shared political consciousness to activists who emerged across the three major eastern cities of Australia in the late 1960s: 'the loose coalition of individual young indigenous activists who emerged in Redfern, Fitzroy and South Brisbane in the period immediately after Charles Perkins' "Freedom Ride" in 1965' comprised the Black Power movement of Australia. These activists had origins in rural areas across Victoria, New South Wales and Queensland, and their vision, concerns and influence were nationwide (Horner, 2004: 167; Robinson, 1994: 50).

There are particular historical, political, geographic and economic links and commonalities in the south-eastern area of Australia which contributed to the meeting of political minds described by Foley (see Barwick, 1963; Boyce, 2011; Burgmann, 2003b; Chesterman and Galligan, 1997; Goodall, 1996). Australia's arable south-east is the most closely settled – and murderously possessed – region of the continent. It makes sense that the Aboriginal leaders who articulate the most acute critique of their condition should have arisen in those parts of Australia where colonization began and where it has been the most genocidal: 'It is history on the rebound' (Pierre Slicer quoted in Ryan, 2012: 327).

A shared political consciousness in the south-east can therefore be understood as a regionally specific phenomenon, yet also as part of the broader history of Indigenous resistance to colonialism across the continent from the time of colonization onwards. The activities of those who began to organize in the major cities of the eastern states of Australia, from Brisbane through to Melbourne, in the late 1960s quite quickly gained the responsive involvement of those further north and west, from Townsville to Ceduna (Foley, 2012: 245; see also Healy, n.d.). The land rights, sovereignty and Black Power activists had pan-Aboriginal concerns and enjoyed pan-Aboriginal support.

The strong, radical voices centred in Sydney, Brisbane and Melbourne brought the modern national land rights movement to prominence. Those who expressed these voices were as involved with the establishment and defence of the Aboriginal Embassy on the lawns in front of Parliament House in 1972 as they were integral to the development of local 'community survival' or 'self-help organizations such as free legal services, medical clinics and housing associations' (Foley and Anderson, 2006: 89; Gillor, 2011; Healy, n.d.; Watson et al., 2007). The protests and the community projects were philosophically intertwined. Speaking in 1988, Foley commented: 'We have a strong united national political movement which not only attempts to bring about political change, but, parallel with that, is actually overcoming specific problems that confront our community' (Foley, 1988: 3). 'Black Power' was expressed in Australia through the rubric of community control, black control of black affairs, a politics of pride in Aboriginal identity and culture, a significant self-help movement, and a belief that engagement with white people and institutions should be based on organized, internal community strength (Foley, 2001; Foley and Anderson, 2006: 88–9; Taffe, 2005: 250).

The self-help projects and organizations started off on a completely voluntary activist basis, 'operating on a shoestring, with mainly volunteer labour, and became an important activist base' (Foley and Anderson, 2006: 89). The first medical services supported other communities to set up their own services (Gillor, 2011).[1] The services that proliferated nationwide in this way joined together into strong national networks such as the National Aboriginal and Islander Health Organization (NAIHO) and the National Aboriginal and Islander Legal Service Secretariat (NAILSS) (Foley and Anderson, 2006: 89; Bill Roberts, interview).

The Aboriginal people whose politics ground this book were participants in – or, if younger, inherited a politics from – this tumultuous and creative era. Members of the political community who embraced 1960s' and 1970s' radicalism actively continued to develop the politics and theorizing of their movement in the subsequent period. While the Aboriginal Embassy is marked by a sense of continuity – it is probably the 'longest protest site in Australia' (Watson, 2000a) – it has accrued meanings during its lifetime. As such, the Embassy is now understood for the dramatic protests of 1972 as well as through its continued focus on – and development of a politics of – sovereignty (Robinson, 1994: 63; Schaap, 2009; Muldoon and Schaap, 2012), a campaign

---

1. Batty (2005) has a different view, claiming that the government established some of these 'Aboriginal' organizations under the policy of 'self-determination'. Burgmann (2003b: 12) says all the health services were 'conceived, designed, established and controlled' by Aboriginal people.

of litigation against genocide (Balint, 2014; Scott, 2004), and a centring of/reference to Aboriginal cultural values within the movement (McGregor, 2009: 344; Muecke, 1998; Watson, 2000a, 2000b). A collection of ramshackle tents, the form of the Embassy manages to evoke the poor conditions in which many Aboriginal people live, while also serving as an embarrassing 'eyesore' for government. Simultaneously, the Embassy's location interrupts the line of sight between Parliament House and the Australian War Memorial in the highly symbolic layout of Canberra, the capital city of Australia, making it function as a living monument to Australia's unfinished business, most particularly the unresolved colonial land wars. All of these meanings are interwoven with a political genealogy stretching back to the early twentieth century, and earlier (Maynard, 2007). Aboriginal political activity has been said to have begun 'in the late 1830s on Flinders Island', Tasmania, and Aboriginal people on Coranderrk reserve near Melbourne were 'probably the first to sustain a political campaign' (Attwood and Markus, 1999: 30).

The radicalism of the late 1960s and early 1970s is firmly and self-consciously linked with past struggles. Key figures in the self-conscious political genealogy of the young Indigenous activists of this period include William Ferguson, Jack Patten and Pearl Gibbs of the APA, and William Cooper and Margaret Tucker of the AAL (Foley, 2012; Taffe, 2008). APA and AAL jointly organized the 1938 Day of Mourning. The activism and philosophies of Fred Maynard and the AAPA in the 1900s and 1920s were part of this genealogy, as archival records and family connections through to the young activists make clear. A key example is the connection between Fred Maynard and Gary Foley's great-grandfather Jim Doyle (Maynard, 2007: 86).

Apart from their favour for more confrontational approaches than their immediate forebears, these young radicals did not represent a break with older Aboriginal people or prior struggles per se. They had links with older community members and political leaders. Yuin warrior Chicka Dixon is recognized as a figure who joined with and mentored this younger generation in Sydney (Foley, 2001, 2012; Goodall, 1996; Robinson, 1994: 50); his experience as a wharfie and unionist endorsed and encouraged their appetite for 'street struggle' (Chicka Dixon, interview). Chicka Dixon saw himself as being more closely aligned in strategy to the new generation of Aboriginal people who took to the streets during the 1960s than he was to the 'old APA' who 'wouldn't *dare* dream of street struggle' (interview). Bill and Eric Onus and the younger Bruce McGuinness, their nephew (Horner, 2004: 140), as well as Bob Maza in Melbourne (Foley, 2001), and Kath Walker (later Oodgeroo Noonuccal) and Don Brady in Brisbane are regarded similarly as mentors to the Black Power/Aboriginal Embassy generation and the younger members of the Brisbane Tribal Council (Watson et al., 2007: 43, 44). The young radicals were also influential on some older Aboriginal community members. Alma Thorpe, who is the best part of a generation older than Foley, counts him and Bruce McGuinness as her mentors (interview). Gary Murray's father Stewart Murray worked closely with Alma's mother Edna Brown on the Aboriginal Funeral Fund. Like pastor Sir Doug Nicholls, to whom Gary Murray is related through his mother, Stewart Murray was deeply involved in the Victorian Aborigines Advancement League (VAAL), the Federal Council for the Advancement of Aborigines and Torres Strait Islanders (FCAATSI) and the National Tribal Council (NTC).

Both men are important to many Aboriginal people active in Melbourne today. That said, there are important nuances in the politics of the older generation mentioned, with those who understand their political lineage as running through the 'Onus line', anchored by Bill Onus, Chicka Dixon and Bruce McGuinness, identifying the 'Nicholls line' as relatively more conservative in agenda and strategies (Howell, 2013: 14).

The political consciousness expressed by Indigenous people of the south-east of Australia in the twentieth century, with its roots in the nineteenth, is both particular to its historical and political context, and part of a continent-wide story of Aboriginal resistance to colonialism. Indigenous struggles throughout Australia have employed diverse strategies, and have generally displayed pan-Aboriginal solidarity (Maddison, 2009; Robinson, 1994). Anthropologist Francesca Merlan (2005: 476) observes in two examples from the Northern Territory (documented in 1958 and 1963) forms of response to colonization that are more 'ritual' than 'protest'. While finding a contrast between the two forms (i.e. ritual vs protest), Merlan (2005: 474) notes the differing circumstances of their expression, and understands them both as being within the category of 'movement' (or 'indigenous mobilization'). Chicka Dixon has identified the political community I focus on not so much by their political views, but according to their particular strategies, which took account of their relative geographical proximity to the seat of federal power: 'How you *fight* it is slightly different ... We took the lead because we had quick access to Canberra. And we could embarrass the bastards' (interview).[2]

---

2. The tactic of targeting national celebrations and sporting events in order to gain

Historiographical debates

There is a substantial literature on the history of Indigenous struggles in Australia from the time of invasion onwards, including histories and biographies (for instance, see Briscoe, 2010; Goodall, 1996; Huggins, 1998; Read, 1990a; Reynolds, 2006). But history writing is a contested field. The politics of the writing of history (and of the teaching of history) and relationships with the academy are key concerns of Aboriginal people from the political community with which this research engages (Atkinson et al., 1985). For some, the struggle for Aboriginal rights has included both an activist and a research or academic practice. Writing and interpreting history from an Indigenous viewpoint is key to the agendas of Indigenous peoples across the globe, and in particular key to Indigenous peoples' research agendas (see also Foley, 2001; Green, Sonn and Matsebula, 2007; Kuokkanen, 2003; Smith, 1999). While Indigenous academics view this as a core concern and one which is repeatedly dismissed by the academy, there are nevertheless some non-Aboriginal academics who have acknowledged the politics of history writing and history teaching (Paisley, Cole and Haskins, 2005). Historiographical debates in this field are not concerned with abstract questions; rather, they have real consequences for contemporary land rights politics (Vincent and Land, 2003).

Let's consider the issues at stake in this debate as it plays out in relation to Indigenous struggles in south-east Australia. The first issue concerns the political character of the Aboriginal movement over the twentieth century, and whether

---

national and international media attention for the movement has continued to enjoy success (Horner, 2004: 159–60).

the relative emphasis on civil rights and land rights is a sign of evolving political priorities among Aboriginal people, or a sign of conscious strategy and externally driven limitations on their demands. The second concerns the 'onset' of an 'organized Aboriginal political agenda', and the long-held belief that this was in the 1930s.[3] Third, historians' treatment of Aboriginal agency and political sophistication is contested. Finally, Maynard and Foley in particular argue that certain moments in the Aboriginal struggle and/or their historically significant qualities have been ignored.

On the first element of the debate, John Maynard questions the interpretations by various historians of the publicly articulated agendas of 'Aboriginal protest groups of the Cooper, Ferguson and Patten era'. Many have judged them to have been primarily interested in equality, citizenship rights and absorption into mainstream Australia, and not so much in cultural distinctiveness and 'Aboriginal rights, particularly in relation to land' (Maynard, 2007: 4–5). Maynard emphasizes the factors which might have constrained the ways they articulated their agendas and upholds their relative radicalism (Maynard, 2007: 4, 5). Foley and Tim Anderson accept Heather Goodall's argument that the land rights and civil rights movements can be understood as 'intertwined' (Foley and Anderson, 2006: 88; Goodall, 1996). Like Briscoe (2004), McGregor (2009) and Muecke (1998), Foley and Anderson conceptualize the Aboriginal movement in a series of phases. For Foley and Anderson (2006: 84), the first two phases include

---

3. Maynard's (2007) important research in this area also illuminates the genealogy of Aboriginal people's engagement with international struggles and philosophies, particularly black consciousness, tracing this to 1907–08.

civil rights, land rights, self-determination and internationalist black consciousness in various measures. Crucially, they note that the demand for the return of stolen land was more central in organizations where Aboriginal community control was greater (Foley and Anderson, 2006: 84). Indeed, for Briscoe (2004: 192) the 'Aboriginal advancement' phase of the 1950s and 1960s in which organizations like FCAATSI were central is one of *'paternalism* and reform'. This suggests that the land demand was suppressed within organizations like FCAATSI, as will be discussed in the next chapter. The third 'phase', from the 1980s onwards, is seen as a bureaucratic era: 'the bureaucratization of Aboriginal services and funding dependency slowed these campaigns in the 1980s' (see also Foley, 1975; Foley and Anderson, 2006: 84).

On the question of pre-World War I Aboriginal activism, John Maynard cites a 'simple lack of research', as well as possibly a lack of fortune in archival research, for the longevity of the theory that William Ferguson and the APA (a 1930s' organization) represented the 'onset of an organized Aboriginal political agenda' (Maynard, 2007: 5). To Maynard, it is rather the AAPA which should be recognized as 'the precursor of the Aboriginal political movement. Yet for several decades the deeds and struggles of the AAPA were largely ignored, misunderstood, forgotten and hidden, its legacy fading into oblivion' (Maynard, 2007: 2). This is linked to Foley's argument that the achievements and influence of the 'urban, militant activists of Redfern, Fitzroy and South Brisbane' of the 1960s' and 1970s' land rights and Black Power movement have been 'trivialized, marginalized and dismissed' by the 'historical and anthropological establishment' (Foley, 2001).

Foley and Anderson identify works by Frank Hardy and Heather Goodall as among the non-Aboriginal-authored historical accounts which they consider properly attribute agency to Aboriginal people in the conduct and development of their own movement (Foley and Anderson, 2006: 99). This is in contrast to the more numerous non-Aboriginal works, which they contend focus disproportionately on the role of 'mission managers and non-Indigenous advocates, in particular Labor politicians' (Foley and Anderson, 2006: 99). This critique is linked to the debate over the character of the first two 'phases' of the Aboriginal movement and the question over how distinct they were from an Aboriginal point of view. On this, John Maynard's book dispels the 'misconception' that the early Aboriginal political movement was 'both unsophisticated and strongly Christian (or White) influenced', instead revealing how they engaged with internationalist black consciousness (Foley and Anderson, 2006: 85; Maynard, 2007).

Foley, who wrote the preface to Maynard's book on the AAPA, finds that the book 'confirms' why the work of scholars like himself and Maynard to 'introduce an Indigenous voice and perspective' into academic history is 'so important' (Foley, 2007: v–vi). The story Maynard tells, according to Foley, has been ignored, or its significance not appreciated by 'generations of Australian academic historians' (Foley, 2007: vi). This has amounted to a silencing and suppression of Indigenous voices and important events by the academy (Foley, 2007: vi).

Indigenous academics from the land rights, Black Power and sovereignty community have engaged in historiographical debates over issues they see as important. Knowledge of the legacies of past struggles and solidarity is important in the contemporary politics of solidarity with south-east Indigenous struggles; it follows that familiarity with critiques of how histories of these events are written is important too.

My characterization of the political community, anchored in important developments in Fitzroy, Redfern and South Brisbane in the late 1960s and early 1970s, has necessarily entailed engaging with the contested historiography of twentieth-century Indigenous activism in Australia. The history of these struggles and the politics of their telling are crucial to making sense of key events – such as the contest over control of FCAATSI and its political agenda. These contests are important parts of the background for relationships between Indigenous and non-Indigenous people engaged in contemporary south-east struggles. In fact, self-conscious engagement with the history of non-Indigenous support for Indigenous struggles in any particular area is key to the contemporary politics of solidarity by those of colonial backgrounds with Indigenous struggles in that area.

TWO

A political genealogy for contemporary non-Indigenous activism in Australia

Non-Indigenous people attempting to support Indigenous struggles in Australia today do so in relation to a history of efforts by non-Indigenous groups and organizations to advance the cause of Aboriginal people; yet this is a history of which they may not be aware (Boughton, 2001). In some cases, efforts by non-Indigenous people to support the Aboriginal cause were paternalizing, or were undertaken without any dialogue with or knowledge of Aboriginal activists and intellectuals, or appreciation of their agendas (Maynard, 2007; Paisley, 2000). The character of these efforts is remembered by Aboriginal people and organizations. In interviews with 'Indigenous and non-Indigenous activists' who have collaborated on 'environmental campaigning', Pickerill observed that the background to all of their 'dialogues' and processes of negotiation 'is a long and often contested history of interactions' (Pickerill, 2009: 72). She noticed that 'Interviewees invoked memories of iconic campaigns [including Jabiluka] as both inspirational and problematic.'

The infamous FCAATSI 'split' of 1970 (Briscoe, 2010; Goodall, 1996; Horner, 2004; Read, 1990b; Taffe, 2005), the 'internal dynamics' of the Jabiluka campaign of 1997–2000 (Paasonen, 2007), the contest over the politics of Defenders of Native Title (DONT) and Australians for Native Title and Reconciliation (ANTaR) (Spindler, 2007), and the non-Aboriginal and Torres Strait Islander response to the request for specific kinds of support made by Aboriginal and Torres Strait Islander people at Camp Sovereignty in March 2006 (Black GST, 2006) are part of the contested history of interactions that comprise the background for contemporary Indigenous and non-Indigenous activists engaged with south-east Indigenous struggles (see also Foley, 2000). Such contests are part of the collective memory of Indigenous and non-Indigenous people who were involved at the time (Taffe, 2005), but not necessarily of newly involved non-Indigenous people. Awareness of such a genealogy must be developed if non-Indigenous people are to understand their current efforts in relation to what has gone before (Anderson, n.d.).

While there are a lot of cautionary tales to be drawn from problematic 'black–white' interactions in past campaigns and organizations during recent history, there are also many inspiring and instructive histories. Writers of Indigenous political history have written about the incredibly rich and inspiring histories of Indigenous resistance and political struggles since the onset of invasion and colonization. I find it important to know these histories as well as to draw upon, know and celebrate pro-Indigenous actions and efforts by non-Indigenous people. This awareness can function politically to show that historical examples of paternalistic behaviours may not be excused as simply being 'products of their time', because alternatives were being lived out publicly in the same period.

A self-conscious genealogy of political solidarity with Indigenous struggles can include histories of white anti-racism,

Western anti-imperialism, and support of Indigenous struggles by non-Indigenous individuals of conscience, as well as by people acting collectively and through organizations.[1] It can include the actions of first- and second-wave feminists, the organized left (including trade unions and the Communist Party of Australia), organizations such as the Australian-Aboriginal Fellowship, the Victorian Aboriginal Advancement League and FCAATSI, as well as students, church groups, environmentalists and, most recently, the movement against corporate globalization.[2] It could also try to capture the sometimes eclectic mix of supporters who have stood by certain Aboriginal political actors for a variety of reasons that are not so predictable. As Foley has pointed out, his generation in the Black Power movement replicated 'the strange array of political affiliations and alliances of some of their predecessors', whose supporters in the 1930s and 1940s included communists, bohemians and members of the Australian nationalist movement (Foley, 2012: 125, 284). The 1960s' generation engaged with an 'interesting range' of social and political progressives, 'unconventional thinkers, drinkers, artists and poets in the Capital city urban Aboriginal centres of south-eastern Australia' (Foley, 2012: 126).

It is important to be familiar with the work of those who have made significant contributions, and as well as those whose practices have been either particularly problematic or particularly positive.

---

1. See Gandhi, 2006; O'Donnell and Simons, 1995; Thompson, 2001.
2. See Burgmann and Burgmann, 1998; V. Burgmann, 2003b; Curthoys, 2002; Horner, 2004; Paisley, 2000.

Indigenous peoples' solidarity with each other

It is crucial in any discussion of supporters of Indigenous struggles to foreground Indigenous peoples' solidarity with each other's struggles, and with anti-racist and anti-fascist struggles (Limb, 2008: 939; Smith, 1999: 108). Indigenous people are of course conscious of the need to build solidarity with each other: as Margaret Tucker, one of the key conveners of the United Council of Aboriginal Women, formed in the late 1960s, spoke about the need for Aboriginal people to cooperate with and help each other, as well as to gain white people's help (Hemingway, 2012: 44). Sina Brown-Davis has drawn attention to the past and continuing solidarity that Indigenous people of the Pacific have shown to each others' struggles (e.g. solidarity between Indigenous peoples of Australia and Aotearoa/New Zealand), reminding non-Indigenous people that they/we are certainly not the only ones to act in solidarity with Indigenous peoples' struggles (Land, 2011a). Also noteworthy is the protest against the rise of Nazism organized by Yorta Yorta elder William Cooper in 1938, which received belated public recognition (Attwood and Markus, 1999; Foley, 1997a; Koutsoukis, 2010; Lyons, 2010; Tatz, 2004). Pilbara pastoral workers marched to Port Hedland under the banner of the Anti-Fascist League in 1944 (Hess, 1994). The young Indigenous militants of Redfern were among many who took direct action in support of the South African anti-apartheid movement's call to boycott the tour of the Springbok Rugby Team (Foley, 2001, 2012; Limb, 2008; Mita, 1983). Among other south-eastern Aboriginal leaders, Bill Onus publicly supported post-World War II Indigenous struggles, such as the 1946 Pilbara stock workers' strike in northern Western Australia (Foley and Anderson, 2006: 86).

That strike was also supported by Aboriginal leaders from the south-west, including Tommy Bropho 'of the Perth Aboriginal Community' (Hess, 1994: 75). In the 1960s Aboriginal leaders from many parts of Australia supported the struggles of the Gurindji at Wave Hill (Northern Territory), the Yolgnu at Yirrkala (Gove Peninsula, Northern Territory), the people of Mapoon (far north Queensland) and the people of Lake Tyers (Victoria), as did FCAATSI (Horner, 2004: 74–8). Aboriginal people have arguably been each other's most reliable supporters.[3]

Support by 'individuals of conscience'

Among non-Indigenous supporters of south-eastern Indigenous struggles there are several individuals who stand out and rela- tively few organizations.

One outstanding individual (who deserves a mention even though he worked in the north-west of Australia) was Don McLeod, a fencing and well-digging contractor with anti-fascist and communist beliefs. He had employed up to ten Aboriginal people on uncommonly good conditions in the Pilbara area of north-west Western Australia before eventually working closely with Aboriginal pastoral workers who staged a major strike against slave conditions on pastoral stations in 1946 (Hess, 1994: 71). The high regard in which McLeod was held by the workers and their own organizers – Dooley Bin Bin and Clancy McKenna – is evident in Hess's account (see also Noakes, Roberts and Williams, 1987).

---

3. This is despite 'divide and conquer' tactics by colonizing governments, whereby Aboriginal people have sometimes questioned each other's authenticity (see Maddison, 2009). This government tactic is not peculiar to Australia (see Harp, 1994).

Another 'friend of the Aborigines' was Mrs Anne Bon, who went to live near Melbourne in 1858 and became passionately committed for the rest of her life to supporting and arguing for the rights of the Taungurung and Woiwurrung-speaking peoples of the Coranderrk mission near present-day Healesville (Matthew, 2003; Reed, 2005). Associated with the same communities was John Green, a much-loved 'friend, and brother' of the people of Coranderrk, who served as 'manager' of the station during its period of self-sufficiency in the 1880s. He was the 'only one they wanted over them' (Barwick, 2005; Broome, 2006).

Maynard makes mention of two individual white supporters of the AAPA during the 1920s: Elizabeth Hatton and John Moloney. Maynard focuses particularly on Hatton, saying that in her work 'taking the matter of Aboriginal issues to the wider public forum ... she was very much a forerunner of feminist activists such as Mary Bennett, Joan Kingsley Strack and Jessica Street', who were prominent in the 1930s (Maynard, 2005; 2007: 46). Maynard assesses Hatton as having uncommon knowledge of and contacts with Aboriginal people (Maynard, 2007: 47). It was not only Hatton's connections with Aboriginal people that was uncommon but also the way she demonstrated that she heeded their knowledge and political analysis of their own situation and way forward (Maynard, 2007: 40, 86–8). Maynard described Hatton's willingness to reassess her preconceived policy ideas through dialogue with AAPA leaders as evidence of 'a major shift in thinking that was decades ahead of its time' (Maynard, 2007: 40). Hatton remained a promoter of the AAPA and its policies, but was never a member of the organization, which was all-Aboriginal (Maynard, 2007: 88).

The AAPA had four years in the public spotlight (Maynard, 2007: 55), and its spokespeople were on the public record, for instance in major newspapers, as active Aboriginal political leaders. Maynard (2007: 40) implies that non-Indigenous people who 'came forward with ideas ... to "help" Aboriginal people' should have known about such Aboriginal leaders. He dismisses 'the majority' of those individuals who came forward to 'help', 'from the earliest point of settlement onwards', as undermining their own well-intentioned efforts with their own 'deeply ingrained assumptions and perceptions of European superiority' (Maynard, 2007: 40).

Another individual whose action in solidarity with radical black politics deserves mention because of its high degree of international significance is the white Australian athlete Peter Norman. Murri artist Richard Bell's mural *A White Hero for Black Australia* acknowledges Peter Norman for his quiet act of solidarity with courageous US athletes Tommie Smith and John Carlos, who staged a Black Power salute on the dais at the 1968 Olympic Games in Mexico after the three won medals in the 200-metre sprint. The salute was regarded as highly controversial by Olympic officials and US media, and predictably and instantly became world-famous. Norman indicated his support by wearing a large badge from the Olympic Project for Human Rights, the umbrella project for the action by Carlos and Smith. He also agreed with their proposal to enhance the symbolism of the protest by omitting the customary handshake between medallists while on the dais. The critical view of Norman's gestures by some in the Australian sporting hierarchy meant that he suffered professional repercussions for the rest of his life.

Norman's ability to make a quick decision to embrace the opportunity identified by Carlos and Smith to attract worldwide attention for black liberation was probably due to his family background, which was both relatively progressive and staunchly Christian. He 'was a believer in civil rights' and had been 'taught through the Salvation Army to love everybody'. Norman commented after the medal ceremony that even though he was not in total agreement with Black Power methods, 'It took a lot of guts to do what they did ... I thought this was a good opportunity to have a white man show himself on the Negro side' (Johnstone and Norman, 2008: 44–5, 64).

Don McLeod, Peter Norman and the little-known Anne Bon, John Green and Elizabeth Hatton can generally be understood in the terms Davis applies to one type of contemporary activist: the 'individual of conscience'. These are people who 'operate on the sheer energy and commitment of the parties involved, with minimal financial or institutional resources' (Davis, 2010: 7). McLeod was the most closely associated with organized politics, although his degree of association with the CPA is contested. John Green was a lay preacher and Peter Norman was part of the Salvation Army. The factors which seem common among all five are engagement as individuals with publicly political Aboriginal (or black) people and leaders, and respect for them as political actors. These dispositions were manifested in their support for Aboriginal agendas. Belinda, a member of the Melbourne Kungkas collective of young women who supported the Kupa Piti Kungka Tjuta, made a connection between solidarity activism and political flexibility, seeing the value of not identifying with a politics that is more specific than 'general "leftist"' (Melbourne Kungkas, group interview).

Solidarity by groups and organizations

Many groups and organizations have engaged with Indigenous struggles, and they have generally been socially and politically progressive or Christian. Among them, the Communist Party of Australia (CPA) and Action for World Development (AWD) have been relatively poorly recognized outside Aboriginal political circles (and ASIO) despite their relatively significant contribution. While better documented, it is appropriate to take note of the support of the New South Wales Builders Labourers Federation (NSWBLF), as well as to analyse key elements in the story of FCAATSI. Also outlined below are some contributions by students, feminists, reconciliation groups and environmental campaigners.

The Communist Party of Australia

Oral history shows how important the CPA was as a supporter of Indigenous struggles in Australia (Alma Thorpe and Gary Murray, interviews; Foley, 2012). Bob Boughton (2001) provides a detailed account of the extent and character of this communist support from the 1920s to the 1970s and suggests why historians have largely ignored and downplayed this (see also Hess, 1994: 82). Boughton also observes that the CPA was ahead of most other organizations in its embrace of Aboriginal agendas such as land rights and self-determination and its opposition to assimilation. He attributes this to policy directives from the international movement to which the CPA belonged, the Communist International, and its black American delegates, as well as the CPA's genuine awareness of Aboriginal peoples' struggles and links to Aboriginal activists – some of whom were CPA members in their own right (Boughton, 2001: 265–6).

Boughton (2001: 264, 287) describes a 'vibrant tradition of working-class and community activism in support of indigenous rights', arguing that it is to this tradition that groups like Australians for Native Title and Reconciliation (ANTaR) and the contemporary 'Reconciliation movement' should properly trace their 'roots'. The general prevalence of anti-communism is no doubt partly responsible for the underemphasis of the CPA's contribution. However, an understandable 'concern to emphasise the agency of indigenous peoples themselves' may also be at play here (Boughton, 2001: 284).

As he recounts the history of the CPA's support for Indigenous struggles, Boughton touches on an episode which is suggestive of an attitude of engaged respect for Aboriginal people as orchestrators of their own struggle. He notes that criticism in the CPA press of APA and AAL's eloquent and well-remembered 1938 Day of Mourning action coexisted with substantial support for the action by the CPA and trade unions. That is, while the CPA press '*criticized* the Aborigines for excluding whites' from their all-Aboriginal meeting on the day, the CPA was still willing to *support* the action (Boughton, 2001: 269). This indicates a certain maturity on the part of the CPA, and a robust sense of self-belief on the part of the APA and the AAL in persisting with the strategy they had chosen.

Boughton identifies three factors in the CPA's reduced relevance as an ally to the Aboriginal movement by the late 1960s. First, conflict within the CPA regarding events in the USSR led to a major split in the party; second, the Aboriginal movement 'found a new ally in the radical student movement developing on university campuses, which was also not without its connections to the CPA'; and third, 'the fruition, ironically, of the Aboriginal movement's aspirations for autonomy which it had worked hard to promote' (Boughton, 2001: 282, 292). In addition, Boughton (2001: 282) cites the growing importance of 'new social movements' in relation to such developments (see also Burgmann and Burgmann, 1998: 126–7).

Solidarity by church-related groups: Action for World Development

The constraining influence of the white Christian element within Aboriginal advancement organizations of the 1950s and 1960s, and the generally conservative influence of Christian beliefs where they were held by Aboriginal leaders as a result of colonial missionary work (Foley, 2012: 159), have meant that for radical black activists the connection between church-related groups and Aboriginal struggles is problematic. In relation to FCAATSI and the referendum which came to be its *raison d'être*, Black Power activists came to ask, 'Christian-influenced methods might have brought about the 1967 referendum, but what had that achieved?' (Foley, 2012: 132). However, there have been some significant contributions made by people associated with more progressive branches of some of the Australian churches (see Lewis, 2010). The church-related organization that stands out in terms of its formative influence on a number of highly informed and committed allies for Aboriginal struggles in the south-east of Australia is the ecumenical organization Action for World Development (AWD). Bill Roberts, Chris Twining, Barry Mitchell and Lorelle Savage trace their long-term engagement with Indigenous struggles to formative experiences with AWD. Looking back on the early days with the organization, says Lorelle Savage, 'I still think we had it right then in terms of the principles of being an ally' (Margaret, 2013: 77).

AWD was formed in 1971 'as a joint venture of the Australian Council of Churches and the Roman Catholic Church' (Rugendyke, 1991: 9). Its founding is illuminated by situating it in the context of the politicization of NGO activity in Australia between 1965 and 1980 (Rugendyke, 1991: 7–8). This shows how NGOs, as well as students and organizations like the NSWBLF, were influenced by and engaged with a set of interrelated political developments in the 1960s and 1970s. During this period 'a series of international events ... demanded a response from Australian NGOs': first, Australian military involvement in the American war in Vietnam (also known as the Vietnam War); second, the tour of Australia, Aotearoa/New Zealand and other countries by South African sporting teams such as the all-white Springboks rugby team; and finally, the East Timorese coup against Portuguese administration and the subsequent invasion of East Timor by Indonesia in the latter months of 1975 (Rugendyke, 1991: 7–8).

Opposition to examples of racism overseas, as well as awareness of colonialism, Australia's neocolonialism and liberation movements overseas, formed the backdrop for NGO and student responses when Aboriginal activists in Australia pointed out to them the hypocrisy of a purely outward-looking concern for human rights (Foley, 2001; Greer, 1972; Limb, 2008: 923).

AWD involved at least 150,000 people nationwide in an education campaign, instigating the formation of networks of groups of ten or so people, who undertook a study programme. It focused on the politics and practice of aid and development, poverty within Australia, Aboriginal land rights, international solidarity (South Africa, East Timor, Latin America) and nuclear disarmament (Ryan, 1991: 124). AWD's education campaigning and activities prospered in particular until around 1983, when the anti-communist wing of the Catholic Church (organized as the National Civic Council, a group led by the notorious Melbourne-based B.A. Santamaria) began a campaign against the organization as having 'links' with 'communist groups' (Ryan, 1991: 125).

AWD looked for ways to 'ensure the accuracy and appropriateness of it efforts' (Ryan, 1991: 129): 'Work undertaken by AWD which relates, for instance, to Aboriginal issues is checked by appropriate groups within the Aboriginal community. This avoids paternalism and misrepresentation' (Ryan, 1991: 129). Many people involved in AWD in the 1970s cited AWD's critique of colonialism overseas as the prompt for their engagement with Indigenous struggles in Australia. AWD was rooted in a critique of colonialism, cognizant of structural issues and adopted a practice of responding to requests from 'groups which consider themselves oppressed'. It is a noteworthy, if underappreciated, organization in the genealogy of non-Indigenous solidarity with Indigenous struggles in south-east Australia.

New South Wales Builders Labourers Federation

The NSWBLF was one of the most significant supporters of Aboriginal struggles in New South Wales in the 1960s and 1970s when the Aboriginal population of Redfern and inner suburbs of Sydney skyrocketed and where (along with Melbourne and Brisbane) a newfound energy and political mobilization emerged (Foley, 2001). In terms of how it instructs the politics of solidarity, the NSWBLF should be recognized for the longevity of its engagement with Indigenous struggles and the fact that this was grounded in a significant Indigenous membership. The engagement of the NSWBLF with Indigenous struggles is evidenced two decades before the most public years of its 'radical action in the interests of others' (Burgmann and Burgmann, 1998: 124), the most well known of which were the 'green bans' on certain property developments in Sydney in the early 1970s. The NSWBLF had a significant Aboriginal membership, including Ray Peckham in the 1960s and Kevin Cook in the 1970s, who both became NSWBLF organizers (Cook and Goodall, 2013). Peckham was heavily involved in the union's support of FCAATSI – to which it committed around 1962 – and was the convener of FCAATSI's trade-union subcommittee (Burgmann and Burgmann, 1998: 133–5). During a similar period, Chicka Dixon was a member of the WWF and its representative within FCAATSI; significantly earlier, around 1908, Fred Maynard and Tom Lacey (who went on to found the AAPA) worked on the Sydney waterfront and were likewise politically active, for instance in the international black consciousness organization UNIA (Maynard, 2007). NSWBLF was closely involved with the 'Sydney black movement' from the late 1960s onwards, including support for the Aboriginal Embassy and the black moratorium in July 1972, and support which helped secure housing in Redfern for Aboriginal people under Aboriginal control in 1973. The NSWBLF recognized that police were harassing Aboriginal people in Sydney and routinely provided bail for people arrested (Burgmann and Burgmann, 1998: 136). It also called on the federal government to negotiate a treaty (Burgmann and Burgmann, 1999).

Several factors situated the NSWBLF, in the era in which it was led by Bob Pringle, Jack Mundey and Joe Owens, as an important ally of Aboriginal struggles. First, the NSWBLF had already secured industrial success in the form of wage rises and improved conditions on behalf of its members. Second, it had the power to effect social change through the withdrawal of labour from key locations in the economy. Finally, the membership accepted the philosophy that it must speak up on 'all issues affecting the life of ... all Australian people', and that they should apply their labour to 'socially useful' or 'socially beneficial' ends (Burgmann and Burgmann, 1998: 12, 124–5; Mundey, 1998). The NSWBLF's importance as an ally of the Aboriginal movement came to an abrupt halt when its radical leadership was ejected in a controversial intervention by the federal BLF in 1974–75 (Mallory, 2005: 132; Mundey, 1998: 35).

FCAATSI: black and white together?

The Federal Council for the Advancement of Aborigines and Torres Strait Islanders (FCAATSI) is important in the genealogy of support for Indigenous struggles in Australia for two key reasons: first, its national membership and influence; second, the infamous contest over Aboriginal control within the organiza-tion. It is crucial to understand that the contest over Aboriginal control related to the question of how Aboriginal agendas were recognized within FCAATSI and that the contest within FCAATSI cast a shadow over relationships between activists for a long time after 1970.

FCAATSI was established in 1958 (as FCAA) and operated until 1978, becoming 'a major player in Aboriginal politi-cal reform' during that time (Briscoe, 2010: 121). FCAATSI drew together most of the individuals and organizations active in 'Aboriginal advancement', built further involvement and achieved national influence. Its paying affiliates included trade unions and labour councils, local and state Aborigines Advancement organizations and leagues, state branches of the Australian Council of Churches, and women's leagues and unions. Affiliates sent delegates to FCAATSI's annual conferences. Most of the non-Indigenous people involved were from the Australian Labor Party or the CPA or were Christians (Foley, 2012: 109). Many strong Aboriginal leaders were also involved, but they were in the numerical minority. Several members of FCAATSI gained prominent positions within the Whitlam ALP government elected in 1972, and within the newly formed Department of Aboriginal Affairs (Taffe, 2005).

FCAATSI's most famous achievement was its successful campaign to hold and then win the 1967 Referendum.[4] The success of the Referendum was significant for two key reasons. First, it was one of only a handful ever won in Australian history; the voting population has generally displayed conservatism regarding constitutional change. Second, the 90.77 per cent 'Yes' vote was an overwhelming expression of support, the highest ever recorded in a federal referendum, and somewhat surprising for a country with a majority white population founded on genocide and federated on immigration policies designed to make and keep Australia white. However, it is also notable that support was garnered for a rather amorphous idea

---

4. This resulted in two amendments to the Australian Constitution such that the Commonwealth would be able to make laws in relation to Aboriginal people, who would also be included in 'reckoning the numbers of the people in the Commonwealth' (Taffe, 2008).

rather than a detailed policy: the campaign slogan was 'Vote Yes for Aborigines'.

Immediately following the Referendum win, FCAATSI entered a period of internal turmoil. During the lead-up to, and in the aftermath of, the 1970 annual conference at which the delegates voted down an 'Aboriginalization' proposal, confrontation loomed over issues of greater voting and decision-making rights for Aboriginal people within FCAATSI. This was predicted, observed and urged by some, and ignored and resisted by others. Some members were concerned about the possible loss of political power if the Aboriginalization motion alienated white supporters such that they withdrew from FCAATSI (Horner, 2004). Some read FCAATSI as an organization that 'White and Black Australians' entered 'on equal terms' (Horner quoted in Taffe, 2005: 262). However, historian Sue Taffe finds that despite some measures which by 1967 had increased Aboriginal and Torres Strait Islander numbers on the executive, 'power effectively remained with the non-Indigenous Melbourne executive' (Taffe, 2005: 242, 237). Eventually, unable to resolve these issues to the satisfaction of the Indigenous instigators through a direct vote on the matter, several well-supported Indigenous members of FCAATSI (Doug Nicholls, Stewart Murray, Chicka Dixon, Kath Walker) led the way in quitting the organization to form the all-Indigenous National Tribal Council. John Newfong followed about a month later, for integrally related reasons, as did Barrie Pittock – who had been the strongest white supporter of Indigenous power within FCAATSI (Taffe, 2005). In the years that followed this split the organization was weakened, gradually sidelined and eventually disbanded (Taffe, 2005).

At the same time, the community services which evolved out of the Black Power movement's self-help projects 'came to represent the grassroots of Aboriginal opinion', and it was those services which government agencies began liaising with 'in order to gauge Aboriginal needs and expectations, rather than the FCAATSI coalition as had previously been the case' (Hemingway, 2012: 88).

The grounds for the split remain a matter of contest. Taffe rightly notes the broader political context at the time. She suggests it had become unacceptable to 'strong Indigenous leaders' within FCAATSI to work with white members who 'refused to relinquish control'; most of these leaders were 'now working in organizations which were run by Aboriginal people' (Taffe, 2005: 286). In newly established medical services and legal services, white doctors and lawyers served, but 'did not make the rules' (Taffe, 2005: 267). It was obvious that 'relationships between Aboriginal and Islander people and those non-Indigenous activists who wanted to assist them had to be renegotiated' (Taffe, 2005: 267–8). In 1970 the Victorian Aborigines Advancement League (VAAL) rescinded a successful 1969 vote asking whites to resign, an indication that debate over these matters was ongoing (Burgmann, 2003a: 11).

However, the split was not attributable only to the principle of Aboriginal control and leadership, nor to the rising consciousness within FCAATSI of criticism of white people's roles in the civil rights movement in the USA (Taffe, 2005: 250; Thompson, 2001). Nor was the split only 'indicative of the development towards Aboriginal autonomy' (Burgmann, 2003b: 57). Alongside these trends and principles a more complicated tension was developing over the contrasting political priorities of 'blacks and whites' working together in FCAATSI (Taffe, 2005: xi). Astute observers attached these contrasting priorities to the positionality of those holding them. In his 1968 report on 'Aboriginal and European leadership in FCAATSI', Pittock suggested that 'the movement had been run by educated middle-class people who had focused on legislative injustices, whereas economic injustices were what held many back, and that the provision of land was necessary to provide an economic base' (Taffe, 2005: 242). Kath Walker also pointed to politically and economically similar goals as a condition for a 'healthy coalition' between blacks and whites – who also must accept each other as 'co-equal partners' (Taffe, 2005: 251–2).[5] At stake were the aims and priorities of FCAATSI and the ability of Aboriginal people to have their agendas prioritized.

It was the key and undying issue of land rights that was pivotal in the mood among many for renewal in FCAATSI (Briscoe, 2010: 121–5; Goodall, 1996). Heather Goodall's research into 'Aboriginal politics in the public arena in NSW from the 1880s to the 1940s' revealed undeniable and striking evidence of the 'continuity in Aboriginal statements of a strong interest in land and place' in the archives (Goodall, 1996: xvii). Goodall is concerned with the ways in which Aboriginal people formulated their concerns and expressed their interests, often in relation to the concerns of their non-Aboriginal supporters. She notes that in the late 1960s, 'major activity in New South Wales' was represented 'largely in terms of civil rights and the need for legislative change' (Goodall, 1996: 312). Following the

---

5. Foley (2000) finds this in his examination of several campaigns in south-east Australia. The struggle to reopen Northlands Secondary College in defiance of Jeff Kennett's Liberal state government school closures in Victoria was the only campaign in which Koori and non-Koori people involved had a shared goal.

FCAATSI split, there was 'a major reassertion of the land issue on to the State and federal agenda in the early 1970s' (Goodall, 1996: 312–13). While some were sceptical about this, suggesting that young radicals were essentially inventing land rights demands, Goodall judges this reassertion as entirely congruent with the 'persistent demand for land among Aboriginal people from the time the invasion violence ended' (see also Briscoe, 2010: 121–5; Goodall, 1996: xvii). It seems the FCAATSI referendum campaign was an example of when Aboriginal concerns, though consistently asserted, were sidelined.

It is important to see the contest over Aboriginal control within FCAATSI in its historical context. While existing scholarship tends to cast as 'radical' those who advocated Aboriginal control of FCAATSI, the domination of FCAATSI by non-Indigenous people for its first fifteen years can be seen as an aberration, given the existence of effective all-Aboriginal organizations in the 'inter-war' period as well as the early 1900s–1920s (Maynard, 2007).

The 1970 split had an impact beyond FCAATSI:

> On a deeper and more personal level, the damage done at the 1970 Easter conference would affect future relationships between activists within and outside FCAATSI. The bitterness and sense of grievance continued. (Taffe, 2005: 265)

The FCAATSI split can be understood as a case in which the loss of a national support organization, and for some the long-term personal sense of grievance that also resulted, had to be weighed against the negative consequences for Aboriginal peoples of being unable to address their core political demands within that organization.

The evolution of the role of students in the late 1960s

University students became more important as supporters of
south-east Indigenous struggles from the late 1960s onwards
(Boughton, 2001; Robinson, 1994). Student radicalism is
understood as an example of new social movement activism,
which in the 1960s and 1970s grew in significance relative to
traditional trade unionism as a force for social change (Marks,
2009; Burgmann and Milner, 1996). The NSWBLF was an
important exception; it has been described as an exemplar of
'social movement unionism', which did not arise elsewhere until
the 1990s (Burgmann and Burgmann, 1998: 122).

Like people involved in AWD, students were attentive to
struggles against apartheid in South Africa and to the war in
Vietnam and were active in both movements. Further, in the
lead-up to the 1967 referendum, campaigning of a distinctive
character, and by a younger generation than those involved
in FCAATSI, was occurring in rural New South Wales. The
Freedom Ride was staged by the Sydney University group
Student Action for Aborigines, a group which included Aboriginal students Charles Perkins and Gary Williams (who were
among the first Aboriginal students in Australia to enrol at
university). The Freedom Ride took its direct cue from similar
campaigns against segregation in the USA and was supported
by white university students (Curthoys, 2002; Read, 1990a;
Burgmann, 2003b: 56).

Perkins emerged as leader of the group.[6] It was between the
first and second towns on the Freedom Ride that 'Perkins, who

---

6. Gary Williams 'did not feel comfortable protesting on other Aboriginal people's
land without their active involvement in the planning of the protest' (Howell, 2012,
citing Curthoys).

had not been particularly noticeable at University, took on a steadily more prominent role' notes Read:

> His personality, experience, age and Aboriginal contacts put him at the head, but there was something more. As the only Aboriginal student, Perkins had to be leader. Without him the students were fighting somebody else's cause. With Perkins at the head the students were transformed, as if symbolically, to a unity greater than the parts. It had become an Aboriginal struggle, with the White students now the troops in support of a leader and a cause. (Read, 1990a: 103)

Read further observes that 'Only the students seemed to have no problem with Black leadership, but by 1968 SAFA itself was dead' (there is no apparent causal connection between these two observations) (Read, 1990a: 123). The observation that students were comfortable with Aboriginal leadership is noteworthy, given the conflict developing within FCAATSI at a similar time. Further, ANU students played a significant role in non-Indigenous community support of the Aboriginal Embassy during 1972, and were again observed to be both comfortable with deferring to Aboriginal leadership and actually helpful (Robinson, 1994; Foley, 2012).

The contested history of non-Indigenous feminist solidarity

The history of non-Indigenous women's interactions and relationships with Indigenous people and non-Indigenous feminists' political connections with Indigenous women in Australia is already the subject of a significant literature. Non-Indigenous women organizing on 'maternalist' and other issues in the interwar period, and as women's liberationists in the 1970s, have engaged with Indigenous women's interests with varying degrees of knowledge, interaction and comprehension.[7] Germaine Greer is one of the women's liberationists who can be identified as productively engaged with the politics of the Black Power movement in the early 1970s, as demonstrated by her volunteering on the Redfern Black Power breakfast for kids programme and in her writings of that period (Greer, 1972; Foley, 2012). Aileen Moreton-Robinson's important book *Talkin' up to the White Woman: Aboriginal Women and Feminism* (2000) demonstrates white women's complicity in the oppression of Indigenous peoples in Australia, sets out the distinct and at times opposing political agendas of Indigenous and white women, and critiques the operation of whiteness in the middle-class women's movement. Future research focused on the relationship between Indigenous and non-Indigenous women engaged in lesbian politics might reveal important nuances to these debates.

Some activists have attempted to reckon with challenges to feminist groups made by Indigenous women. Political scientist Barbara Sullivan gives an account of one attempt to respond to such challenges. Her account itself includes an engagement with notions of a self-conscious political genealogy for non-Indigenous solidarity with Indigenous struggles in Australia. Sullivan identifies 'the debate about Indigenous land rights that occurred in 1997–1998' as one of the 'top-priority issues in Australia during the 1990s' (Sullivan, 2007: 39). This debate occurred 'in the wake of the Australian High Court decision in the case of *Wik*' (handed down in December 1996) (Sullivan, 2007: 39), which itself followed the important 1992 *Mabo* case

---

7. See Burgmann, 2003b; Cavadini et al., 1972; Foley, 1998; Lake, 1999; Paisley, 2000.

and subsequent highly contested Native Title Act 1993 (Sullivan, 2007: 41–2). In July 1998 the Liberal–National coalition government headed by then-prime minister John Howard passed a cluster of amendments (known as the 'Ten Point Plan') to the Native Title Act 1993 in response to the *Wik* decision (Sullivan, 2007: 42).

Sullivan finds that although feminists engaged in the *Wik* debate, and while they were not particularly influential, they did not attempt to 'gender' the issues at stake (i.e. to draw out the impact of the government's policy on Indigenous *women*). The primary reason for this is that it was clear the 'rights of all Indigenous people were under threat and … it would have been an inappropriate feminist strategy to "gender" the *Wik* debate' (Sullivan, 2007: 50). Women for Wik, formed from within ANTaR in 1997, and described as a partnership between Indigenous and non-Indigenous women, 'mobilized support for Indigenous rights *by* women (but *for* Indigenous men and women)' (Sullivan, 2007: 54–5). According to Sullivan this strategy 'represents the fruit of a long-standing debate between white feminists and Indigenous women in Australia', in which Indigenous women have fought to get white women to understand their struggles and analyses, and challenged 'the unwillingness of white women and feminists to come to terms with the inheritance of racism and the oppression and exploitation of black men' (Sullivan, 2007: 55).

The contest over white and/or middle-class feminist efforts to engage with Indigenous women continues. Yet developments like that outlined by Sullivan demonstrate the potential for partnerships between Indigenous and non-Indigenous women that address issues central to the contest. This underscores the importance of engaging with the historical background or genealogy of related efforts today.

'White support groups' affiliated with the Council on Aboriginal Reconciliation and ANTaR

In the 1990s, many community groups were established throughout Australia with an explicit focus on supporting reconciliation and native title in what has been described as a 'boom' in white support groups (Foley, 2000). The government-appointed Council on Aboriginal Reconciliation (1990–2000) had been encouraging non-Indigenous people to form community reconciliation and self-education circles since 1990. However, the timing of the greatest upsurge of white support groups in the *late* 1990s was the manifestation of 'a backlash against the backlash' (Burgmann, 2003b: 91). Activist-turned-historian Verity Burgmann says the 'extraordinary upsurge of grassroots mobilization in support of reconciliation only really started in response to the Howard government's obvious hostility' (Burgmann, 2003b: 85) to reconciliation, the apology to the stolen generations, and native title. Evidence for this is that following Howard's infamous performance at the May 1997 Melbourne Reconciliation Convention (Barta, 2008) (at which he was judged to have 'hectored' the audience, many of whom turned their backs on him), the number of reconciliation groups jumped from 20 to 'more than 260' (Burgmann, 2003b: 91). The number of groups continued to rise, so that by 2002 there were at least '396 local reconciliation groups dispersed around the country' (Burgmann, 2003b: 95).

The boom in white support for reconciliation – of which the 'bridge walks' of the year 2000 are often invoked as the high water mark – has been greeted with both pleasure at its extent, and criticism at its lack of efficacy in bringing about substantive changes to Indigenous–state relations. Further, Yorta Yorta man bryan Andy[8] has questioned whether the huge crowds of non-Indigenous people were inspired by a sense that the issue was trendy, rather than by a genuine, deep-seated commitment (bryan Andy, interview; see also Gooder and Jacobs, 2000). The organization Defenders of Native Title (DONT), and its successor ANTaR, a national network of local groups, have been criticized for their focus on supporting native title, the weakness of which as a form of land tenure is a far cry from freehold land rights, which have been the persistent Aboriginal demand. Despite these critiques, the willingness of non-Indigenous people to sign up in large numbers was also regarded as proof of a reservoir of goodwill held by non-Indigenous people towards Indigenous people. The phenomenon of a 'backlash against the backlash', which Burgmann deployed to explain the boom in white support groups in the late 1990s, probably applies in reverse in the wake of the apology delivered by prime minister Kevin Rudd on behalf of the Australian Parliament in 2008. The government at that moment appeared less hostile to Aboriginal peoples, and – anecdotally – community action in support of Aboriginal struggles lost urgency.

Greenies' close but contested relationship with Indigenous struggles

Indigenous people and communities have worked closely with certain actors within the environmental movement on specific land-related campaigns. Issues involved have included logging,

---

8. bryan Andy prefers to spell his name lower case (interview).

the nuclear industry and mining. According to Verity Burgmann, 'environmental and indigenous movements have a closer
relationship than most other social movements'; the campaign
against the Jabiluka uranium mine is 'an example of [that] fact'
(Burgmann, 2003a: 15). Pickerill (2009) and political scientist
Karl-Erik Paasonen (2007) nuance this picture by drawing out
some of the kinds of conflicts that have characterized coalitions
between environmentalists and Aboriginal people.[9] In their
campaign against the Jabiluka uranium mine the Mirrar people
gained the support of major environmental organizations and
networks (Burgmann, 2003b). However, sources of support
were not limited to environmentalists. The Mirrar people were
successful in gaining support in the form of a national network
of Jabiluka Action Groups which had many members who did
not identify primarily as environmentalists, and from many
pre-existing groups including churches, unions, minor political
parties and anarchists (Burgmann, 2003b: 185, 187). Importantly,
non-Mirrar Aboriginal people, including Jacqui Katona (executive officer of Mirrar's Gundjehmi Aboriginal Corporation),
Christine Christopherson, Gary Foley and Michael Anderson,
supported the Mirrar campaign (Burgmann, 2003b: 186, 187;
Paasonen, 2007). Gaining and maintaining the support of other
Aboriginal landowners in the Kakadu area was an important
feature of Mirrar strategy and proved integral to the success
of the Mirrar campaign (Paasonen, 2007).

---

9. In Pickerill, an example is the attitude of some environmentalists towards 'nature'
as wilderness unaltered by human agents, which clashes with Indigenous understandings
(Pickerill, 2009). In Paasonen's analysis of the Jabiluka campaign, it was key to understand
the Mirrar people as operating from a 'situation of crisis' as distinct from non-Mirrar
supporters, who operated from a 'situation of affluence'. These contrasting situations
produced divergent collective identities and logics of action (Paasonen, 2007).

Friends of the Earth (FoE) is unique among the major environmental organizations in Australia in that it has an explicitly pro-sovereignty policy and a relatively long-held focus on Indigenous land and rights (Cam Walker, interview). FoE activists formed an Indigenous Solidarity Group in 1996 and went on to organize two significant gatherings in Melbourne in March 1997 and December 1998 (Amis, n.d.). A large delegation of Ngarrindjeri women attended the 1997 gathering to raise issues relating to the Hindmarsh Bridge dispute, and in 1998 a large delegation of senior Aboriginal women from Coober Pedy, the Kupa Piti Kungka Tjuta (KPKT), attended to garner support for their campaign against the national radioactive waste repository in northern South Australia (Amis, n.d.). The KPKT issued a 'call-out to greenies' to assist in their campaign (Crombie et al., 1998). Some members of environmental activist networks have encouraged other activists to recognize that they live and campaign on 'sovereign Aboriginal lands', and that 'environment related campaigns *always* enjoy increased power (legally and politically) when in partnership with Aboriginal People' (emphasis in the original). It is perhaps 'ferals', unkempt-looking but highly committed members of the broader environmental movement, who have shown the capacity to appreciate with most clarity the agendas of Aboriginal sovereignty campaigners (Robbie Thorpe, interview). In Caleb Williams's view, this 'protester category' (ferals) comprises a 'numerically small, but knowledgeable and highly mobile group of activists', many of whom are committed to protest activity and 'an anarchist/alternative culture/deep ecology lifestyle' that resists the logic of the conventional world of full-time work (C. Williams, 1998: 8).

Developing areas of support

Indigenous activists in Australia and overseas have found some commonalities with the values and politics of the anti-corporate globalization movement and anarchist groups. Indigenous engagement, alliances and/or common cause with others engaged in these political communities or philosophies have grown in importance in the early years of the twenty-first century. The Carnival Against Capital protests in Seattle, which disrupted the 1999 meeting of the World Trade Organization, marked the beginning of a series of similar such confrontations. The inauguration of the World Social Forum in 2001 in Brazil as a counter-gathering to the WTO demonstrates this convergence of interests on the global stage. Anarchist modes of organizing have featured in some of the biggest mobilizations yet this century, in particular the anti-corporate globalization movement (Sheehan, 2003), in which Indigenous struggles have been firmly represented, and even the Arab Spring (Lasky, 2011). While there is an apparent clash between the anarchist politics of 'no rulers' and the Aboriginal assertion of sovereignty, there is a match in terms of a common politics of small, self-organized, local community structures and action. That said, if in Aboriginal sovereignty the law is of the land, not of a ruler, there is no clash. Further, there is a values match in the do-it-yourself ethic of anarchism and the history of successful self-help action by Aboriginal people. The value of independence from government and white control – which are synonymous in Australia – seems shared. This philosophical overlap between some sovereign Aboriginal voices in favour of what Robbie Thorpe has referred to as the 'sovereign initiative' and anarchists who reject the 'politics of demand' (Barker, 2010) could lead to positive, proactive action on local Aboriginal agendas and struggles if alliances develop. Mohawk scholar Taiaiake Alfred – who promotes Anarcho-Indigenism – contributed to theorizing in this area in his 2005 work *Wasase: Indigenous Pathways of Action and Freedom* (Lasky, 2011). It is worth exploring the philosophical tensions between anti-colonial anarchism and decolonization, so that some of the complicities in relation to land, power and privilege that can be enabled by anarchist perspectives can be brought into view, and deeper solidarities developed (Awakening the Horse People, 2014).

Indigenous people have mounted critiques of economic neo-colonialism with and through decentralized networks comprised by anarchist groups, pacifists, farmers, trade unionists, environmentalists and others. First World anti-corporate globalization activists have both found inspiration in the possibility of alliances with Indigenous activists and, in the context of increasing concern about climate change, started to regard the struggles of Indigenous peoples as important for the future of all people (Sheehan, 2003; Venkateswar and Hughes, 2011). Importantly, Indigenous struggles are located slightly differently in this developing context: not so much as struggles that other groups can be seen as supporting, but as something closer to a touchstone for other groups. An example of this is the Idle No More movement, in which a grassroots movement of Indigenous and non-Indigenous women mobilized thousands of Canadians. Idle No More was sparked in 2012 by urgent concerns about parliamentary bills that would erode Indigenous sovereignty and environmental protections in order to facilitate tar sands developments and associated oil pipelines (Wallace, 2013). To support Indigenous treaty and constitutional rights was to support Indigenous peoples' ability to protect land and water on behalf of all.

Indigenous struggles in settler nations of course date from the time of territorial invasion, specifically from the moments it became apparent that invaders were there to stay and intended to gain exclusive access to land. The forms that Indigenous people have adopted for these struggles and their accompanying rhetoric are politically and historically specific, reflecting both the limits imposed by the dominant culture in particular times and places, and the agency of Indigenous people in pushing those limits to the greatest extent possible. This agency can be seen in the tactics of the Aboriginal Embassy activists, who read the political landscape, revised the strategies of the older generation, refused to negotiate on the terms of the dominant culture, and achieved substantial policy changes through protests of unorthodox style and form (Foley, 2012: 208). Maori academic Hine Waitere discerns a further development, one demonstrated by a greater centring of and reference to Aboriginal cultural values within the movement: a shift by Indigenous people from talking on behalf of oneself 'through the frameworks of our dominant counterparts' to talking about oneself while 'in-oneself' (Venkateswar and Hughes, 2011). This has probably always been desirable but is now more politically feasible due to Indigenous peoples' successes in gaining recognition and in shifting colonial consciousness.

Uneasy alliances

The discussion so far has treated as self-evident the proposition that Indigenous people desire political support from non-Indigenous people. In general, Indigenous people outnumbered in settler-colonial nation-states have worked hard to nurture their support bases, believing the realization of their political aspirations rely on the ability to win significant non-Indigenous support (Burgmann, 2003b; Simpson, 2010: xiii). Yet the question of how much to prioritize the project of engaging with and educating non-Indigenous people continues to be a subject of debate for Indigenous people. Yorta Yorta woman Monica Morgan has deliberated over how to balance working with her own community and politically educating Indigenous young people, on the one hand, and, on the other, working with non-Indigenous allies, in the hope that change can be effected that way (Monica Morgan, interview). In a related reflection, Robbie Thorpe mentioned that he sees two projects as crucial: educating Aboriginal people and educating non-Aboriginal people – it's hard to know who has been more deprived of education! Many Indigenous people have stated that they regard it as crucial to somehow gain political support from non-Indigenous people in Australia (Gary Murray, interview; Wayne Atkinson, interview; Targan, interview). This supports Foley's view that a key role for non-Indigenous people seeking to be politically supportive of Indigenous people is to educate themselves and other non-Indigenous people, to lessen the demands on Indigenous people to do this educating.

Despite suggestions that Black Power advocates were driven by separatism, groups such as the NTC – established by the Aboriginal leaders who supported the Aboriginalization of FCAATSI – in fact always called upon non-Indigenous people to support them as allies, adding 'not as masters' (National Tribal Council, 1999). The loved and respected community member and leader Bruce McGuinness (who served as president of VAAL and director of VAHS) expressed what Burgmann reads as a 'compromise position' on separatism (where separatism was associated with US Black Power politics). According to McGuinness, 'if a non-Aborigine wants to devote hours of his leisure time to help and give technical advice to us then we must not turn our backs on them ... Let us, the Aborigine, assist the non-Aborigine to aid us...' (Burgmann, 2003a: 11). Burgmann finds that 'White help, it was felt, could be received, but on Indigenous terms' (Burgmann, 2003a: 11). Black Power activists pursued those they thought could assist them, such as lawyers and doctors: people with skills as well as institutional status who were in a position to assist them to realize their self-help projects (Foley, 2012; Hemingway, 2012: 82).

Despite these policies and statements, commentary on the impact of Black Power in the 1970s suggests that the 'Black Power mood disturbed many of the white supporters of Aboriginal causes' (Burgmann, 2003b: 57). Perhaps reactions to this disturbing 'mood' have clouded understandings of why Aboriginal control of the movement was seen as necessary. It was not just the principle of Aboriginal control that was at stake in contests with feminists, with DONT and within FCAATSI. Rather, to institutionalize Aboriginal control seemed the only way to ensure that the efforts of non-Indigenous members of, or supporters of, the movement were directed to Indigenous priorities: economic injustice, land rights and racism.

THREE

Identity categories: how activists both use and refuse them

When non-Indigenous people and Indigenous people come together in pro-Indigenous, pro-land rights political spaces they are establishing a relationship based on a critique of colonialism. This is a setting in which individuals' social locatedness in relation to colonialism is salient: for instance, Indigeneity matters in terms of who has a claim to restitution based on the theft of land. Therefore it makes sense to talk in terms of categories such as colonizers and the colonized, Indigenous and non-Indigenous, dispossessed and beneficiary. It also makes sense in these settings to be attentive to how structural categories are so often emulated in the way people interact and to use strategies to avert this: this is where talking in terms such as 'Kooris' and 'supporters' functions to suggest how political direction and strategy should be decided and what roles are available.

Yet one of the most powerful expressions of a colonial mindset is to establish and police a sharp divide between 'Indigenous' and 'non-Indigenous' (Gandhi, 2006). Indeed, Alma and Robbie Thorpe questioned the way I framed my questions along the lines of Indigenous versus non-Indigenous (interviews). It is not only that the idea of a discrete binary with total purity on each side is both ridiculous and impossible; the Indigenous–non-Indigenous distinction and the treatment meted out in accordance with that distinction is one of the most pernicious manifestations of colonialism (Gandhi, 2006: 2). To routinely think in and uncritically invoke these terms is to be beholden to colonialist logic.

The identity categories that are used to mount a critique of colonialism's unjust consequences can play back into its hands on the level of discourse (Foley, 1997b; Gandhi, 2006; Hoskins, 2012). People engaged in decolonizing and pro-land rights politics negotiate this dilemma by at times using and at times refusing these categories. Further, Indigenous theorists working in the academy, the community or both have offered crucial innovations against this dichotomy.

A number of ideas and writings are informative for people new to or grappling with this dilemma. I combine critical theory with the scholarship and insight of Indigenous theorists and community practitioners in presenting a new framework for identity and relationships to inform those interested in de-colonizing solidarity.[1] This framework builds on the contribu-tion of postcolonial criticism, which revealed how the 'imperial binarism' that insisted on a distinction between Indigenous and non-Indigenous cannot be sustained (Gandhi, 2006: 2–4). This was proven by historical research which highlighted, for example, the many instances of interaction and intimacy between the two sides and the internal diversity within each (see Bhabha, 2004). Such an approach has also been taken

---

1. Critical and Indigenous theories have some theoretical commitments in common, and others in conflict. American Indian scholar Sandy Grande brings to bear a sovereign stance on critical theory, enabling a concise critique of the dominant theoretical commit-ments of the 'Left'. The major points of tension she identifies with revolutionary critical theory are its failure to address Indigenous sovereignty and the complexity of Indigenous subjectivity; and its anthropocentric relationship to land. However, she is constructive, always looking towards eventual solidarities (Grande, 2008: 238).

up by critical anthropologists (Lea et al., 2006). Within that discipline an ascendant focus on 'relationality' – in particular the recognition that Indigenous people's lives are shaped by interaction and change – has challenged approaches which regarded these lives as if lived in a separable realm.[2]

I highlight new forms of relationality which go beyond a critique and dissolution of the 'us' and 'them' identity thought of imperialist culture on that culture's own terms. Critique and dissolution of identity thought have led many scholars towards the notion of hybridity. There are better destinations to end up at than that in thinking through this issue.

Undoing the ideological work of colonialism

Newly involved non-Indigenous people who are relatively privileged[3] will either be asked, or will find it profoundly important, to come to terms with a number of propositions. Some of these are more possible to understand and reckon with early on and some more so as time goes by. Middle-class or white non-Indigenous people often need to go through a process of

- coming both to see and to deeply know our/their social location and its implications. The implications are multiple: psychological (both conscious and subconscious), material, structural and legal (Bailey, 1998; Harris, 1993; Pallotta-Chiarolli and Pease, 2013);

---

2. Moreton-Robinson (2006: 219) observed that Australian anthropologists' struggles to make sense of non-remote native title claims accelerated this shift (see also Hinkson and Smith, 2005).

3. Privilege is relative: 'To different degrees every colonizer is privileged, at least comparatively so, ultimately to the detriment of the colonized', and 'this can be read by the relation of each group's concrete economic and psychological position within the colonial society' (Memmi, 1965: 77, 79). There are multiple forms of privilege: raced, gendered, classed, embodied, Western and heterosexual (Pease, 2010b).

- coming to see that how we see ourselves and whose interests we share has been constructed and inherited (Roediger, 1999);[4]
- coming to see how the idea of racial difference has been created and made real – as reflected in harsh lived realities.

To come to terms with these propositions is to gain insight into the strategic and psychological dilemmas that colonization has created for those challenging it. One part of the challenge for white people is to see ourselves/themselves both as individuals of conscience and as members of a group with unearned privileges and a history of colonialism with which to reckon (Kendall, 2006). From there, the variety of ways to approach, manage and resist internalized colonialist views of difference and identity come into view.

To critique, resist and respond to socially constructed racialized realities on decolonizing terms involves re-centring and listening for Indigenous cultural resources and knowledge as they are deployed by Indigenous people engaged in this politics (Hoskins, 2012; Moses, 2010; see also Bradley and Seton, 2005). It is a process of pulling a way of being 'out of the grip' of colonizing modes (Povinelli, 2006).

I have suggested that people with relative privilege are more likely than others to need to come to terms with the notions about race outlined above. This is because it is more difficult to notice that race matters and recognize that it confers privilege to white people when one is white and relatively privileged than it is when one stands outside privilege. Those who are

---

4. And, further, in the case of whiteness, over time converted into a form of property (Harris, 1993).

located outside privilege and feel the effects of its exclusions are better placed to have a clearer view of its workings (Bailey, 1998; Collins, 2004). Coming to terms with privilege and finding an alternative way to be and act therefore involve learning from the knowledge generated by people outside of it: the critical social theories generated by emancipatory movements (Bailey, 1998: 36). The study of whites and whiteness was initiated by non-whites.[5] Those who have had to – 'in order to accommodate to or challenge White privilege' – have been keen observers of whiteness (Seidman, 2004: 239).

For white non-Indigenous people in particular, to understand our relation to Indigenous people is to learn from Indigenous critiques of systems of white supremacy and the privilege that accrues to white people. This is intended not as an argument to accept a view of non-Indigenous and white people as homogenous, but as a strategy for bringing unacknowledged white privilege into view and informing strategies for challenging it. As Bailey (1988: 37) suggests, 'An integral moment in understanding my relation to people differently situated from me comes in learning to see how I am seen by outsiders.' This 'relation to people differently situated from me' is vital: to understand one's *relation* to Indigenous people – to work towards greater clarity about one's privilege and one's complicity – is linked to an imperative for action.

To understand one's relation to Indigenous people or any other group is a process of locating oneself in the social relations of domination and oppression. Indeed,

---

5. A genealogy of scholarship in this area would acknowledge non-white critiques such as those by Albert Memmi (1965), Frantz Fanon (1968) and W.E.B. Du Bois (see Lake, 2007), as well as the feminist tradition (Seidman, 2004: 239). Ruth Frankenberg produced one of the first books to interrogate whiteness from within (1993).

Most people live their lives with access to privilege in some areas, while being subordinate in others. Thus we are never just a man or a woman or a black person or a white person. We all experience these intersections in ourselves. (Pease, 2010b: 23)

The study of how gendered oppression intersects with race was initiated by African-American feminists, Third World scholars and Indigenous women. Such theorizing has pointed out how middle-class white women's feminism has been inadequate for addressing the complexity of the impact of class and race on women's (and men's) lives (Moreton-Robinson, 2000; Pease, 2010b).

The idea of a matrix of social relations in which domination and subordination intersect enables people to locate themselves in terms of both privilege and oppression in one or more dimensions. It also enables people to acknowledge complicity with other dimensions of domination and subordination (Pease, 2010b: 23). Yet the interplay of oppression and privilege for people privileged in some dimensions and oppressed in others is not simple or able to be determined mathematically: 'this places the onus to change on those with access to multiple levels of privilege' (Pease, 2010b: 23). Crucially, people with access to multiple levels of privilege can also use their privilege in order to contribute to social change (see also Keefer, 2007; Pease, 2010b: 24).

It is important to be able to take an intersectional view of privilege and oppression because it is true to lived realities, and because it informs a broad moral and political framework for non-Indigenous people's support for Indigenous struggles. In this view, solidarity with Indigenous struggles is put in the context of working towards meaningful social change 'not just for [Indigenous people], for everybody' (Foley, cited in Land, 2011a: 51). The importance of this is its link to non-Indigenous people not seeing their efforts as being about helping Aboriginal people (which produces many annoying dynamics and problematic behaviours) but rather seeing their/our interests served in solidarity work, to the extent that to change the system that oppresses Indigenous people is to change the system that also oppresses some non-Indigenous people in one dimension or more. That said, it is crucial to be attentive to and to challenge the tendency of white people to appropriate the position of victim in order to avoid confronting complicity with colonial and racial oppression. The challenge is 'to "own" whiteness without "masking" that privilege through ressentiment (weakness) supplied by other subject positions' (e.g. 'woman', queer, working class) (Probyn, 2004: para. 22).

The lives of supporters of Indigenous struggles in southeastern Australia are shaped along many dimensions of oppression and privilege, such as the workings of Indigeneity when it is displaced to another setting; sexuality, gendered lives and women's only space; embodied privilege; male privilege; age; and educational background. The way that differences cut across each other – sometimes aligning to multiply privilege, and at other times contradicting each other – is apparent. In addition, these dimensions are complicated through place, colonialism and culture, such that aspects of identity are valued differently in (and among) some Aboriginal social worlds from how they are valued in dominant culture. Intersectionality is even more complex, contingent and shifting when its workings within and between distinct social worlds are brought into view.

Using binary identity categories

To use the words 'Indigenous' and 'non-Indigenous' is far from neutral. For instance, to use them can reproduce stereotypes, do regressive discursive work, and create certain traps. The Indigenous/non-Indigneous binary imposed by colonialism has rightly been harshly critiqued by many scholars who have identified the inbuilt ideas of superiority and inferiority in such ways of thinking (Collins, 2004).

Some scholars have also harshly criticized the way (Indigenous) anti-colonial nationalists have invoked the binary in their own service: '"Identity" thought, the idea that there is an "us" and a "them"', has been 'the hallmark of imperial cultures *and* those cultures trying to resist' (Gandhi, 2006: 4, stress added). The narrative of anti-colonial nationalism, or nativism, has inverted and reinstated imperial manicheanism in a kind of 'counter-politics of exclusion' (Bhabha, 2004; Gandhi, 2006: 4).

Like Gandhi in her critique of oppositional cultural nationalism, Foley shows that Aboriginal activists have at times been beholden to hegemonic and colonialist discourses of race and purity, to their own strategic/political detriment. Referring to the 'Koori political upheaval' of the late 1960s and early 1970s, Foley describes the emphasis of some Koori activists on 'bloodlines' as a trap, because it was essentialist, biologically untenable, and embraced 'genetic base notions of race' (Foley, 1997b). To promote Aboriginal cultural identity as 'authentic, homogenous and stable' is necessary in certain political and historical contexts and for claims upon and negotiations with the state that are framed in that way, while at the same time the problems with such simplifications are acknowledged (Hoskins, 2012).

Strategic and political dilemmas for movements based on 'collective identification' and 'identity politics' may include an inherent tension between pride in identity and exclusion of 'outsider' identities (those lacking the 'appropriate identity'), as well as an unproductive 'ranking' of one form of oppression over another (Bystydzienski and Schacht, 2001: 6). Further, while there is strategic advantage in demonstrating that, for example, women as a group are subordinated, there is much diversity within this group. Indeed, most people have more than one social group characteristic. What about internal power dynamics within an identity-based group? What about 'oppressors' who want to change? Must they be rejected from the identity-based group? Who wants to 'join a group wherein one is identified as the enemy'? 'What reasonable group would invite individuals into their ranks who are seen as having the identity of the "other"'? (Bystydzienski and Schacht, 2001: 5). Finally, there is the risk that strategically asserted identity categories (used by people well aware of their drawbacks) become 'glued to firm moral positions – white positions are suspected of exploitation and assimilation, Indigenous positions are assumed true and immune from critical analysis' (Lea et al., 2006: 6; see also Hoskins, 2012).[6]

But how can critics of colonialism talk about the politics and lived realities of colonialism without describing the contrast in treatment that the state has meted out according to these categories?

---

6. In the effort to understand the colonial production of injustice and interrupt its reproduction, it is not productive to apply mechanically a Marxist or structuralist analysis (Hoskins, 2012; Roediger, 1999: 187).

The terms 'Indigenous' and 'non-Indigenous' (which, to my mind, can be twinned with the structural categories 'colonized' and 'colonizer', yet not with the racial categories 'black' and 'white') helpfully foreground the colonial relation of the two groups in Australia. This distinction has clearly been a fundamental structuring principle of the (colony, then the) nation from colonization onwards (Wolfe, 1994; see also Moreton-Robinson, 2003: 37). To document and discuss the way race plays out in people's lives can of course be held in tension with a critical view of the 'mode of thought' from which race categorization springs, and the injustices that attend it (Cowlishaw, 2000). Crucially, the binary I at times invoke aligns with political and historical categories, not racial, biological ones. Whiteness, too, 'is not a biological category but a political one' (Ang, 1995: 69).

It is not possible to sustain an uncritical use of an indigenous/colonizer binary, and it is necessary to clearly identify the advantages and drawbacks of using these terms (Jones and Jenkins, 2008: 475). For instance, the term 'Indigenous' may be deployed by Indigenous peoples as a basis for 'internal collaboration and a politics of strength', despite the colonizing work the term does in 'brushing over national and tribal differences' (Jones and Jenkins, 2008: 475). Further, the binary reflects a material, historical reality (a 'social fact') for many people: to use it keeps in view a socially constructed division that has real consequences for many people (Grande, 2008: 238). What Franz Fanon called 'the fact of blackness' has remained 'spectacularly apparent to Aborigines and others deemed black … When we deny it, we whitefellas deny the history that made us white' (Cowlishaw, 2004: 10).

Clearly there are differences among Indigenous peoples in terms of language, education, histories and cultures, and likewise there are many differences among colonizers. Indigenous cultures have influenced colonizers, and Western cultures and languages have affected Indigenous peoples. Further, colonizer and Indigenous peoples 'often do not understand themselves in these terms', despite invoking them as highly salient in some contexts (Jones and Jenkins, 2008). There is a distinction between the interrelationships in the world of Jones and Jenkins's study (collaborative academic inquiry between an Indigenous and a colonizer academic) and interrelationships 'in the social and personal world' (Jones and Jenkins, 2008: 476). Like Jones and Jenkins I have observed that there is an 'assertion, at some crucial points, of an indigenous political and social id/entity distinct from that of a colonizer subject. For indigenous subjects, this is a necessary distinction and disjuncture; for collaborators, it is a necessary "between"' (Jones and Jenkins, 2008: 476).

In the south-east of Australia it is the case that colonialism imposed an Aboriginal–non-Aboriginal dichotomy; it is in congruence with this divide that glaring injustices have been perpetrated. The people and communities around which this research is formulated are, on the one hand, Aboriginal people who may mount claims for land rights, sovereignty and Aboriginal control of Aboriginal affairs based on their inherent rights stemming from prior occupation of this land, as well as their collective marginalization, morbidity and mortality compared to the population of Australia as a whole.[7] On the

---

7. Bradley and Seton (2005: 38–9) describe the return, embrace and acculturation of members of the Stolen Generation (Aboriginal children separated from their families) by the Yanyuwa people and how this was managed by them in relation to a land claim.

other hand, there are non-Aboriginal people who support these claims yet would not gain materially from their realization (Gandhi, 2006).

The question of where non-white non-Indigenous people fit into this structuring and this dichotomy is the subject of some discussion. As background to that discussion, the history of restricted immigration to Australia and the persistent numerical predominance of people of Anglo-Celtic origin in the population is one factor which sustains a focus on 'white' non-Indigenous people as particularly responsible for dispossession. On the one hand, if the maintenance/invoking of the structural binary is read as 'excluding' non-white non-Indigenous people, it functions to support a white nationalist move to centre white people as the ones who are related to and as the ones who manage 'multicultural' elements (Ang, 1995; Hage, 1998). It also attempts to head off the possibility of relationships, conversations and solidarities between Indigenous people and non-white non-Indigenous people. Ang's discussion of how Australian feminism is implicated in a 'white settler subjectivity' in which '"white" is the constitutive centre' includes the observation that 'white Australia constitutes and asserts itself by demarcating itself from the immigrant on the one hand and the indigene on the other by racialising and/or ethnicising both, naturalising its own claim to nativeness in the process' (Ang, 1995: 70–71). On the other hand, the 'inclusive' position – that anyone who is non-Indigenous is a colonizer, as Moreton-Robinson argues (2003) – functions politically to invite an interrogation of non-white complicity with colonization (although equally it could be seen as conscription into white possessiveness; see Nicoll, 2008). Like the 'firm view' that Tom Clark and Ravi de Costa take in the Canadian context, I accept the need for 'all newcomers' to understand that Australia is 'built on the territories of existing communities' without their consent, and also 'that the original expropriation must always mark our response' (Clark and de Costa, 2011: 330). Anti-racism struggles conducted by non-Indigenous people of colour in settler nations are asked to begin with and reflect on those nations' originary genocide, and to act as allies to Aboriginal activism against settler domination (Amadahy and Lawrence, 2009; Lawrence and Dua, 2005).

An *uncritical* use of a binary distinction between Indigenous/ non-Indigenous and colonized/colonizer is unsustainable. I maintain that it is necessary to invoke them and that when I invoke them it is as political, structural categories, not 'natural', 'racial' ones. I also maintain that such a framework is appropriate for my study, which focuses on a political practice and space in which structural categories are less important in locating people than the way colonized and colonizer interests are identified and served.

Borderlands and hybridity

Scholars who argue against invoking the Indigenous/non-Indigenous binary and who foreground instances of its failure will often instead promote hybridity (Paradies, 2006). Postcolonial theorist Homi Bhabha demonstrated the 'epistemic and existential impossibility of colonial division' through his address of the 'tropes of "hybridity," "interstitiality," "mimicry" and the "in-between"' (Bhabha, 2004; Gandhi, 2006: 3). However, Gandhi finds 'postcolonial orthodoxy' susceptible to a 'subtle determinism' in that it relies (in a 'concealed rhetoric') on a perceived inevitable dissolution of the colonial division over time: 'a matter of temporal unfolding, an evolutionary effect of the laws of biological mutation' (Gandhi, 2006: 5). There is an implication that 'the existence of hybrid spaces would provide the hope that these spaces would increase in size and significance until the awkwardness of difference disappeared' (Cowlishaw, 2000: 113). The problem with this way out of the problematic colonial division is that it is Indigenous and colonized people who are expected to do 'all the hybridizing' (Hoskins, 2012: 87).

This is where American Indian scholar Sandy Grande locates a key point of tension with some postcolonial and revolutionary scholars. Linked to Gandhi's critique of susceptibility to 'subtle determinism' of 'postcolonial orthodoxy' is Grande's critique of the seminal work of Gloria Anzaldúa on *mestizaje* subjectivity. Grande notes that revolutionary scholars, rejecting the postmodern take on identity, now advocate the postcolonial notion of *mestizaje*. However, Grande finds 'the transgressive *mestizaje* functions as a potentially homogenizing force that presumes the continued exile of tribal peoples and their enduring absorption into the American "democratic" Whitestream' (Grande, 2008: 240).

The theoretical debate over hybridity is inseparable from political concerns (Moses, 2010). As such, non-white groups have been reluctant to let go of identity categories as central organizing principles. For historian of twentieth-century and settler-colonial genocides A. Dirk Moses, this is particularly understandable in Australia, where Indigenous people are currently a minority of the population overall, and in most geographic areas. The political/strategic danger associated with discussion of hybridity comes, if we follow Gandhi, from the way hybridity is postulated as inevitable. For one thing, this view forecloses agency by Aboriginal people, because hybridity is happening/will happen on someone else's terms. Also, a deterministic view regarding the increase of hybrid subjectivities (seen as coupled to biological hybridity, and the complexity of social worlds) is attended, politically, by the threat that the legitimacy of claims for measures of justice (redistribution of land and/or political power) on the basis of rights inherent to Indigenous people exclusively will be diminished.[8] Further, demands that Indigenous people embrace a hybridist approach to identity appear as a double standard, given that 'white' people don't have to. Hybridity in white people is not demonized in the same way as it is in Indigenous people in colonialist discourse. Riding on this, Robbie Thorpe said to me: 'God knows what you've got in you!' (interview).

Gandhi's complaint regarding postcolonial orthodoxy is not devoted so much to engaging with its 'elision of agency', as to 'its relative neglect of, or [lack of interest] in, anticolonial actors, especially such as might have performed their political vocation impatiently from within imperial culture, unwilling to wait for its eventual hybridization, actively renouncing, refusing, and rejecting categorically its aggressive manicheanism' (Gandhi, 2006: 5). Supporters of Indigenous struggles in settler nations are likewise anti-colonial actors; focusing on how

---

8. The distinction between land rights and native title is relevant here: land rights (including compensation for unreturnable land) are based on redistributive justice according to the need for land, and that right is therefore held by people who are members of a category defined structurally/materially; whereas native title is based on bloodline entitlement and survival of certain markers of 'tradition'. Note that this links to Foley's 1997 discussion.

identity categories are used, refused and innovated against in such scenes brings helpful frameworks into view.

Refusing and innovating against available categories

The choice between the two approaches already introduced – either habitually invoking the binary towards anti-colonialist ends or relying on the postmodernist hybridity approach to identity – is unsatisfactory. Those 'unsatisfactory theoretical choices' led Gandhi to search out people similarly situated to those in my study, and are grounded in stories of 'crosscultural collaboration between oppressors and oppressed' (Gandhi, 2006: 6). Gandhi focuses on British critics of Britain's own empire, calling these people the ones who 'stood with'. That is, the 'internal' (British, non-Indigenous) critics of empire who stood with the 'external' (Indigenous, e.g. Indian) critics. In seeking out people so located because of theoretical interests, Gandhi's work is informative for a decolonized theoretical framework for solidarity.

Gandhi notes that, despite the important political work of postcolonial scholars who critique 'identity' thought, a relative neglect of those who 'stood with' – such as the metropolitan anti-imperialists of nineteenth-century London she consequently decided to study – has meant that a key politics has also gone relatively unnoticed by theoreticians. That is, the very 'struggle for independence' is a site for the breaking down of the binary at stake in this discussion (Bhabha, 2004: 278). The collaboration between Indigenous critics of empire and the ones who stood or stand with them blur the colonizer–colonized boundary through their practices. When members of the colonizing culture act to further the interests of the colonized while standing to gain no material advantage from this themselves, their relationship to their structural location changes (as class location is read from the class interests that are served). Essentially that relationship changes from one of loyalty to one of treason; for Gandhi (2006: 2), 'betrayal', 'departure', 'flight', 'treason'. This transformation can also be understood through the notion of identifying and resisting or reducing complicity.

Grande, too, finds something interesting in the activist work of Indigenous and non-Indigenous scholars: the space that is theorized and called into being by red pedagogy. To explain: red pedagogy is 'a space of engagement. It is the liminal and intellectual borderlands where indigenous and non-indigenous scholars encounter one another, working to remember, redefine, and reverse the devastation of the original colonialist "encounter"' (Grande, 2008: 234).

The scene I have studied is usefully understood not so much as borderlands (in which two spaces mix or meet) but as a new/different space which departs from the binary (Gandhi, 2006; Grande, 2008; Povinelli, 2006). According to Moses (2010: 19) it is brought into being by Indigenous innovation: the application of 'fundamental principles' of local 'traditional knowledge' to the colonizing situation. That is, in the face of the colonial encounter, Indigenous people did and still do the work of accommodating new people.

Ways of managing difference:
Indigenous innovations in the encounter

Colonization created and then policed difference in its own interests. Concurrently, from the first colonial encounters through to attempts to address the mess created by colonization, Indigenous peoples have used various strategies to respond to and manage the presence of outsiders – drawing, of course, on Indigenous culture and values to do so (Bradley and Seton, 2005; Martin, 2008).

It is instructive to note the contrasting ways in which colonialist and Indigenous cultures have read and managed difference, assimilation and acculturation. In the south-east of Australia, colonialist approaches at first demonized and later forcibly promoted the biological intermingling of Aboriginal and colonial peoples. This latter policy, known as assimilation, was aimed at eradicating Aboriginal people as peoples. Under both approaches, people deemed 'half-caste' were singled out by colonial authorities for specific forms of bureaucratic and genocidal attention (see Land, 2006). It is instructive to see how elsewhere 'hybridity' is at times talked of in terms unfamiliar in an Australian context. A formulation like 'transcendent and harmonizing persons who are of blended ancestry' (Raweno:kwas, 2010: 38) reminds us that the framing of 'hybrid' as pejorative is grounded in specific ways on account of the particular Australian historical context. Further, it should be recognized that Indigenous people have at times found ways to manage relationships with outsiders through the expression of cultural ethics, diplomacy and political agency (Hoskins, 2012; Povinelli, 2006; Santos-Granero, 2007).

A study of legal decisions in North America reveals how dominant settler-culture attitudes towards group identity and hybridity can be deployed flexibly in order to consistently favour white interests (Harris, 1993). In the particular case of the Mashpee people of Massachusetts (north-eastern USA):

> The Mashpee absorbed and managed, rather than rejected
> and suppressed, outsiders; yet the court erased their identity,
> assuming that, by virtue of intermingling with other races, the
> Mashpee's identity as a people had been subsumed. (Harris, 1993:
> 1765)

In the face of the colonial encounter, Indigenous people continue to innovate in approaches to containing and/or accommodating incursive people. Further, to borrow a comment on contemporary globalization, 'Both physical and mediated contacts between representatives from all parts of the globe have increased, with the result that new etiquettes for mutual interaction are being devised all the time' (Bell and Coleman, 1999: 5). As Maori scholar and community practitioner Te Kawehau Hoskins has written, Maori cultural ethics, such as emphasizing relations with and responsibility and obligation towards others, notwithstanding what they may have done, have much to offer to the theorizing of political relations (Hoskins, 2012: 85, 90–91). While strategic essentialism along the lines of the oppositional colonized/colonizer binary has been important in opening up the political space in which Maori claims for restitution can be heard and their moral basis established, it does create ethically questionable exclusions: 'A politics informed by Maori cultural ethics glimpses a different, certainly riskier, but ultimately more radical and productive politics' (Hoskins, 2012: 85).

As such, in 2003 Robbie Thorpe, in a reworking of the colonialist re-enactments of the first landing on the beach favoured in dominant-culture celebrations of Australia Day/ Invasion Day, announced to soldiers and convicts on the First Fleet, 'If you are prepared to abide by our law, go through our customs and pay the rent, you're welcome to stay' (goori2,

2011). This suggests 'how whites should have behaved.' As Foley says, it's 'an alternative ... to Australia Day' for those who 'feel that they want to make some sort of amends' (goori2, 2011).

In a move that can be understood as responsive to this politics expressed by Robbie and Foley, Jane Belfrage composed a 'Request for Permission to Live on Country as an Interim Permanent Resident' (see Appendix IV), in which she stated that 'in every sense I have emigrated from colonial white Australia and immigrated into south-east aboriginal Australia. I would like my emigration/immigration to be legitimate and recognisable.' This reflects a personal process of reckoning with a colonizer identity along with the search for a mechanism to recognize Aboriginal sovereignty and to switch allegiance. It could be seen as a way for those located as colonizers to break the 'bonds of solidarity with the perpetrators' of dispossession, our ancestors, and to open up the political space for restitution and reparation of those injustices (Maddison, 2011: 26). This activist-based theorization speaks to the suggestion of political scientist Sarah Maddison that 'The ways in which we identify with our group as white Australians, non-Indigenous Australians or just as Australians' matters for 'our experience of collective guilt' and our capacity to 'take collective responsibility for historical injustice' and 'to seriously develop a restorative, decolonizing response' (Maddison, 2011: 15, 22).

Learning about difference

A structural view of difference and colonial relations is crucial, yet so is a process of complicating this view. This is about making sense of lived experience and developing a practice for operating within a world in which the mechanical application of this view does not suffice. According to Helen, a keen and reflective observer of her own and other non-Indigenous people's interactions with Indigenous people,

> Aboriginal people I know sometimes complain that white people only want to relate to them as far as their Aboriginality goes ... especially where people meet in ... activist sort of settings, and meetings and conferences and stuff. The Aboriginal person is always related to because of their Aboriginality. Sometimes idolized, sometimes – often even at the same time – copping prejudiced, racist, inappropriate stuff.

Helen's observation suggests that the conditions of the activist setting can produce particular tensions. The idea is that most white people – and, as Helen contends, *particularly* activists – are relating to Aboriginal people on the basis of their Aboriginality.

Members of dominant groups often have problems responding to difference without reifying, appropriating or attempting to erase it. As Sullivan (2006) points out, there are different kinds of difference: easy ones like exotic food and culture are what white people like to appropriate. Contentious ones like social, economic and political differences white people like to deny or control. As an alternative, those positioned as colonizers could focus on 'learning (about difference) *from* the Other, rather than learning about the Other' (Jones and Jenkins, 2008: 471). One of the members of the Melbourne Kungkas reflected on what she learned about difference from the Kupa Piti Kungka Tjuta:

> Belinda: One thing that really happened for me over time, those five years or so, was ... that I came to really revise how I thought about ... the Kungkas and what was different about them to me and my experience. And ... I really remember lots of lessons in them resisting, or just disrupting any attempt to – for us to seek

out the exotic and the culture and all that. The first time [was
when Mrs Smith named a greenie's dog 'Lassie' instead of giving
it a Yankunjatjara name].[9]
  Then and lots of other times – sometimes I thought what
we were encountering was, you know, class difference or ...
a difference in age and you know ... there were lots of things
about them that were different to me, but they weren't
necessarily because they were like traditional senior Aboriginal
women. And that was really instructive.

Here Belinda describes revising earlier thinking about difference; this speaks to the project of learning *about* difference as
Alison Jones and Kuni Jenkins set it out. The questions which
inhere in encountering the 'Other' have, of course, animated
many Western scholars; I find Jones and Jenkins refreshing on
this. As Sullivan notes, there is a well-rehearsed argument that
it is natural for humans to have biases, and, in their encounters
with the strange, to react with antipathy or aversion. Related
to such claims is the suggestion that there is a symmetry
between the way white people see others (as 'strange') and how
others see white people: 'For black people, white people are
not so much unusual or new as they are terrifyingly familiar'
(Sullivan, 2006: 40). This is explained by the non-optional
'world'-travelling forced upon non-white people (Lugones,
1987), resulting in extensive familiarity with the lives and
manners and worlds of white people (Sullivan, 2006: 39–40).
So theories of the encounter with strange others might best
be seen as a white viewpoint, since the strange/unfamiliar
view is perhaps an address to the world by white people who
have not travelled to other worlds (account of Lugones in
Sullivan, 2006). Sullivan cites favourably the suggestion of

---

9. This case is cited in Chapter 5.

early-twentieth-century sociologist W.E.B. Du Bois that 'it is intimacy and familiarity, not foreignness, that tends to produce anger and hostility towards others'; remembering Du Bois's claim that 'black people often have and have had' intimate knowledge of white people (Sullivan, 2006: 40). Sullivan's engagement with the scholarly debate about ways to address difference finds, as Jones and Jenkins have, that 'the idea that increased familiarity is a desirable solution to the "problem" of the disruptive strange' should be questioned (Sullivan, 2006: 41).

Perhaps the sense of 'wonder' in the face of difference that some have argued for (Sullivan, 2006: 39) can take most usefully as its object difference itself: wondering about difference, learning about difference with or from the encounter with the other, not learning about the other per se.

After freedom: brother, sister, friend

Anthropologist and theorist Elizabeth Povinelli, in a discussion of Fanon's essay 'Concerning Violence' (in *The Wretched of the Earth*, 1967) discusses a struggle to 'pull a way of being out of the grip of the Western dialectic of individualism and tribalism, contract and status' (Povinelli, 2006: 231–2). Fanon was considering what a '"genuine eradication" of the colonial order would consist of after a "real struggle for freedom" had taken place' (Povinelli, 2006: 230). This would be to decolonize the social order, to decolonize the discourses that Povinelli reveals as being at work (discourses which, problematically, insert 'European history into an indigenous social imaginary'; Povinelli, 2006: 231). In Fanon's view there would be new vocabularies, new relationalities: namely, 'Brother, sister, friend' (Povinelli, 2006: 230; see also Giibwanisi, 2013). Self-criticism would inhere in this kind of relationality: Fanon will not be mistaken for an 'anthropologist of naive communalism'. Povinelli (2006: 231) notes that the 'hail of a friend is in this assemblage a form of stranger sociality made intimate'. *Made* intimate – note that Indigenous people have made it so. This is a decolonizing move based on the application of those 'fundamental principles' to which Moses refers. Indigenous people have agency in this framework, contrasting with the hybridity approach. As Povinelli says of this work of Fanon and of other theorists and activists, including in Australia:

> They were ... struggling to pull a way of being out of the grip of the Western dialectic of individualism and tribalism, contract and status. They insisted that this dialectic of individual freedom and social determination was Europe's history of itself and its brutal exploitation of the colonial world. (Povinelli, 2006: 231–2)

The theoretical framework for analysing ways of being and relating offered here has come out of holding two frames in tension and being urged to listen for Indigenous agency and innovation. Several Indigenous people I interviewed displayed no discomfort in discussing non-Indigenous ancestry, as well as describing themselves as Aboriginal, and their lives as shaped by racial categories (Alma, Lisa and Robbie Thorpe, Gary Murray, interviews; see also Cowlishaw, 2000: 105), and rather more discomfort with the way I framed my questions along Indigenous versus non-Indigenous lines (Alma and Robbie Thorpe, interviews). Importantly, in his opening, proactive statement as we began our interview, Robbie Thorpe remarked: 'I don't see it as Indigenous and non-Indigenous for starters. It's: if you've got issues with the crime of genocide, well, I'd want to know you.' Later, Robbie talked about seeing blackness and whiteness operating only between the ('white') state and the ('black') Aboriginal people – not between individuals 'at the community level'. Robbie also spoke about non-Aboriginal young women as 'the best warrior-esses', and how he sees non-Aboriginal people who support his politics as being on the 'same track':

> I'm going to this destination, and I've just got to get there some way. So if you can help me do that, I'll help you do what you need to do, too. We're on the same train, on the same tracks. (Robbie Thorpe, interview)

Robbie brings his allies into the category 'warrior' (a term he also uses in the interview to describe his place in his community) in a way which for me reads as an innovation against the 'filial' project of Western political thought, which 'rarely announces itself without some sort of adherence to the State, to the family, without ... a *schematic* of filiation, stock, genus or species, sex (*Geschlecht*), blood, birth, nature, nation' (Gandhi, 2006: 27). Robbie brings allies with no blood/caste/kin relationship to him into a category named through Indigenous-identified language ('warrior'), and therefore into a space that sidesteps the colonialist division 'Indigenous'–'non-Indigenous'. This also functions to confuse, critique and transcend the binary between family (filial relationships) and friend (relationships with outsiders, strangers). The warriors in this space are not united by filial ties (to blood/kin/caste), but are united by a loyalty to ideals that is filial in its degree.

There is both an irredeemable difference between people in the scene with which this book is concerned (read in 'social facts', and in a deep and necessary acknowledgement of the personal and communal histories of each person) and a difference that is partially overcome by the acting out and pursuit of a certain set of (anti-colonial) interests. When non-Indigenous activists serve anti-colonial interests, they manifest a subjectivity that refuses the colonial logic that rigidly treated people according to the ascribed categories of Indigenous and non-Indigenous. In order to understand the logics and consequences of settler colonialism, it is necessary to see how this colonial formation metes out fundamentally different treatment to colonizers and indigenes (Wolfe, 1994), which is why I so often invoke these categories. Yet, within the social world of people pursuing social justice against the workings of settler colonialism in the south-east of Australia, these categories are at different times used, refused and critiqued, and, crucially, innovated against: not so much blurred as departed from. Their use reflects 'social facts': that is, their social and material consequences. The way that critics of empire negotiate their/our use of these terms reflects the struggle to resist such powerful discourses from within their force field (that is, the area in which they operate).

The logics of binary thought and of elimination of Indigenous people and appropriation of land are that against which 'new relations' and 'new meanings about identity' are invoked (Moses, 2010: 20) and in which anti-colonial resistance is generated. This new/different space, which departs from the binary, is brought into being by the application of 'fundamental principles' of local 'traditional knowledge' to the colonizing situation (Moses, 2010: 19).

My way of addressing this binary is to see it as the object of critique, for the colonizing work such binaries have done, as well as to acknowledge the social facts in the colonizing context of south-eastern Australia. To sum up: I don't resolve the tension by coming down on one side or by finding middle ground, using little bits of each frame to construct my own view. Rather, I see this tension as reflective of an imperfect (because colonizing) world and the challenges and dilemmas produced by it. I see its realities accepted by, and actively negotiated by, those I interviewed. This is a difficult process of confronting 'the state within the self' (Lea, 2008: 235). I see this process as generating a grounded, innovative set of possibilities for radicalized/transgressive ways to relate (and ways to understand relating). This new way of relating includes non-Indigenous people seeing their interests as linked in with those of Indigenous people, though not in a way which appropriates Indigeneity.

Conclusion

I have revealed in this chapter my relative sensitivity to a range of ideas and writings that provide perspectives on key tensions in the endeavour of supporting Indigenous struggles in settler nations. I have also identified emergent politics and relationalities, presenting productive directions for people working in or supporting Indigenous struggles. Understanding these can help to inform and encourage activists' endeavours to recognize and undo the ways in which we/they have internalized colonialist ideas. The framework I suggest for decolonizing solidarity in theory and practice reflects some elements of a debate between modernism, structuralism, redistribution and materialist analysis, on the one hand, and postmodernism, post-structuralism and the critique of binaries, on the other.[10] Related to this is the

---

10. I hold these competing frames in tension while acknowledging that many theorists have come down on one side or the other. Nancy Fraser (1995) has been influential for scholars who have also adopted such a position in these debates. Her work on recognition and redistribution instigated a significant literature debating her approach and a trend to

contentious engagement with 'hybridity' among postcolonial scholars, and alongside all these considerations is the importance of intersectionality, which is particularly complex in a cross-cultural, settler-colonial context. To understand one's social locatedness and to centre Indigenous conceptions of identity and difference are key to the project of decolonizing solidarity.

engage with both postmodernism and structuralism. Fraser (1995) cited 'race' as one of the axes of injustice that are simultaneously cultural and socio-economic, and in which recognition and redistribution struggles are intertwined. Marilyn Lake (2003) engages with Fraser's view.

FOUR

Collaboration, dialogue and friendship: always a good thing?

One of the consequences of the political autonomy asserted by the Aboriginal Embassy in 1972 and manifested by the establishment of Aboriginal community-controlled organizations (legal services, health services, childcare agencies) in Australia in the 1970s and 1980s was a change in the basis of relationships between Aboriginal people and government agencies. Aboriginal people were in a position to reject blatant paternalism and coercion, to claim the right to provide their own services to meet their own needs. Community-controlled services called on government to hand over funding for Aboriginal welfare. Aboriginal Health Services in particular were in a strong position to make this demand, given their greater success and efficiency in meeting Aboriginal health needs compared to state health departments (Howell, 2013).

However, in answer to the assertion of sovereignty and calls for self-determination by the Aboriginal Embassy and the self-help movement, governments have consistently manoeuvred to bring Aboriginal people and activists into roles, consultative structures and institutions that are within or controlled by government (Hemingway, 2012: 214–15). Likewise, Aboriginal self-help organizations have been forced to govern themselves according to dominant culture practices; governments have refused to see Aboriginally governed organizations as 'legally recognizable' and insisted they become incorporated to receive funding (Hemingway, 2012: 208). Manoeuvres such as the creation of bodies designed to deliver Aboriginal voices to government – but always in a consultancy or advisory role, never in a decision-making or executive policymaking role – were quite successful in diverting energy and attention away from Aboriginal aspirations at key points in the 1970s, 1980s, 1990s and 2000s (Castejon, 2002). Each of the bodies created (National Aboriginal Consultative Committee, National Aboriginal Conference, Aboriginal and Torres Strait Islander Commission) were, in turn, dissolved by government. While appearing to accommodate Aboriginal demands for a changed relationship, this response by government has in effect been a method of reasserting control (Mansell, 2003).

In the late 1990s, drawing on international and community development thinking, 'capacity development' gained currency as a policy approach in Aboriginal Affairs at the national government level in Australia. However, soon enough, coercive Shared Responsibility Agreements and 'mutual obligation' welfare reforms were brought in, manifesting the most regressive possibilities of the concept of community capacity-building, rather than the more empowering possibilities of a critical approach to community development (Makuwira, 2007; see also Hunt, 2005).

The prevailing political climate of the new millenium, according to south-east Indigenous campaigners and supporters such as Gary Murray, Monica Morgan, Wayne Atkinson, bryan Andy and members of the Melbourne Kungkas, is characterized by a general acceptance of the need for Indigenous people to be 'upfront' in decision-making and as spokespeople. This owes a lot to the era in which Black Power politics provided a framework for greater community strength, and 'Aboriginalization' policies were employed to force the issue. However, the imperative for Aboriginal people to be seen to be upfront can easily become an opening for tokenism. Tokenism is a criticism frequently made against government and bureaucratic practices. It can just as frequently play out in supposedly community-controlled settings. For example, Gary Murray has condemned government failure to educate and train Aboriginal people in the last few decades, and described how the 'Lack of black experts and people with qualifications' plays out in Aboriginal co-operatives and corporations today. Gary suggested:

> If you went around to, say, Bairnsdale, Morwell, Ballarat, Heywood, Mildura, etc. etc., and if you did an analysis of how many non-Indigenous staff compared to Indigenous staff, what you'd find is that the non-Indigenous staff are in all the positions of power, usually higher salaries, so they'll be from the CEO, to the accounting staff, for sure.

However, compounding this problem is the attempt to hide it. Gary continues:

> But you know, you sort of notice they keep reasonably low-key, and you'll get an Indigenous person on the media doing the business, but who's pulling the strings, and who's doing the work and who's getting paid for it are just as important as the decision-making stuff.

Working in the context of power imbalances

Aboriginal–state relations, the dynamics of which are particularly evident in relation to government funding agreements and increasing bureaucratization, have shaped the development of the community-controlled sector (Foley, 1975; Foley and Anderson, 2006; Gillor, 2011; Hemingway, 2012). Despite this, Aboriginal people have succeeded in gaining significant moral authority and wide recognition of the importance of community control (Barkan, 2000). It is increasingly impolitic for non-Aboriginal organizations of any variety to dabble in Aboriginal Affairs in the absence of relationships with local communities.

Many positive-sounding words have come into use to describe relationships between Aboriginal people and communities and settler individuals, groups, organizations and governments and the processes that hold them together. Partnerships, collaborations, alliances and coalitions might be sought, and they are seen to be held together by dialogue and especially by trust.

There are plenty of lessons to be learned from theorists, including community practitioners, who have considered the challenges of working in the context of power imbalances, and have tried to work out ways to deal with difference that does not reproduce colonizing dynamics (Bell, 2008; Wallace, 2013). Ideas informing white anti-racist practice and community organizing suggest how complexities relating to trust and accountability can be managed. In south-east Australia this could be more honestly described as a process of trying to do good work in disputed sovereign space, or transacting under colonizing conditions.

Relationships between people contributing to south-east Indigenous struggles can take many forms, for example collaborations between individuals across Indigenous–non-Indigenous difference, or the relationship between a non-Indigenous activist group and an Indigenous leader or member of a community. Relationships might be maintained for the purpose of communication between collective efforts made in parallel, rather than as part of directly working together. An example of parallel efforts relevant to south-east Indigenous struggles in Australia is Aboriginal-run land rights or community survival projects, operating separately from but indirectly supported by non-Indigenous efforts at self- and community education and at challenging interpersonal and institutional racism. No matter what the form or function of the relationships, attentiveness to notions of representation, voice, difference, dialogue and power is key to reflective practice. It is important to consider a variety of perspectives on collaboration, dialogue and difference in order to foreground the contradictions inherent in collaboration and dialogue across difference.

One of the most important things to enshrine for people working together across difference is that supporters should be located or should locate themselves so that they may be challenged by those they are supporting: Indigenous people or, in parallel situations, the people most directly affected by the social justice issue (Jensen, 2005).

Indigenous people, in their diversity, may take different approaches to managing relationships with supporters. Some approaches are quite optimistic and risky, and others are more pessimistic, with risk managed through structures and boundaries which are put in place. There is a tension between the long track record of white untrustworthiness and the need for Indigenous people to be optimistic about the possibility of developing trusting relationships with allies (Robbie Thorpe, interview; Tony Birch, CRG meeting; see also Hoskins, 2012). Optimism keeps alive the promise of collaborations towards meaningful social change.

How could positive qualities like friendship, knowing and sharing possibly be a problem?

Non-Indigenous people may come to solidarity relationships with Indigenous people bearing a number of assumptions. For example, they might assume that they will be gratefully and enthusiastically welcomed, and may not anticipate being held in suspicion by Aboriginal people initially, for quite some time or forever. They might think that they will gain friends among Aboriginal people they work to support politically, or work with towards some political goal.

Anti-racist trainer Frances Kendall and social worker Stephen Burghardt have questioned the assumption that friendship is part of cross-race ally relationships in the USA. Both have critiqued what they see as misplaced desires for friendship in such contexts. For example, Kendall (2006: 140) is careful to preface a chapter on 'How to Be an Ally if You Are a Person with Privilege' with the statement 'This is not a chapter about friendship'. She rejects cross-race friendship as the 'goal' of doing racial justice and anti-racism work. Rather, the goal of an ally is 'to address racism and white privileges in the institutional communities of which you are a part'. That said, friendship can be an unexpected bonus coming out of years of 'racial justice and antiracism work' for some activists (Kendall, 2006: 140). Burghardt mentions friendship when he discusses the work involved in negotiating relationships across social inequality:

> It's important to emphasize that such work need not culminate in deep friendship to be meaningful, either; such an assumption is too personalistic to be realized with everyone we come into contact with, including all those with whom we work. That's

not the point of these efforts. The point is that such work, like all labor born of choice and mutual determination, can be deeply worthwhile. (Burghardt, 1982: 133)

Burghardt suggests a focus on deriving satisfaction from the labour of anti-racist work, not from some hoped-for friendship. Related to the non-Indigenous desire for friendship are other, related desires. Many of these desires are, ultimately, about eliminating difference: wanting to be black, or the same, or as one, or co-inhabiting a self-identical reconciled community. There are more productive and progressive ways to approach or understand anti-racism and ally work, and they still leave room for positive sentiments: seeing such work as an expression of love in a wider public sense (Lynch and Walsh, 2009), and love for 'guests, strangers and foreigners' (Gandhi, 2006).

In the context of contemporary Australian politics the desire of a non-Indigenous person to be friends with or to be loved by an Indigenous person (any Indigenous person) may be a depoliticized impulse associated particularly – though not exclusively – with the parliament-generated discourse of reconciliation (Barta, 2008; Gooder and Jacobs, 2000). Indigenous people from the south-east Australian political community have made concise critiques of government-sponsored reconciliation, seen as an agenda to empty out or depoliticize Indigenous demands for justice and truth. In Gary Foley's words, 'Reconciliation is not justice.' Yuin warrior Chicka Dixon (interview) has pejoratively labelled the 'reconciliation mob' the 'kiss and make up tribe':

Chicka: I will not thank Australia for introducing weapons of mass destruction, including musket, cannon, syphilis, gonorrhoea, smallpox and numerous other diseases. I *will* not thank them.

Clare: And that's what you saw was part of reconciliation.

Chicka: Yes.

In Australia, state policies of forced assimilation inflect the meaning of friendship across Indigenous–non-Indigenous difference.

How do we deal with expressions of social love across difference politically and in particular political contexts? The desire of colonizers for reconciliation, collaboration and dialogue with the colonized is often directed to achieving a 'shared understanding' and 'talking with one voice' (Jones and Jenkins, 2008). Related to this, Ien Ang (1995) and Maria Lugones (1987) both critique the idealization of 'unity' in feminist texts attempting to engage with difference. Lugones raises this in a piece which develops insights into 'non-imperialistic understanding between people' (1987: 11). Reaching an understanding does not necessarily involve 'learning about the Other' but rather 'learning (about difference) *from* the Other' (Jones and Jenkins, 2008: 471). Jones and Jenkins critique the imperialist enthusiasm for 'getting to know the Other' as one-way sharing that benefits only non-Indigenous people. Teacher educator Nado Aveling (2004) highlights what could be read as appropriative impulses, and an address to Aboriginal people who are assumed to be passive, in interviews with twelve non-Indigenous women. Aveling reports women saying: 'I'd really like to learn from them'; 'I'd love to get them in here and involved in looking after the land and teaching us what they know' (2004: 64). Rauna Kuokkanen, a Sami scholar of Native Studies based in Canada, regards modes of addressing difference as crucial and sees the 'entire project of knowing the other' as 'suspect' (Kuokkanen, 2003: 268, citing Gayatri Spivak).

Imperialist ways of addressing difference include indulging the urge to discover the strange and novel as familiar, or trying to erase or negate difference (Gandhi); aiming for unity or sameness, for self-identical community (Gandhi; Lugones); even trying to get to 'know' the Other (Jones and Jenkins; Kuokkanen).

More promising are the radical possibilities of adopting a politics of friendship. Gandhi claims the phrase 'the politics of friendship' for the friendship, fellowship and collaboration between Indian anti-colonial nationalists and radical Britons/ metropolitans in late-nineteenth-century London. Her naming of this politics is built on the narratives of those under-acknowledged friendships and collaborations in the late nineteenth century; and, further, it privileges the trope of friendship as 'the most comprehensive philosophical signifier for all those invisible affective gestures that refuse alignment along the secure axes of filiation to seek expression outside, if not against, possessive communities of belonging' (Gandhi, 2006: 10).

In the politics of friendship, filiative bonds are no longer primary; instead, 'a love for guests, strangers and foreigners' motivates political solidarity (Gandhi, 2006: 29). A principled distaste for racially exclusive worlds inspires an ethic of loyalty to strange friends. This is where the variety of dissent that would gain no material advantage – dissent of metropolitan critics of empire – is recognized as 'political' (Gandhi, 2006: 2). This variety of dissent was shared by the subcultural community of Gandhi's study, who stood to gain no material advantage from the diminution of imperial power yet who had in common their view and diagnosis of imperialism as a 'peculiar habit of mind'. They critiqued the system which relentlessly mapped 'hierarchies of race, culture and civilization upon relationships between genders, species, classes' (Gandhi, 2006: 7).

The scene of Gandhi's study could be seen as a mismatched 'negative' community of the marginal and excluded (homosexuals, vegetarians, socialists, feminists, suffragists). However, Gandhi finds that these exiles from Western civilization held in common an anti-imperialist, utopian socialist politics as well as anarchist sensibilities. They yearned for other-directed ethics and politics and to depart from the 'fetters' of inherited communities. Read in a positive light this community was one which preserved and was marked by difference.

Yet, as Londoners, as metropolitans, these Western misfits and critics of empire are located as hosts in their politics of hospitality towards 'revolutionary exiles and émigrés' from Europe and Indigenous people from the colonies. How does this work where the setting is Aboriginal land, thought of in the terms of the colonial project as the 'periphery' rather than the metropolis? What does it mean to be a Western critic of empire not at home (in the metropolis, London), but in the colony?[1]

In the south-east of Australia, Aboriginal people have taken the lead in accommodating incomers of various persuasions and attempting to inform them of the customs and laws of the land (goori2, 2011). This has been and is an expression of sovereignty, and of care (see Birch, 2007; Georgatos, 2012). A politics of friendship in a settler colonial context is possible

---

1. Note that Gandhi considered the criticism of empire by the English Anglican priest Charles Freer Andrews (1871–1940) in India. Yet note that the particular colonial formation in that case is a franchise colony rather than a settler colony (see Wolfe, 1994).

where Aboriginal people continue to assert radical title and continue to express concern for the rights of all people (Foley, cited in Land, 2011a: 51; Hoskins, 2012). This generosity – this ethic of unconditional love – is evident and humbling for those who will see it.

The politics of reducing 'social distance'

Questioning the idea of colonizer–colonized friendship was part of my thinking for a long time prior to commencing the research for this book. Experience as a student activist volunteer in East Timor of friendships that seemed easier led me to identify more clearly how burdened analogous relationships were in Australia.

As part of time spent in contact with Aboriginal people as an activist, I started to see that as a non-Aboriginal person I live in a different social world, separate from Aboriginal community life in Melbourne. This led to wondering what is to be done about the fact that my social circle of friends and extended family is quite racially exclusive.

Sacks and Lindholm (2002: 146) advocate overcoming the 'social distance' between 'ourselves and those who are marginalized' rather than always spending time with those of 'our own kind'. They quote a white, male, wealthy, American college student who thought that changing those with whom he spent time could help him to *feel* rather than 'know to know' (Lea et al., 2006: 7) that racism is wrong.

I have sometimes wanted to address the whiteness of my social world through gestures of 'inclusion', based on the idea that I could add Aboriginal people as guests at a dinner party or gathering with my middle-class white friends. However, following Sullivan (2006), I believe that the objective should be to change the shape of my life, spending and investing time and energies differently, so that over time my life and social world become more reflective of my values. An example of investing time and energies differently is to volunteer with anti-racist and non-white community initiatives. Further, because of the danger that white attempts to reduce social distance could reiterate processes of forced assimilation, appropriation, gentrification and intrusion (Sullivan, 2006), spending time with people not of my 'own kind' needs to be on others' terms, rather than on mine.

'The constant barrage of questions that you get'

It is important to realize that some contexts for working relationships have been experienced by Aboriginal people as anathema to friendship. Wayne Atkinson, a community and university educator with a long ancestral history of land rights claims, has spoken about the impact on him of working with non-Indigenous people: 'It can be overwhelming.' He talked about how he needs his own space, to get away from it. Dr Atkinson then talked about 'the constant barrage of questions that you get ... Practically on a day-to-day basis':

> Wayne Atkinson: Even when I go back home sometimes, I might go into a pub and see some old mates. And it's there, you know. You're just waiting for something to come out. Some image that's conjured up in their mind about a particular issue that they'll be then using to test on you, so that you can enlighten them, or turn it around, and set them straight on it.

> Clare: And you find that that's something that you wait for. You know that it's gonna come up, even with supporters or people you've known for a long time.

> Wayne Atkinson: Yes... The onus then comes back on
> Indigenous people to educate, to confront these misconceptions.

I asked Wayne Atkinson whether it was a case of 'counting on one hand, or not being able to count at all, the number of non-Indigenous people you can be with and relax and you don't feel like they're gonna come up with something?' He replied, 'Yes, well, that's a good question, that's relevant to this whole examination...' He went on to talk about the very few people who have become, over a very long period, someone he could trust. These are usually 'people you've grown up with', not people met through activism. There were certain contexts for Wayne Atkinson which made friendship with white people impossible: one was within Government Aboriginal Affairs bureaucracies, and another was in the academic setting:

> I was very antagonistic towards – when I was working in government – towards the amount of white gubbahs[2] ... that you were subordinate to. It was an antagonistic relationship ... The tension was always there. I just hated being subordinate to a gubbah person in what is essentially my own affairs. But you had these relationships, and you had to – you sort of adjusted to them. But I just don't have any friends, close friends that I made [from that time in government] ... And likewise probably in academia is much the same. There's not many non-Indigenous people that inspired me, in terms of teaching Indigenous studies.

An account of Charles Perkins's time in the Department of Aboriginal Affairs, in which friendships were limited, resonates with Wayne Atkinson's experience. According to Peter Read (1990a: 131), 'Perkins found no friendship in the office.' Perkins said:

---

2. Gubbah: whitefella, or non-Koori.

[T]hey were nice blokes ... they did the right thing all the time. But the one weakness in their armour was that the personal touch wasn't there with the people like myself who at the time were crying for it ... I could never feel with them that they believed in me as an Aboriginal person ... And they laid down the terms of reference for that relationship. (Read, 1990a: 144–5)

These accounts suggest that in some contexts the conditions are not right for friendship between Aboriginal and non-Aboriginal people. They are also further evidence of the problems with 'knowing' and 'sharing', and the cumulative effect on Aboriginal people of being asked questions or presented with stereotypes to turn around. In the context of forming working relationships or partnerships between organizations, a huge amount of Aboriginal peoples' effort is often expended explaining or answering 'all the questions mainstream organizations have about Aboriginal culture':

Mainstream organizations need to take responsibility for training their own staff about Koori history, culture and values, and about the local Koori community. Before planning a collaboration, mainstream organizations should ensure that they have allowed time and allocated funding for cross-cultural training. (Waples-Crowe and Pyett, 2005)

Who desires and who benefits from collaboration?

The work of Pakeha scholar Alison Jones with Ngati Porou scholar Kuni Jenkins to rethink collaboration is instructive. Albeit writing from a university setting, they critique the 'desire for collaborative inquiry understood as face-to-face, ongoing dialogue between indigenous and settler colleagues or students' (Jones and Jenkins, 2008: 471). Writing from Aotearoa/ New Zealand, Jones and Jenkins ask: who desires and who benefits from collaboration? They reflect on their pedagogical experiment in dividing a university class according to ethnicity in response to Maori students stating that they 'preferred to study their histories, knowledges and experiences separately from their Pakeha (White) peers' (Jones and Jenkins, 2008: 476). Maori students enjoyed the programme, finding it a welcome relief from prior disheartening experiences of coming together and sharing with settler students in the classroom. These prior experiences had entailed constantly having to explain themselves and dealing with cultural ignorance and even hostility from Pakeha classmates. In the other half of the programme, many of the white students were furious about being denied the opportunity to 'learn' and 'share' (Jones and Jenkins, 2008: 477). This is an example of how coming together for the apparently benign purpose of sharing and learning can be revealed as delivering benefits to only one side. Maori students 'did not feel the need to be recipients of sharing'; nor did they want to 'reduce difference' (separation was seen as 'reinforcing difference' and this was ascribed a negative value by white students) (Jones and Jenkins, 2008: 477). In light of this, and their reflections on their experiences as academics, Jones and Jenkins see settler 'enthusiasm for dialogic collaboration' as a phenomenon to be critiqued and consider 'how this desire might be an unwitting imperialist demand' (Jones and Jenkins, 2008: 471).

Possibilities and limits in collaboration, dialogue and conflict

Nicholas C. Burbules and Suzanne Rice (1991: 395) consider 'whether dialogue can be maintained across differences, whether it is desirable to try, and what conditions might make it possible'.

They note that 'any concrete discussion of difference implies *sameness*': a comparison of any two things is only useful when 'there are at least some respects in which they are similar' (Burbules and Rice, 1991: 403, stress in original). They urge sensitivity to how 'the "same" thing might look and feel quite different to members of different cultural groups', and that this should 'make us err, if we are going to err, on the side of crediting and respecting a group's self-understanding when it seriously conflicts with our own – especially when dealing with a group already at a disadvantage' (Burbules and Rice, 1991: 405). In a book addressed to social workers and/or political organizers, Stephen Burghardt argues that objective differences in lived experience underscore the need for attentiveness to questions of how power operates in situations of dialogue and collaboration:

> If a person is willing to accept [the limitations created by social differences] and can learn to work with them on a combined basis of legitimate differences (black experience necessitating careful scrutiny of whites, women of men, etc.) and simultaneous mutuality (shared needs for good working conditions, more effective methods of practice, etc.), then both personal and political growth are possible. (Burghardt, 1982: 111)

Overall, Burbules and Rice argue for optimism:

> there must be *some* forums in which such discussions are seriously undertaken, and there must be *some* individuals from each group who are prepared to take on the burden (and risk) of attempting some degree of communication and translation across the gulf that divides them. (Burbules and Rice, 1991: 404)

If it were not for optimism about the prospects of effecting change (and the possibility of trustworthy relationships), what would drive any struggle for social justice, or any collaboration?

To attempt dialogue across difference is not to presuppose either understanding or reconciliation; nor is the only goal of dialogue to reach a convergence of meanings. To attempt dialogue is not to presuppose the attempt will succeed; nor is it to be naive regarding the risk of further harm. Failed dialogue or conflict might still produce greater understanding. Certainly it is not aimed at eliminating difference or the domination of one particular perspective. The politics of solidarity which this book discerns and discusses entails attentiveness to the many possibilities and limits in collaboration, dialogue and conflict. Having established some reasons to think twice about seeking collaboration, it is time to turn to some strategies for managing support relationships.

Aboriginal people's strategies for managing support relationships

It is important for would-be allies to question and learn from the existing repertoire of frameworks that are available for understanding our/their work. This includes questioning apparently unproblematic frameworks and values such as friendship and dialogue, as well as learning from Aboriginal people's suggestions regarding how to manage dynamics that commonly arise within solidarity contexts.

Initiation, participation and control

The first, most repeated and strongest principle that Foley instilled in me as a newcomer to pro-Aboriginal politics in 1998 was that you don't do anything unless you've been asked to do it. I told Robbie about how this guided my solidarity activism from the beginning:

Clare: I felt I was invited to go to Jabiluka to be in the blockade, like everyone was invited, to support. And I wanted to go to Timor because we were invited and we'd been told by Foley you don't do anything unless you've been asked to do it, obviously.

Robbie: Yeah, yeah.

Clare: And it's community controlled. So.

Robbie: Yeah.

Clare: So I obviously jumped at that.

Robbie: And that's been good advice?

Clare: Yeah. That's been ... yeah, very, very guiding for me.

That Aboriginal people must initiate a project or collaboration is one of the three key ingredients of genuine community control, as conceptualized at the Victorian Aboriginal Health Service in Fitzroy in the 1970s and 1980s. As Bruce McGuinness has said, initiative, involvement and participation together ensure that there is community control of Aboriginal business (McGuinness, n.d.). For Foley (2012: 143), it is 'psychologically extremely important for the Aboriginal people to solve their own problems', adding to pride and self-confidence in the context of denigration and oppression. The presence of white people as members of black political organizations can subtly render the organization 'automatically less effective. Even the best white members will slow down' black people's arrival at a proposal to solve their own problems (Malcolm X, 1968: 495). The principle of Aboriginal people initiating and being in control of their own struggle is politically, concretely important. It is not just arbitrary exclusion based on identity politics.

*Conditions are not always right
for dialogue and collaboration*

Members of the political community whose struggles frame the
relationships of concern in this book are very much cognizant
of strategic questions relating to power, dialogue and collaboration. A Black Power text by Stokely Carmichael and Charles
Hamilton which was widely read by FCAATSI members in the
late 1960s contained the premiss: 'before a group can enter the
open society it must first close ranks' (Taffe, 2005: 250). Also in
the late 1960s, Noonuccal leader Kath Walker was working on
articulating some of the tensions inherent in coalition politics:
'Coalitions cannot work effectively, she argued, "nor can they
be sustained on the moral, friendly or sentimental conscience of
white behaviour patterns"' (Taffe, 2005: 251). The black–white
FCAATSI coalition had relied on assumptions like those Walker
critiqued; many argued that this laissez-faire approach to the
operation of power resulted in Aboriginal people's political
priorities being underplayed. The alternative model Walker
proposed was that when 'black Australians' became a 'solid,
determined fighting unit', they would be able to 'dictate their
own terms for advancement' and 'determine where white Australians could be of assistance' (Taffe, 2005: 251). Alliances with
non-Indigenous people and groups could be better negotiated
and entered into on the basis of internal Indigenous community
strength and organization. Disagreeing with these proposals for
strategic reasons, other Aboriginal people within FCAATSI
believed that for the rights and advancement movement to
have 'any hope at all', alliances with the greatest number of
white organizations were needed (Taffe, 2005: 256). The distinct

positions Aboriginal people took on the FCAATSI coalition reflect key strategic dilemmas and tensions.

Depending on the conditions, separate work might be more appropriate than coalition, collaboration or dialogue. Irene Watson (2005: 41) poses questions about whether safe conversational spaces and encounters are possible, given the unwitting, cannibalizing character of colonizer subjectivities in Australia. Bearing this in mind, it is clear that 'no marginalized group should be *expected* to go into partnership' (Tamasese et al., 1998: 61, stress added). It follows that people, groups or organizations wanting to enter a partnership should consider the question of whether the marginalized group is 'in a place where it is right for them to participate in the partnership?' (Tamasese et al., 1998: 61).

Aboriginal people are at times forced into dialogue in situations of overt power imbalance, for instance in meetings with government bureaucrats and politicians over matters such as native title negotiations and cultural heritage site clearances. Discussing such situations, multi-clanned traditional owner Gary Murray argues:

> We've got to have a conscionable relationship. You don't want an unconscionable one where the blackfellas are sitting on one side of the table with no resources, and no expertise and no articulateness, and all that sort of stuff, and the whitefellas are on the other side and the whitefellas see that and it's all one-way traffic. Right? You want to avoid that.

In order to achieve some influence in situations like this, Murray talks about the strategy of invoking traditional sources of authority, unsettling the sources of authority from which the room full of whitefellas draw their power. In such a context, power is relatively openly contested. However, even within a situation of collaboration and solidarity, rather than forced dialogue, the workings of power and contrasting relationships to colonialism eventually reveal themselves.

Trust, cooperation and inequality

There is clearly much that precedes Indigenous–non-Indigenous interactions: the legacy of Australia's colonizing past and present as it manifests in relationships between Indigenous and non-Indigenous people working to transform relationships between each other and the state. This is a context where the state is understood as existing within the self, not just outside of and imposed on its critics (Lea, 2008: 235). This context must be expected to prefigure possibilities for trust, which is elsewhere assumed to be a necessary starting point for working together.

Dealing with this in practice means that non-Indigenous people must strive to be trustworthy (and enter into constructs for enforcing this), but not expect to be trusted in return. This acknowledges our colonizing past and present, as well as the riskiness of trust across colonizing power differences.

In considering possibilities for working across differences in people's location with respect to colonization, it is important to acknowledge that, in a society 'where sexist and racist assumptions are an integral part of the upbringing and way of life', these deep-seated assumptions will inevitably manifest in day-to-day interactions, despite non-Indigenous people's (or men's) good intentions (Tamasese and Waldegrave, 1996: 52). Such an acknowledgement leads to questions about the workings of trust under colonizing conditions.

In the experience of Chris Twining, who has thirty years' experience working in community development and community education (including racism awareness consultancies), encounters between an Indigenous person and a non-Indigenous person carry more than just personal interaction: 'You come in one to one but basically you're both of you taking 200 years with you, you know ... I'm wearing all that baggage from 200 years of whitefellas as well' (interview; see also Hardin, 1996: 27). Chris talks about some of the dynamics she has observed: 'I think that's the hardest thing ... for non-Aboriginal people working with Aboriginal people: it takes so long to build up that trust' (interview). She is pointing to the way over 200 years of colonizing history plays into present interactions.

Burghardt (1982) writes of what he sees as the 'not-so-hidden realities of race, class and sex' in social work practice. He believes that

> a white person must understand that he or she can be deeply
> involved in fighting racism and still be viewed as a racist by
> blacks; indeed you *will* be. We shall examine why and how
> a white person can accept this and can understand this as a
> necessary perception for blacks to have about most whites (or, in
> varying degrees, women about men, gays about straights, etc.).
> Coupled with this awareness, of course, is a greater potential for
> effective practice. (Burghardt, 1982: 110–11)

There's no such thing as partnership between equals

Aboriginal people have developed strategies for managing relationships with supporters across a range of contexts, from activist settings to agencies and government. These can be seen in the way Aboriginal people negotiate deliberate but informal relationships, in the expectations placed on non-Indigenous people working within community-controlled organizations, in the adoption of formalized partnerships, agreements, MOUs (memoranda of understanding), contracts, protocols and treaties. Monica Morgan provides an important view of the idea of partnership as 'between equals':

> Absolutely not. Ours is as a sovereign people. If you come in as an activist, and you come in to support Indigenous people, you must understand that they're First Peoples. And when you're talking about supporting them to gain rights to country then you're doing it recognizing them as sovereign people. So you haven't got the same rights, no ... There's no such thing as partnership between equals, because the fact is whitefellas have got their own power through the system and the structure. (Monica Morgan, interview)

For Monica, the fundamental inequality in power between Indigenous and non-Indigenous individuals or organizations that collaborate means that agreements must enshrine Indigenous rights rather than equal rights.

Foley makes the following suggestion for any 'white supporter' of the 'Koori struggle for self-determination':

> Join a support group and take one step at a time, learning as you go. Make sure, however, that the group you join is one that genuinely supports Koori control of Koori affairs, and is in some way affiliated with, or taking guidance from, the local Koori traditional owners and/or local Koori community. (Foley, 1999)

Another strategy is evident in the way the community-controlled Victorian Aboriginal Health Service (VAHS) conceptualizes its engagement with non-Indigenous volunteers and workers. I discussed this with Alma Thorpe – a Gunditjmara elder, who was founding administrator (and later a director) of VAHS, and who was integrally involved in the development of the Aboriginal community-controlled health movement through NAIHO. Alma talked about the way VAHS spelled out how non-Indigenous people were expected to help out, making them very conscious of working under community control and direction: 'doctors and workers were very well screened, and they were educated under that scheme that we had going.' She also talked about the important screening and monitoring role that Bill Roberts came to play at VAHS. Bill first presented at the Victorian Aboriginal Health Service in Fitzroy, Melbourne in 1974, when they were looking for help to establish a dental service. He ended up working there for twenty-five years, eventually as director of medical services, and in time became the only non-Aboriginal member of the executive of NAIHO. Alma noted that 'Bill would monitor certain people'. The processes employed at VAHS attested that non-Indigenous people were working in a community-controlled setting, something that they could then be held accountable for. Further, Bill Roberts accepted the role of leadership in relation to other non-Indigenous people; members of the Barmah–Millewa Collective at pro-sovereignty environmental organization Friends of the Earth also accepted such a role (Margaret, 2013).

A partnership between the Victorian Aboriginal Community Controlled Health Organisation (VACCHO) and several mainstream community and social service organizations is an example of more formal arrangements (see Land, 2011b; Waples-Crowe and Pyett, 2005). In the context of pro-sovereignty environmental campaigning, Cam Walker talks of 'creating an architecture for communication' to enable traditional owners to 'guide what you're doing' (interview).

It is important that Aboriginal people – as the non-dominant group – are the ones who dictate the terms of any partnership, agreement, contract, protocol, alliance or treaty and are believed when they say this has been breached. This is because 'agreement between those of unequal power is inherently suspect' (Baier, 1986: 246; Hardin, 1996: 102). As Robbie Thorpe has said in a related discussion, treaties and agreements must be 'internationally scrutinized' in order to redress the inequality of bargaining power between Indigenous peoples and the state (see also Brennan et al., 2005).

Accountability: being located as easy to challenge

Deliberate arrangements to ensure the accountability of members of dominant groups to members of marginalized groups can enable 'the building of trust with the group with whom trust has been broken' (Tamasese and Waldegrave, 1996: 61). The Family Therapy Centre (FTC) in Aotearoa/ New Zealand has been particularly influential in its approach to what it calls cultural and gender accountability, which it has trialled and documented for others to consider taking up.[3] One of the few non-Indigenous groups that took up accountability processes to guide an engagement with Indigenous struggles in south-east Australia was AWD. AWD developed accountability processes after a study tour in Aotearoa/New Zealand in the early 1970s (Barry Mitchell, interview). This took the form of introducing Indigenous monitors into AWD's anti-racism

---

3. Various organizations have attempted to translate the accountability processes outlined in 1996 by Tamasese and Waldegrave, who addressed the challenges for adopting these processes in a subsequent publication (see Tamasese et al., 1998; see also Huygens, 1999).

workshops (Margaret, 2013). Pro-feminist men's groups have also applied these practices (Pease, 1997).

Accountability, in the FTC model, includes the absolute commitment of the agency to seeking a satisfactory solution to cultural and gender issues that arise. This seems to be lacking in the bureaucratic culture Tess Lea (2008) has described in the Northern Territory Government. Lea's observations highlight the importance of accountability processes through a description of a context embodying the opposite. She observes a now-ritualized institutional practice of accusation and flagellation, in which Aboriginal staff in the Territory Health Service predictably and at regular intervals raise grievances about racism (cast by Lea as 'berating') and non-Aboriginal people obediently flagellate themselves. This appears as a dystopic, bureaucratized, rehearsed, familiar interaction which is clearly non-transformative (in that nothing changes and the whole ritual is repeated to no avail), and in fact, as Lea shows, is part of the enculturation of new bureaucrats and of the circular logic of intervention that drives and sustains the bureaucracy. Her observation of the way in which accusation and flagellation are played out in this bureaucratic context provides an interesting counterpoint to the approach of Jensen (2005) and Kendall (2006), both of whom write in the US context. Jensen (2005) writes of coming to know his own racism and of his attempts, as a white male academic, to operate in an anti-racist manner. He attributes his moral and political growth to his engagement in political activity 'with people across identity lines' and to putting himself in situations in which others can 'easily challenge' him. He says 'comrades whom I trust can hold me accountable ... propel me forward' (Jensen, 2005: 79). There are a number of differences between the 'challenge' situations which for Jensen give rise to transformative conversations and reflections, and the bureaucratic culture in which Lea finds accusations of racism and responses to this to be ritualized and profoundly stifling. Transformation seems to be linked to the ability of the accuser to hold people accountable, and the willingness of the anti-racist to be held accountable and reach a satisfactory outcome. Kendall argues that honest, hard conversations about race are impossible under white, polite organizational cultures. She relates how African American women are accused of manifesting an unprofessional communication style and are further marginalized as a result of attempting to discuss issues around racism (see Williams, 1998). Because of a lack of ways to conduct productive conversations about race, grievances can come to be expressed in the form of a long-overdue 'unruly' outburst, for which the non-white person is then punished in various ways (Kendall, 2006: 73). The difference between the approach of Jensen and that of the FTC is in their relative formality. Jensen locates himself as easy to challenge in what appear to be informal ways, whereas in the FTC accountability processes are institutionalized. Members of the dominating culture or gender are held to the commitment to work through problems of racism or sexism under an institutionalized agreement to ensure people can work together equitably.

Accountability constructs can be formal or informal but must be real. Activist contexts may be suited to less formal processes than those of the Family Therapy Centre. Foley's suggestion for activist contexts is for white support groups to affiliate to or seek guidance from the local Koori traditional owners or Koori community. His suggestion brings together the important notions of group-to-group relationships (based on collectively expressed voices) and the non-Indigenous group being located as easy to challenge. The other notion raised in the account of the work of VAHS and Bill Roberts, and echoed in the discussion of the Family Therapy Centre approach, is the importance of developing relationships of collective responsibility among non-Indigenous people.

Relationships of collective responsibility among non-Indigenous people

When non-Indigenous people develop relationships of collective responsibility with each other they potentially reduce the burden on Aboriginal people of such education work. In addition, this can increase allies' political sophistication in both recognizing and dealing with racism through experiential learning; and create a structure for critical self-reflection towards reflective ally practice, which should both encourage and extend this work.

Kendall (2006: 93) encourages white people to take responsibility for other white people, a process which includes the perhaps uncomfortable step of acknowledging them as 'my people'. However, there are some dangers inherent in the practice of white people taking responsibility for each other's developing practice.

Reinscribing white privilege?
Leadership within dominant caucuses

The whole point of accountability processes is to facilitate the responsibility of dominant groups to deconstruct their dominance (Tamasese et al., 1998: 53). Yet there is a danger that discussion within dominant group caucuses could function to reinscribe privilege. Leadership of such caucuses is crucial to any success.

Leadership is needed due to the fact that well-meaning members of dominant groups tend to need strong assistance to stay on task when caucusing on their own racism. For instance, they may avoid responding to reports of discrimination in transformative ways. Instead, responses are often of a 'paralysing', 'individualizing' and 'paternalizing' type (Tamasese and Waldegrave, 1996: 52–3). White peoples' responses will typically

> shift the focus back to us, even when the conversation is not about us. A classic example of this is white women crying during conversations about racism because they feel guilty about being white and women of colour having to put their pain aside to help the white women who are crying. (Kendall, 2006: 72)

Anything occurring within the accountability process which works to replicate domination is to be guarded against. Chris Twining's experiences as a non-Indigenous co-facilitator of anti-racism workshops and consultancies illustrate this. Chris knows she must provide a leadership role against a racist scripting (Bailey, 1998) into which she is aware that she herself has been educated. Chris spoke of the challenges of trying to identify and confront white and non-Indigenous people's racism:

> I don't do it lightly ... [Racism is] so much part of who I am as well ... people can say something, and it could be really patronizing stuff but because I'm part of who they are as well, it sounds right to me – you know what I mean? So you really have to be on the ball all the time and pick up those things when people say them. (Chris Twining, interview)

Chris also feels that working alongside an Indigenous co-facilitator provides a measure of accountability. This co-facilitated structure developed out of earlier accountability constructs used by AWD members in which an Aboriginal person would be present as a monitor during anti-racism workshops. Other members of AWD continue to use this construct (Chris Twining, interview; Margaret, 2013: 74).

Leadership of a 'dominant' caucus or workshop must be clear and consistent, and needs to prevent paralysis and individualizing, avoid replicating domination and 'encourage self-reflection that aids the deconstruction of power relations'. Further, the onus for monitoring should not fall only on the marginalized culture or gender. The members of the dominating culture must work to '"self-start", to recognise and call a stop to certain sorts of behaviours' (Tamasese et al., 1998: 53). This is just the sort of role Bill Roberts came to undertake as part of his role at VAHS; other health services at times asked Bill to help sort out similar issues (Bill Roberts, interview).

For accountability processes, just as for the politics of solidarity more broadly, it is important to maintain both the practice of critical self-reflection and public political action. Working on dismantling privileges must happen on systemic as well as interpersonal levels (Tamasese et al., 1998; see also Burghardt, 1982: 111; Jensen, 2005). Further, staying 'focused on the big picture' – of working together in relation to bringing about change in communities and the broader society – as well as doing accountability work within one's own organization is important for maintaining energy. Accountability structures entail the risk of pessimism and long internal processes, which, while valid, can take on a life of their own (Tamasese et al., 1998: 62).

Approaches to trust among reflective non-Indigenous people

Many community and international development practitioners, and those who are concerned with work in cross-cultural settings more generally, are convinced that establishing trust is a prerequisite for effective dialogue and cooperation (Rhodes, 2014: 207, 214). Yet, in the specific context of solidarity with south-east Indigenous struggles the strategy of establishing trust and the idea of being trusted by Aboriginal people were not uniformly embraced by reflective allies.

'Never trust a whitefella, no matter who he is'

The key elements of Bill Roberts's ideas on trust were that he trusted the Health Service; he didn't trust himself; and that the Health Service grew to trust him over time. Bill had come to the Health Service with an analysis of colonialism developed through his involvement with AWD, as well as an awareness of Paolo Freire's work on the oppressed, and recent exposure to Quaker values of listening. He was active in supporting the East Timorese struggle against invasion by Indonesia. Vigilance and self-effacement were part of Bill's practice.

Bill Roberts agreed to work under community control, and saw that principle being genuinely manifested throughout the Health Service, where he worked closely with Alma Thorpe, Gary Foley and Bruce McGuinness. This meant that he could trust the direction he got from his bosses at the Health Service – the administrator and the chairperson. In the activist setting, in supporting Indigenous leadership of their own struggle, non-Indigenous activists place trust in Indigenous community campaign leaders in very significant matters such as being committed to their cause in the collective interests of Indigenous people, and pursuing this commitment with integrity and sound strategy.

Bill's approach from the outset of his work at VAHS in 1974 was to listen. An early experience in which the VAHS chairperson Bruce McGuinness asked Bill to start out by making dentures for older Koori people was challenging for Bill, because it was the 'total opposite of what you learned at dental school'. However, the experience ended up validating Bill's determination 'that I would only carry out work after I'd *listened* to what the Aboriginal people wanted'. Bill's dental training had taught him that 'going in as a dentist to a community that has lots of dental problems … the prime thing you concentrate on in those circumstances is the children. Well now, that was my intent.' But, as Bill said, he followed McGuinness's direction:

> I pursued that and made more dentures in that next two years than I'd ever made in my previous forty-five years or whatever. But what that did was it gave the community a trust in me to deal with their children. So it ended up being a very suitable and a very right starting point.

Bill kept his promise to himself to listen, which for him meant holding back any expression of his views. He did this for at least eight years:

> Because of my mindset that it was important to listen to the people and regard their perception of their needs, it became quite reined in, so that at conferences or at board meetings I'd just present what was necessary, and well, ninety-nine times out of a hundred I didn't even feel like getting into an argument, because it all flowed well anyway. But that hundredth time I'd restrain myself over the early years, you see. Well, then it probably got

to the – it would have been at least the eighth year before I'd challenged anything, you see. Or just began a discussion. (Bill Roberts, interview)

Bill gave an example of a single instance at NAIHO when he did strongly argue a viewpoint and saw it prevail. The issue was an important strategy question regarding government funding. Bill's view was shared by the national coordinator of NAIHO Denis Walker,[4] but contradicted that of VAHS chairperson Bruce McGuinness and the NAIHO executive. Bill's view prevailed. During our interview, Bill said, 'In retrospect, I think, it was the beginning of the wrong decision.' Perhaps this confirmed for Bill his long-held maxim that Aboriginal people should 'never trust a whitefella'. In all but that one case, Bill withheld his opinions on strategy. Part of what made this possible (apart from his promise to himself) was the strong congruence between Bill's deeply felt and practised values and those he saw at work at VAHS. Bill saw the reality of the 'fundamental ideal of the community being in control of the process from go to whoa' at both VAHS and NAIHO. He was happy to accept direction from Alma Thorpe and the board because of their integrity. This is despite the fact that this dynamic was new to Bill, who had 'never worked for a boss before'. VAHS articulated its practice as based on initiation, participation and community control, and Bill saw all members of the Aboriginal community involved in initiating and running the Health Service. For instance, Bill said that 'a number of the gummies [those who are on the grog] were associated in the establishment [of the Health Service]'.

---

4. Denis Walker, a Noonuccal man, son of Oodgeroo, was a founding member of the Brisbane Tribal Council (1969) and founder of the Black Panther Party of Australia (1972).

Bill also noted that, although VAHS did not have enough funding to meet all the needs of the Aboriginal community, and was ordered by the Department for Aboriginal Affairs on threat of losing funding not to serve non-Aboriginal people, the Health Service didn't turn them away:

> One of the first things that I was told, which, again, boosted my thoughts and feelings about these people, was, 'Don't turn anyone away, Doc. Cos anyone who comes to our counter has a need. So do what they need.' So, you know, it was remarkable. Because we didn't have the funds to do what we needed to do.

Further to this, the supportive, selfless attitude of both patients and workers at the Health Service towards Bill's solidarity work with the East Timorese independence movement was, for Bill,

> an incredible revelation of what these patients were like compared with the demands that'd been put on me in private practice. Because they saw anyone who was in a struggle like the East Timorese was worse off than they were, and it was more important that they be served.

At times it was necessary for Bill to take urgent phone calls from politicians or from East Timor. Bill said: 'And patients would be there, and they all had knowledge of what was going on.' And Bill remembers patients saying: 'Doc, go on, take that phone call, don't worry about me, that's more important than we are.' Later in the interview Bill said:

> I was Catholic, I'm still Catholic, but I learned *far* more about the *real* gospel message by working amongst Aboriginal people than I ever had in school or in church or anywhere else. Because they live out 'love your neighbour as yourself'. (Bill Roberts, interview)

Likewise, Alma Thorpe said of Bill: 'He was a true Christian … I always had a good relationship with him. It was his integrity

I think. His *being* actually who he was and how he operated.' Bill describes how 'As the Aboriginal board and chairperson and administrator ... grew in trust of me I was given other duties other than being a straightforward dentist.' These duties ultimately led to Bill 'being a community development officer in the sense of helping communities to get health facilities started, not simply dental facilities' and eventually becoming director of medical services at the Health Service. Having heard of the high regard in which Bill was held by Aboriginal people he worked with at the Health Service, I asked him: 'Did you ever feel concerned that Aboriginal people might trust you *too much*?'

> Bill: Oh, yeah, that was the beginning point. Yes. I always carried that concern. And because I *knew*, well, I grew more and more aware, and conscious of, and had been told orally, and read it through *some* good books – those by Henry Reynolds, and some other whitefellas like him, and then others that have been more recently written by Aboriginal people – I always said, preceding me speaking on an issue for a length of time, not just an everyday thing: 'Never trust a whitefella, no matter who he is.'

This suggests that Bill, in some significant way, did not trust himself not to manifest white dominance. Tamasese and Waldegrave (1996: 62) say as much: 'It is precisely because we are becoming more sensitive to our own biases that we have set up these systems of accountability.' Bill's very awareness of his own potential untrustworthiness as a whitefella probably made him more trustworthy for Indigenous people. Non-Indigenous people come to be seen as more trustworthy at the point at which they regard themselves as less deserving of trust. As Burghart has written:

[O]n the one hand, I am viewed as racist by blacks; on the other hand, I work in certain groups to end racism for my own good. Over time, my activity reveals that I am not as racist as some people may have thought. At the same time, I relearn elements of racism still within me that need greater attention. (Burghardt, 1982: 111)

'The first aspect of working with Indigenous people is to try to build trust'

Speaking in 2008, Frank Hytten expressed a different approach to trust in his work with Indigenous people. Frank could see that in some contexts, 'Maybe given 200 years of *culture* that teaches Indigenous people that we're an untrustworthy bunch of bastards, it's going to take a while before they are prepared to accept someone more intimately...' This is a clear statement of Frank's understanding of the epistemology of Indigenous scepticism about non-Indigenous people generally, and potential allies specifically. However, whereas Bill cautioned 'Never trust a whitefella', Frank expressed the view that the work of building trust was primary in his approach to working with Indigenous people:

> So, the first aspect of working with Indigenous people – or anybody – is to try to build trust. And that can take time. And that's really important because *I* think *mostly* we don't allow time ... So now I've been with the Fitzroy Stars Football Club [an Aboriginal Australian Rules football club] for eighteen months. And I'm only getting to the place, and only now, literally, that I can say 'Look, I *don't* think that's right, I *don't* think we can do that.' Or, as I said in today's conversations, 'We have to act, we can't keep dithering around this issue. We *have* to make a decision.' And on Tuesday I *more* or less sought permission to force the issue. It's about something that matters. It's not earth-shattering. But if we don't get on with it we won't be ready to put a team on the field. Yeah?

Frank understands his work of trying to 'right injustices' as fundamentally guided by 'the community development framework', an approach to trust that is congruent with community development principles. Coming from a background in youth work, unemployment and psychiatric disability, Frank's advocacy work has most recently been in relation to Indigenous people. He was born and grew up in India and says 'my culture is some kind of mixture of Indian, English–British–Raj-y kind of culture, and Australian.' He is university-educated. He has worked as coordinator of ANTaR and as chief executive officer of Reconciliation Victoria.

Frank's belief in the primacy of trust to the project of working together is something he saw as fundamentally important to working with 'anybody', not just with Indigenous people. He also saw the need to reach a state of 'being solid' with each other as the basis for working together, and saw the need to interact as equals:

> On an interpersonal level I think power *has* to be shared. So we *have* to become equals. So I'm *not* there to run around doing people's bidding. I'm there to do that to the extent I need to do that to build the relationship, to demonstrate trust, to demonstrate that I am here for the long haul, to demonstrate that I am prepared to listen, to demonstrate da da da da da. But *ultimately* I'm there as a human being with the same rights as they have. *And* conversely, I'm there to accept *them* as human beings with the same rights that I have. And *that's* where we can start to come to some negotiated peace, and build a relationship. (Frank Hytten, interview)

There is a sense conveyed in these statements that Frank's trust-building practice enables, eventually, his more vigorous input: expressing disagreement and interceding in meeting processes in order to encourage the group to reach decisions.

The trust-building phase of Frank's advocacy work seems to be about allowing the group the time and opportunity to build up knowledge of Frank – his character, commitments, capacities – so that they have some basis on which to assess his trustworthiness (see Hardin, 2002: 114, 126). Once he perceives their preparedness to invest trust in him, he starts to change the nature of his behaviour by becoming more active and more vigorous in his engagement. However, since they have trusted the meek, mild Frank before with no bad result, they might risk trusting the newly revealed Frank. This strategy by Frank is intended to draw the new group into trusting him on more significant matters, in order to enable them to derive more benefits from the skills he has to offer. Frank would see these as including facilitation skills, the ability to realize projects and make things happen, being a go-between in difficult negotiations for the group, and doing 'whitefella' bureaucratic tasks. In Frank's practice, he is the one who pushes the boundaries of trust, always seeking to make any risks the new group takes in trusting him worth their while. A critique of Frank's approach in the light of accountability and anti-racist literatures would be that it places the interpersonal relationship as primary, above the social relations of the colonial, racial order in which people are embedded. Burghardt (1982) is helpful in pointing out that objective differences in lived experience underscore the need for accountability structures. His view suggests a dialectic between difference and sameness: difference in lived, material realities and sameness in 'shared needs for good working conditions, more effective methods of practice' (1982: 111). As Burbules and Rice (1991: 403, stress in original) have written in relation to debates over whether dialogue across difference is possible and worthwhile, 'any concrete discussion of difference also implies *sameness*: two objects, two people, two points of view, and so on, can be contrasted usefully only when there are at least some respects in which they are similar.' Frank's approach to trust is to try to get to the point that the marginalized group recognizes him as a decent, committed person, who is pursuing the same broad political aims, and wanting to work effectively. From this basis, the relationship can develop further, increasing collective capacity to achieve goals.

'I don't trust white people to be aware of our own racism'

Helen, a non-Indigenous activist and writer, described how her lack of trust in both herself and other white people to identify her racism meant that she withdrew from working with a particular Aboriginal community. Helen was born in Australia on Wathaurong land, to migrant (German and Polish) parents. Helen is a writer and a radical lesbian activist who began attending anti-Vietnam War marches at the age of 13. Her lifelong radicalism has included women's liberation, lesbian politics and a very passionate engagement with Aboriginal issues.

> Helen: I think particularly in those outback communities it's really fraught with danger that you're going to be doing things that are counterproductive that you don't even realize you're doing, because I've seen other people doing it, but I don't have enough perspective on myself to know whether I am or not, so I think I'd better just keep out of it too.
>
> Clare: Yeah. So you sort of became aware that you probably wouldn't be able to get that feedback from the Aboriginal people themselves, and it doesn't sound like there were other non-Indigenous people you could check in with and say 'Oh, look, what do you think, how's it going?'

Helen: Yeah, I could, but, you know, I don't trust white people to be aware of our own racism. In my experience we're not.

Helen talks about reaching the conclusion that she'd 'better just keep out of it'. There is a sense in which Helen's distrust of herself and other white people prevents her from continuing to engage with the community she describes. This could be read as reflective of the ultimate privilege, which is for members of dominant groups to keep out of engaging with social justice struggles in order to avoid making mistakes. For Helen, though, the concern is to avoid harming people. Helen also reflected:

I definitely have high awareness compared to most other white people of when I'm doing racist things. But in the past I've done them: looking back *now* I can see things that I've done that I wasn't aware of at the time because I hadn't evolved my consciousness and awareness of it enough ... to see. I can only see it now looking back. So what might I be doing now that maybe, you know, in five or ten years I can see that 'Oh, gee that was really, ah, patronizing or invasive'?

Helen's reflections point to a dilemma in which, at one level, it seems inevitable that a process of learning and consciousness change will occur over time. However, at another level, it is racist to expect Aboriginal people to put up with this igno-rance while white people make mistakes along the way. Helen's question, 'What might I be doing now [that is patronizing]?' expresses her heightened self-consciousness about unknowingly being racist, and her deeply felt awareness of the harm done by racism. As Patricia Williams argues (1998), racism 'is as bad' as physical violence and assault. In Williams's view it is probably worse, and in order to express this she denotes racism as 'spirit-murder'. Accepting this view, if there is a risk of harm in any engagement by white people with Indigenous people, one can argue that engagement should stop altogether. Alternatively, Indigenous people can decide whether or not to take that risk.

Although Helen is a relatively aware white person, she felt isolated and unable to challenge other white people. Helen's difficulty in confronting white people's counterproductive behaviour and her ultimate disengagement from the community were heightened by being a working-class person:

> I've often sort of thought: should I have come out fighting harder, against these white people? And then I feel like I was a coward, because I didn't fight them harder. But I felt I'm not able to.
>
> Some of that's about being a working-class person ... with parents of ... a low social status. I think it is harder for me to take on ... more middle-class, high-status [people. For example,] a university lecturer with a Ph.D. [would be] seen as a high-status person, and I'm a nobody.

Helen's situation demonstrates the importance of a view which acknowledges that privilege and subordination intersect. Helen is subordinated by class, sexuality and gender, while privileged by her white skin.

Elements of Helen's and Bill's practice can be understood as an attempt to hold oneself (and sometimes other non-Indigenous people) accountable. This resonates with the practices of the white anti-racists that Kowal (2010) has observed practising vigilance over their/our own barely repressible (or irrepressible?) habits of white privilege. One problem with trying to hold oneself accountable is that it relies on self-reflection and a lot of guesswork, and can for some non-Indigenous people lead to a sense that it is better not to engage with Indigenous people. I have suggested that collective approaches to accountability could offer possibilities in these situations; such approaches 'encourage you to be your best self and ... help you if you get off track' (Kendall, 2006: 133). A key feature of accountability processes is that they locate non-Indigenous people as challengeable by both Indigenous people and non-Indigenous people.

Helen's comments sparked in me a chain of reflections about the general paucity of trust between non-Indigenous people. To me it seems that non-Indigenous people orient them/ourselves towards establishing relationships with Indigenous people as a condition of or as an aim of supporting Indigenous struggles. Non-Indigenous people derive a sense of legitimacy from having a connection with 'the right' or even just 'any' Aboriginal people or person. Non-Indigenous people crave the approval of Aboriginal people, and disassociate from other non-Indigenous people just in case they are one day accused of racism by an Aboriginal person. This may also reflect 'power plays between allies to be the "better white activist" or the "better non-indigenous activist"' (Margaret, 2013: 91). In these ways non-Indigenous people resist responsibility for each other's racism.

A counter-example to the suspicion in which non-Indigenous people seem to me to hold each other is from the SLJR collective. Members of SLJR strongly identified themselves as a group at the 2000 Olympics protest at Victoria Park, Sydney, by all wearing identical political T-shirts. In retrospect, this seems to have been an expression of a collective identity and a collective sense of responsibility for each other's actions at the protest camp. I had not been part of the SLJR collective in the lead-up to the protest, having been in East Timor for the preceding six months. I remember being reluctant to identify myself with the SLJR collective at the protest.

I have made the point that non-Indigenous people generally tend to disassociate from other non-Indigenous people in order to avoid possible Aboriginal disapproval. Indeed, I personally might be avoiding entering into collective relationships of responsibility with other non-Indigenous people.

What makes activist relationships tick?

In working relationships between people of colonial backgrounds and Indigenous community leaders it is obvious that there should be useful work happening that supports Indigenous agendas. Utility is the *raison d'être* for these relationships, which, approached from the perspective of how friendships work, can also be understood as reflective of some kind of deal (Rawlins, 1992; Vernon, 2005). The deal – the give-and-take – between friends is constantly, if silently, negotiated, and is really only understood from within the logic of the friendship, so that one friend might listen to another's worries, and the other might provide company when needed (as in Jon Hawkes's description, in our interview, of his friendship with Gary Foley). What is the 'deal' between Indigenous and non-Indigenous people as we/they negotiate relationships in the activist context? In certain cases and political contexts, the utility of allies might be understood by Indigenous people as short-term, meaning there is no need to create 'ongoing, deeper transformative relationships' (Wallace et al., 2010: 98–9). Gary Murray clearly expresses the need, as he sees it, for Indigenous people to network with, engage with, draw in and involve non-Indigenous people in political and community development work: 'We *have* to network, that's part of the tactics.' For Gary Murray, on a political, tactical level, a primary need is to 'boost our numbers'. There is also a practical need to engage with non-Indigenous people on certain cultural, community and economic development projects, such as

> the Kurrumarat Project, the Big Cod Project ... to design and construct uniquely culturally looking Wamba Wamba rivercraft and lake-craft ... But in the process of designing that project we *have* to talk to people who've got the expertise. We haven't got the expertise in building those boats, at this point.

What is the 'deal' from a non-Indigenous perspective? Are Indigenous people useful to non-Indigenous people? The deal does not have to be symmetrical; perhaps there is some pleasure, rather than use, to be derived. Is there pleasure in the work, as Burghardt (1982) advocates? Or is involvement in a relationship with Indigenous people about some hoped-for friendship or re-demption, or some assumed dividend (Paasonen, 2007: 90)? For Jane Belfrage, there was meaning and satisfaction to be derived from service. For some non-Indigenous people, activism could be experienced as fulfilling for the way it expresses love in a wider public sense (Lynch and Walsh, 2009). When non-Indigenous people conceptualize social justice work as being about love in a wider public sense, they must also recognize what Maria Lugones (1987: 3–4) suggests for women of colour: 'I recognize that much of our travelling is done unwilfully to hostile White/Anglo "worlds" ... I recommend that we affirm this travelling across "worlds" as partly constitutive of cross-cultural and cross-racial loving.' For several Melbourne Kungkas, the idea of wanting or receiving something seemed inappropriate, something they struggled with.

Conclusion

Authentic relationships across race include the quality that 'both people are self-aware and willing to keep channels of communication open about power and privilege differences' (Kendall, 2006: 144). That said, Kendall is realistic about the difficulty of conducting conversations about race under racist conditions, and about the demands white people put on people of colour to talk nicely about race. She shows how white people expect people of colour to take responsibility for making white people feel safe when they raise issues of race. For instance, white institutions hold people of colour accountable for the 'manner' of their issue-raising – labelling it unhinged, crazy and unprofessional. Like Kendall, Burghardt discusses how 'work' goes into building any meaningful relationship across social inequality in the context of political organizing.

For Wayne Atkinson, to relate to virtually any non-Indigenous person is an exercise in forbearance. For Atkinson, this includes all activist relationships. He persists with the work of working with non-Indigenous people, and has to find ways of personally coping with the stress. To expect Indigenous people to put up with relentless expressions of racism and ignorance is unjust. However, Atkinson expresses a tension between the pain of this and the need to continue the struggle through educating people.

Many reflective non-Indigenous people who have maintained a solidarity practice over the long term, and who are to some extent aware of their privilege, practise a fair amount of benign faking. This is integral to the struggle to unlearn ways of thinking and being: that is, a struggle against those 'unconscious habits of white privilege' that they were coming to know in themselves. Knowing that one's reactions are scripted by a racist world, it seems important to hold back from expressing them. This is a kind of faking, familiar as a strategy within friendships (think of the many little untruths with which friends reassure each other; see Vernon, 2005). However, there is a more sinister type of faking: pretending to be a fantastic ally, but in other worlds conforming to whitely ways. This underscores the importance of personal integrity and courage: the importance of reckoning with complicity, of challenging racism in white settings, of admitting and interrogating the limits to what you are prepared to do in solidarity (see Moreton-Robinson, 2000). I suspect many existing relationships would be impossible without benign faking on both sides. Relating in activist relationships, let alone communicating openly about 'power and privilege differences', as Kendall advocates, involves pain and hard work, particularly for Indigenous people.

There are obvious utilitarian reasons for Indigenous people to engage in political relationships, alliances and solidarities. In the real world, these relationships may be held together by open, honest communication or by letting things slide. My sense is that in the absence of accountability constructs which can enable honest, difficult, necessary conversations about the workings of race and privilege, both sides use dissimulation mainly for the purpose of supporting the relationship. What is unsaid and what is let slide probably *enable* some activist relationships to exist. Even within accountability constructs, dissimulation of the kind that someone uses to hold him- or herself together when experiencing the pain of racism would still be needed to enable difficult conversations.

Coming to more clarity about tensions inherent in activist relationships might assist activists to identify ways to conduct these relationships that do not rely on the strategies of friendship. Rather than relying on dissimulation – which boils down to Aboriginal people having to tolerate racism – accountability processes which support difficult conversations about race and power could be used.

FIVE

Acting politically
with self-understanding

Indigenous people have at times challenged the nature and form of non-Indigenous support for their struggles. It is important to understand the political significance of these challenges.

Albert Memmi (1965) and Bantu Steve Biko – writing from northern African and South African contexts respectively – point out that it is not possible for white people to escape from the 'oppressor camp' because whites are allowed to enjoy privilege whether or not they agree with white supremacy (Biko, 1988: 37). Writing from a North American context, Ruth Frankenberg agrees: '*no* white person is exempt from participation in racist discourse or practice' (Frankenberg, 1993: 170). Yet it is possible for some white people to come to know the various ways in which their lives and actions are manifestations of white privilege and to start to reject or redeploy some of those privileges. Some work can be done from within the 'oppressor camp'. But this relies on the ability of members of dominant groups to move from one place to another within their white, or colonizer, or other dominant subjectivity. As Jane Belfrage says:

> I find my identity as an Australian very, very problematic. And
> I can't say I'm proud to be Australian. Because I have an identity
> as an Australian who is a colonizer. And I'm gonna be stuck with

that. I'm going to move, you know, from one space to another within it. But like ... Irish people that I'm connected to, they just love being Irish. But I can never ever be like that about being an Australian ... but I accept it. Cos that is, you know, who I am in this time and place, in this lifetime. And if this is the only one I've got, well, this is it. So I'm not going to hate it. You know? Ha ha ha.

Jane's changing relationship with her identity was made through critical self-reflection alongside her twenty years of activism in relation to particular land-rights struggles in the south-east of Australia, from Canberra to the south-west of Victoria.

Non-Indigenous people involved in supporting Indigenous struggles in a colonizing society such as Australia must 'always remember that we act from within the social relations and subject positions we seek to change' (Frankenberg, 1993: 5; see also McIntosh, 2006; Tamasese and Waldegrave, 1996). It is not enough to believe oneself to be a political supporter of Indigenous struggles; this intention by no means guarantees that any act (or utterance) by a 'supporter' is a supportive act. There are politics around how to be a supporter.[1]

Prevailing social relations cause unearned privileges to accrue to white people. This is something that white non-Indigenous activists are challenged to work at undoing, having realized that political support does not confer immunity from manifesting the privileges of whiteness (Foley, 1998, 2000; Holt, 1999). There is a range of responses to these challenges: to what extent do non-Indigenous people recognize our/themselves as

---

1. For that matter, even seeing oneself as a 'supporter' – or only a supporter – or an 'ally', or someone standing in solidarity, or a 'partner' has political implications. All of these terms suggest 'us' and 'them' (Margaret, 2010).

addressed by such challenges? And to what extent do we/they accept and manage to work through such challenges?

Non-Indigenous people are being asked to act politically, but to do this on the basis of self-understanding.

Acting politically with self-understanding

These two projects – acting politically and gaining self-understanding – are linked and must be maintained and held in balance over time. This chapter will explore the arguments for balancing 'critical self-reflection and a commitment to action' (Alfred and Coulthard, 2006), showing how they intersect and feed into each other, as well as providing examples of strategies within each project. It will also discuss some of the dilemmas of the strategies outlined. This will establish the importance of acting politically with self-understanding to the politics of solidarity overall.

Members of privileged groups must be in both engaged developing self-understanding through the practice of critical self-reflection and committed to collectivist and public political action if they are serious about working as allies of Indigenous struggles.[2] Commitment to these ongoing projects is the basis on which members of privileged groups can work towards acting politically, with self-understanding.[3]

Coming to recognize the need for greater self-understanding and entering into an interrogation of one's complicity and/ or privilege is challenging for many non-Indigenous people

---

2. The necessity of acting politically with self-understanding is widely regarded as crucial to the political endeavour of concern in this book. See Alfred and Coulthard, 2006; Amadahy, 2008; Burghardt, 1982; Jensen, 2005; Kendall, 2006; Pease, 2002; Tamasese and Waldegrave, 1996.
3. I read Ruth Frankenberg as arguing this (Frankenberg, 1993: 168–85).

(Freeman, 2010: 155). However, this self-understanding is crucial for members of privileged groups who want to challenge discourses or practices in which they are implicated. It involves 'Coming to grips with colonial privilege by acknowledging the role that [we] as settlers play in the maintenance of empire' (Alfred and Coulthard, 2006). For non-Indigenous people this can be thought of as the process of 'decolonizing ourselves' – our own thinking, our own minds. Indigenous theorists identified the need to decolonize themselves; Kenyan writer Ngũgĩ Wa Thiong'o's 1986 book *Decolonizing the Mind: The Politics of Language in African Literature* was an influential expression of this thinking. Ngũgĩ was concerned with finding ways to get free of the effects of imperialism's assault on the 'African mind', its annihiliaiton of 'a people's belief in their names, in their languages, in their environment, in their heritage of struggle, in their unity, in their capacities and ultimately in themselves'. A corresponding task has now been taken up by some non-Indigneous people.

Many scholars and activists have pointed out that while work to develop self-understanding, and to change 'individual consciousness among the privileged', is important, it must be accompanied by 'collectivist and public political action' aimed at addressing structural privilege (Pease, 2010b: 170, 173). As Jensen has argued,

> It is possible to not be racist (in the individual sense of not perpetrating overtly racist acts) and yet at the same time fail to be antiracist (in the political sense of resisting a racist system) ... Because white people benefit from living in a white supremacist society, there is an added obligation for us to struggle against the injustice of that system. (Jensen, 2005: 80)

This ethic applies to institutions as well as to individuals who seek to manifest a commitment to anti-racism. Tamasese and Waldergrave (2006) and others argue that working on dismantling privileges must happen on systemic as well as interpersonal levels. It is in activity – in living out a commitment to end racism through contributing to anti-racist campaigns and causes – that racism can continue to be unlearned (Burghardt 1982: 111).

Developing self-understanding

To develop 'self-understanding' in the context of supporting Indigenous struggles, non-Indigenous people need to go through a process of getting to know our/themselves in historical and political context. It entails working on gaining a clearer view of the workings of race and of white privilege, and of complicity at a personal level and at a structural level. It involves exploring questions such as:

- Where are you from?
- What is your culture?
- What happened to Aboriginal people where you now live?
- How are you positioned in relation to colonialism?
- How are your life and your habits shaped by privilege?
- Why are you interested in being supportive of Aboriginal people?
- What does being an ally mean to you?
- How do you know you are emerging towards non-racism?
- Do you want something in exchange for work as an ally?
- What are the ethical considerations in ally work?[4]

---

4. This list of questions was composed from a reading of the following writings: Acker,

Foley regards critical self-reflection as one of the first steps that non-Indigenous people should take if they are 'serious about wanting to be involved in the struggle for justice' for Indigenous people (see also Freeman, 2010; Nanni, 2010). According to Foley,

> The first thing you need to do is not go and talk to any blackfellas at all, really. You need to look in the mirror. You need to look at yourself. You need to think hard and fast about who *you* are ... In the process of sorting out [any psychological identity problems of your own] you will reach a higher level of consciousness that will make you better prepared, then, to come and work in Indigenous communities. (Foley, cited in Nanni, 2010)

It is notable that the first step Foley suggests actually represents a brake on the impulse to act that many newly cognizant non-Indigenous people often express by asking, 'What can I do?' While admirable and encouraging as a response to Aboriginal people's testimonies of dispossession, this impulse towards a technical response can also be understood as a reflex for managing (avoiding) guilt (Maddison, 2011: 9–10). It is often associated with complaining that the government is not doing enough to fix the situation, itself a strategy for avoiding the harder and deeper work of knowing and confronting one's own complicity. For Aboriginal peoples' status to change, non-Aboriginal people will all need to change.

Critical self-reflection must not only 'precede' actions as an ally but continue to be performed alongside that public political ally work (Kendall, 2006: 150). Critical self-reflection can be explored individually or collectively, by talking with others.

1996; Kendall, 2006; Sullivan, 2006; Foley, cited in Land, 2011a; McIntosh, 1989, 2003; Calderón and Wise, 2012; Bobiwash and Butler, n.d. (1999–2000).

An engagement with the project of developing self-understanding as a non-Indigenous person will include interrogating one's social location as a colonizer, albeit a reluctant one. It should involve interrogating the workings of unconscious habits of white privilege. As theorist Shannon Sullivan argues (2006), these habits are deeply ingrained in people through ongoing transaction with a racist world, yet they are not natural and are possible to shift.

Critical self-reflection cannot be separated from public political action

There is an intersection between critical self-reflection and public political work. Each can be seen to inform the other. Some people from privileged groups have talked about how their public political activism developed self-understanding and resulted in a deeper level of understanding of the issues faced by oppressed groups (Cam Walker, interview). Some have also described feeling that they have become less free to choose not to be involved (freedom to choose the level of activist involvement is understood as a privilege). Pease (2010b) writes from personal experience in pro-feminist struggles about how political work can change one's sense of self, making it seem difficult or impossible to walk away from the issues.

Further, developing self-understanding can also help to direct public political work. Work that enables non-Indigenous people to see more clearly their/our complicity with the structures and logics which they/we purport to oppose can feed political strategy. As Tom Keefer suggests in his analysis of the solidarity work of 'non-native activists' with Haudenosaunee (Six Nations) people in a land reclamation struggle near Ontario,

Canada, developing a clear view of how their own social location implicates them in colonialism provides non-native activists with 'opportunities to disrupt it' (Keefer, 2007).

Public political action

So what does it mean to act politically, to take public political action?

There are many challenges for non-Indigenous people contemplating how to engage in public political work. However, such work can also take many credible forms.

'Long-term struggles need long-term allies'

A key challenge for non-Indigenous people contemplating how to engage in public political work in solidarity with Indigenous struggles is the long-term nature of these struggles. Any assessment of non-Indigenous people's contributions to Indigenous struggles will make note of the high rate of attrition. The short-term or temporary character of many non-Indigenous people's support was a source of frustration among many Indigenous people I interviewed. Short-term involvement may reflect non-Indigenous people wanting or expecting a situation to change quickly, and losing their staying power when they realize that it will be a long haul.

All the Indigenous people I interviewed could talk about their experiences of supporters 'coming and going'. Some discussed their perception that non-Indigenous people who were only involved for the short term seemingly never really cared deeply anyway (bryan Andy); or were once supporters, but then, as a result of actively or passively making conventional life choices, 'blended in' to the system (Monica Morgan); or,

possibly worst of all, went on to get a job in Aboriginal Affairs
using their activist experiences as proof of their cross-cultural
proficiency. On this, Monica Morgan reflected:

> I have known over the last twenty or so years young people
> come in, do their internship or their apprenticeship and then they
> go on, have families, get jobs ... I think to myself: maybe they're
> going to be bureaucrats, or law-makers or academics and they're
> gonna make a change. [Pause] I don't know, I wouldn't have a
> clue ... they flow through. I don't know where they come out at
> the end.

Wayne Atkinson said: 'I often use the analogy "the struggle continues but supporters come, supporters go..."', and
later in the interview observed, 'Along the way you'll have
these differences I suppose, in peoples' commitments and that.
You move on from there ... others come on board and you
start the process again of trying to educate them! Ha ha.' As
pro-feminist activist and scholar Bob Pease has pointed out,
'one of the forms of privilege is the ability to ignore calls for
involvement in social justice campaigns', or to commit but then
change one's mind (Pease, 2010b: 184).

Jen Margaret's discussions with allies in North America
backed up the contention that 'Long-term struggles need
long-term allies.' Parallel to this were many examples in my
interviews attesting to the regard in which long-term non-
Indigenous allies are held by Indigenous people (see also Land,
2011a). That said, Gary Murray offered a unique perspective:

> If you look at that period when Pastor Doug Nicholls was
> running the League [VAAL] – some of them whitefellas stuck
> around from the '40s, '50s right through to the '70s ... But you
> don't see that no more where a non-Indigenous person stayed for
> that long haul. That's because the politics have changed. People's
> values have changed, their dynamics have changed. White people

tend to say, 'Well it's a black issue and black people have really got to run it.' That's why we see people come and go.

Repeat experiences of a short-term commitment from 'allies' means that newcomers – or long-term allies previously unknown to an Indigenous person – might perceive reserve from Indigenous people for some time. As Cam Walker, who works as campaigns coordinator for Friends of the Earth, Melbourne, remarked: 'I really have felt it over the years. There's that: "Well, you know, you might be here for ten minutes, or you might be gone"' (interview). Nina Collins was aware of the issue of attrition, and felt she had received a dismissive reception at times, but decided to take this as a challenge:

> people have blown me off, and said, you know, 'You're young, what would you know?' or 'You're just going to be here for a short time, and then once Indigenous issues have fallen from the headlines and something else is up, you'll be gone' – which I've taken on as more of a challenge than a criticism. But I think they had a point. (Nina Collins, interview)

Frequenting community events is one way non-Indigenous people can show they are committed, according to Frank Hytten (interview). As one participant in a roundtable on relationship-building in Indigenous solidarity work said, 'Listen, take direction and stick around' (Amadahy, 2008).

As a rejoinder to this discussion of long-term commitment I will highlight that some problematic dynamics can emerge over the long term. This is something Lisa Thorpe commented on in our interview. She raised the phenomenon of people working for Aboriginal organizations who start to believe they are Aboriginal, or speak and make decisions on behalf of the community. From her perspective, this 'so often happens.

You'll never be an Aboriginal person, same as we will never be a white person. So let's respect those boundaries to begin with' (Lisa Thorpe, interview).

Boundaries around what you need to know: knowing enough, not all the details

Another key challenge for non-Indigenous people is accepting the complexities and boundaries around what they need to know and find out to inform their political actions. Margaret talks about *knowing enough*, suggesting that what non-Indigenous people might want to know is 'too much' (Margaret, 2010). Non-Indigenous people need to understand that, for instance, there may be intra-Aboriginal politics relevant to a campaign that it is not strategically wise to make public, and that cannot therefore be shared widely with supporters (Paasonen, 2007). There can also be issues within Indigenous communities that make projects go slower, but it may be fair enough that the details of these are not shared with supporters. These issues can range from lived realities like homelessness, numerous funerals, no money, no food, relatives in jail, and conflict and/or politics in communities to community processes needing to be followed. However, non-Indigenous people do not need to know the details of all the issues. Several Indigenous people I interviewed remarked on this issue.

Yorta Yorta woman Monica Morgan observed that non-Indigenous people seem to express some frustration that projects can't happen more quickly. She perceived a sense of urgency among non-Indigenous activists, which existed in tension with the situation of Indigenous people running campaigns while also engaged in a day-to-day struggle to survive:

> Monica: [Some of] them working on the Barmah forest – they're just so one-eyed and so, you know, really focused and they *really* want results. We're saying, 'Well, you have to go through the channels' … and then those channels grind slowly in the Koori community…
>
> So they get frustrated, I know they get frustrated. And I just say 'That's just how it is' … But you don't really need to know about all the ins and outs of it, you just have to know that we've got other things over here that has to be handled while you just keep paddling the canoe…
>
> Clare: Is that something that they find hard to understand sometimes, or…?
>
> Monica: Sometimes they do. Yeah they do, yeah. They can be very persistent, and that in itself can be off-putting. (Monica Morgan, interview)

Monica made reference to community processes relating to decision-making which may involve 'people that are older, have families, responsibilities, other kind of ties, and then you got your elders, and you got personalities'. These things add to the time it takes to go through the proper channels. In a separate interview, Yorta Yorta man bryan Andy talked about the need to deal with the way things are done culturally within a project, and cultural business regarding how to deal properly with death and grieving. He commented that 'Black projects have so much more baggage', saying:

> It seems to be there's so much more work you've got to do to achieve things within the Indigenous community – not that that's a bad thing by any stretch of the imagination, but … there's a whole process that you have to go through that is laborious and time-consuming.

There is a challenge for non-Indigenous people around the need to be sensitive to issues that might make campaigns and projects go more slowly than they would like, and to balance this against the imperatives of campaign strategies as well as their own enthusiasm, energy and devotion.

Undoing privilege, secreting 'personal problems'

The final interview I undertook was with Robbie Thorpe, someone with whom I worked closely during the years of the Ph.D. work this book is based on; we continue to co-present a radio programme. It was during this final interview that I finally recognized as ally work the struggle to transcend the social reality of oppression that Robbie does in working with people like me. That is, the struggle to keep 'personal problems' out of the activist setting: Robbie talks about the necessity for him of keeping 'personal problems' from 'bogging down' the project of working on the 'bigger picture' (interview). During the interview I argued that I saw these so-called 'personal problems' as, more precisely, an unequal distribution of personal problems, and therefore as a manifestation of my privilege and his oppression. Povinelli (2006: 77) finds that the 'uneven distribution' of goods, resources, rights, recognition, and 'life and death' arises from 'structural impoverishment'. Of course Robbie also read the 'personal problems' as political:

> I say, 'No, my personal problems aren't important' ... They are to *me*, but not to the bigger picture stuff ... They are in a sense. You know, the health and happiness of my family is the whole fucking thing I'm wanting to do these things for ... But it's not that easy.
> Most blackfellas have got multitudes, myriads of fucking problems going beyond their birth ... It's because of the institutionalized, racist attempt to destroy us ... We're not in the best of health, our people ... We've got mental problems, problems in our families, fucking you name it, we've got it.

> So that just makes it a bit harder to deal with blackfellas. Our minds aren't there, focused all the time. It's difficult to work with blackfellas.
>
> That's why the most important thing is do that background work first … background studies and things like that … if you want to help Aboriginal people … Because otherwise it becomes a problem for blackfellas. Whitefellas say, 'Oh come on, do this! Why can't you do that?' (Robbie Thorpe, interview)

It was through reflecting on this conversation with Robbie that I finally came to understand the work of reducing the impact of 'personal problems' as parallel to the work of non-Indigenous people to reduce the impact of privilege on our/their way of relating. This is often impossible: even if 'personal problems' aren't talked about, and we get on with 'bigger picture' work, the personal impact of those problems seeps in. As Robbie stated, that 'makes it a bit harder to deal with blackfellas. Our minds aren't there, focused all the time.' The way personal problems *seep in* is perhaps parallel to the tendency of paternalism, which *creeps in*. Both parties are trying to keep these things out.

This reflection on my personal experiences, in conversation with Robbie, suggests one way in which Indigenous people and non-Indigenous people are working in parallel to help relationships work.

Forms for public political action

Having set out the challenges of the need for long-term allies and the need for non-Indigenous people to understand the political complexity that may exist behind the scenes, or the greater 'baggage' involved with black projects, I will now set out some concrete examples of public political action.

'It is important to act and actions can be small'

Margaret (2010) states with great clarity an incredibly important suggestion for non-Indigenous people wondering 'what to do' and what action to take. Margaret is well aware of the potential for would-be allies to be 'immobilized' by feelings of guilt or denial or '"not knowing" what to do'. She notes that 'white people like to be comfortable and "right" in their actions' and offers up for discussion this possible response: 'It is important to act and actions can be small; for example, *sharing with other white people what you have learned*' (Margaret, 2010: 17). She continues with a suggestion that underscores the importance of humility and knowing what has been done in the past: 'Significant actions, such as building alliances with indigenous peoples, are best undertaken, initially at least, alongside other people/groups already active in this work, rather than being forged individually' (Margaret, 2010: 17). While coordinator at ANTaR Victoria, Frank Hytten drew together a matrix of activities, ranging from small upwards, with many suggestions for reflection and action (see Appendix IV).

Bystander anti-racism

Linked to the suggestion of 'sharing with other white people what you have learned', above, is an issue raised by Indigenous people of white people's responsibility for challenging racism, both in settings where Indigenous people are present and in situations where no Indigenous people are present. Non-Indigenous people might intend to challenge racism, but find that they face repercussions from other non-Indigenous people for standing up against it.

Wayne Atkinson has spoken about the importance of notic-ing racism, and standing up for Aboriginal people. He made this point using the example of a trusted non-Indigenous person:

> When we were confronted with that harsh sort of prejudice and hostilities, they were there shoulder to shoulder with you. Yep. And they were also quick to challenge, themselves, any misconceptions and prejudices that were aimed at their mates. At Koori friends … When Kooris were being put down in the pub or something. They'd stand up for ya. Say, 'Hang on, you're talking about my mate.' And so it would go from there. And *they* would confront.

bryan Andy talked about knowing that non-Indigenous people could turn their racism on and off depending on the context.

> I know that happens a lot with non-Indigenous Australians, where they know when it's alright to be racist and when it's not alright to be racist. I'd love to just send some non-Indigenous actors into a bar, film them, and bring up an issue around Sorry Day or Invasion Day and just watch people respond to things … I think Australians are very sophisticated at knowing when to turn it on and turn it off.

For non-Indigenous people who want to challenge racism, punishment of white disloyalty may 'trump' these intentions (Kendall, 2006). Kessaris (2006) has considered how 'non-conforming' white people are punished by other whites if they take an anti-racist stance. As a Blekbala (Indigenous person) reading the writings of Mununga (white people) who 'publicly align their empathy with Blekbala people and society' (2006: 349), Kessaris aims to 'expose what goes on between Mununga … in Australia that contributes to the maintenance of racism' (2006: 347). She finds that 'group racism not only attempts to keep Blekbalas in their place, but it coerces and bullies non-conforming Munungas to remain in their place of privilege' (Kessaris, 2006: 349).

In the face of possible bullying, non-Indigenous activists' intentions to challenge racism are supported not only by having an understanding of the harm caused by racism and the need to share the burden of challenging racism with those who are its targets, but also by remembering that this work is an important part of the raft of strategies needed to influence social norms for the better. Finding a way to respond either in the moment or afterwards can result in eventual changes to institutional culture, policies and practices (Nelson et al., 2011).

Anti-racism work: Organizing white people

Beyond challenging incidents of interpersonal or institutional racism are more sustained anti-racist practices. These are driven by the suggestion that non-Indigenous people – in particular white people – direct their activist energies towards anti-racism work and organizing among their own communities. The need for anti-racism work among non-Indigenous communities can be appreciated by undertaking the small experiment Foley has proposed (Land, 2011a). He suggests that 'white supporters ... go out and find yourself a racist':

> Just go home, to the dinner table. You'll find your racist. Raise the subject of 'Aboriginal...' – you'll find the really hard core racist arguments that are thrown up. And if you can't, as an individual, change the attitudes of someone who's really close to you and you personally care about, then don't think that you're going to be able to do anything about changing the attitudes of the broader society. (Foley, cited in Land, 2011a: 50)

Self-organized reading and discussion groups can build knowledge about racism and whiteness among group members, and this can be extended to more public gatherings with guest speakers. 'Organizing' work can be directed towards 'developing political organizations rooted in each community', which can work as allies of Indigenous organizations, starting by creating links between non-Indigenous people who support Indigenous people, but who in many places are most likely 'unorganized and atomised' (Keefer, 2007). Anti-racism work by experienced allies can take the form of running workshops for non-Indigenous people and consultancies for institutions, as Chris Twining, a Celtic, white Australian woman I interviewed, has done for many years.

This argument for white people to work on and among 'our' own/white people has a long genealogy, having been invoked by Black Consciousness/Black Power thinkers and activists and their allies in various contexts, including South Africa, North America and Australia (Aal, 2001; Biko, 1988; Keefer, 2007; Kendall, 2006). If white people are creating a problem (by perpetuating dominant-culture colonialism and racism), then the dominant culture, rather than those it relegates to a position of subordination, should be the target of activists' energies. This framing of the problem and the strategy to redress it can be seen in the Black Power politics of informing white activists that their place is not to work with black organizations, and that if they really want to help they should to do that by 'organizing' their own white communities (Thompson, 2001). Tom Keefer has argued the same point, noting problems with the relatively widespread non-Indigenous activist protocol of 'taking leadership' from Indigenous people in a specific context in Canada. A key problem in the context Keefer described was that the relevant Indigenous people, the Six Nations people, did not actually consider themselves to be 'giving leadership' to their non-native allies. According to Keefer, waiting for 'leadership' meant 'crucial opportunities to build non-indigenous support ... have been missed' (Keefer, 2007). Addressing a different aspect of the politics of leadership, Canadian-based white activist Stef Gude has commented: 'There is a middle ground between taking the lead and waiting to be told what to do. It's a balance – taking responsibility and not burdening already stressed-out, overworked indigenous leadership, but also taking guidance from them' (Amadahy, 2008: 27). Anti-racist organizer/educator William Aal explains why activist work needs to target white people: '[I]n order to eradicate racism activists and organizers need to start working with those who benefit most from racist structures and who play the biggest part in maintaining them' (Aal, 2001: 295).

Despite the wide acceptance of this view among those influenced by Black Power politics, many have observed reluctance on the part of white people to do this. Essentially, working with white people is regarded as less exciting than working with black people (Thompson, 2001). Further to this, Steve Biko – well-known anti-apartheid activist of the 1960s and 1970s in South Africa – decried a tendency he observed among white liberals to seek to work directly with black people, finding it indicative of suspect motivations:

> Since they are aware that the problem in this country is white racism, why do they not address themselves to the white world? Why do they insist on talking to blacks? In an effort to answer these questions, one has to come to the painful conclusion that the liberal is in fact appeasing his own conscience, or at best is eager to demonstrate his identification with the black people only so far as it does not sever all his ties with his relatives on the other side of the colour line. (Biko, 1988: 79)

As implied above, Biko did believe white liberals had roles to play: to concern themselves with white racism (1988: 37); to fight for their own freedom; to 'educat[e their] white brothers' about the history of the country; and to 'serve as a lubricating material so that as we change the gears in trying to find a better direction for South Africa, there should be no grinding noises of metal against metal' (1988: 40).

To return to Margaret and Foley, the seemingly modest action of talking to friends or family about colonialism may reveal itself as a challenging task, and may lead to more insights, including the likelihood that the would-be ally does not know enough to be able to argue against the racist opinions of others.

Self-education and community education by non-Indigenous people can be conceptualized as a way of sharing with Indigenous educators and organizers the burden of redressing non-Indigenous people's 'knowledge deprivation' (Wayne Atkinson, interview) or inexcusable ignorance (Barker, 2010). Indigenous people I interviewed (Gary Murray, Robbie Thorpe) testified to the repetitive nature of this education work (see also Land, 2011a). It is important for non-Indigenous people to engage in self-education using existing resources and opportunities rather than burdening Aboriginal people individually.

One difficulty that a non-Indigenous organizer of community education initiatives has voiced is that non-Indigenous audiences like to hear from a 'real live Aborigine', yet there are not enough to go around (Land, 2011a: 53). This points to one of the challenges faced by allies answering the call to work with white communities. Aboriginal people can't meet all the needs out there; white people need to make it part of their work to explain this and still find ways to keep audiences engaged with the issues. This is a difficulty that perhaps needs to be addressed *together*. Perhaps Indigenous people will still have to do some educating and non-Indigenous activists will have to do some of the hard work of convincing other non-Indigenous people that their expectation is too challenging (Kuokkanen, 2003).

What happened to the local mob?

Linked to the strategy of going home or to one's circle of friends to find 'a racist' to convert is Foley's exhortation: 'What do you know about what happened to the people who lived on the place that you live on now?' (cited in Land, 2011a: 52). Both of these suggested actions are characteristic of decolonized solidarity. Considering 'what happened to the local mob' leads to an engagement with local struggles.

Attentiveness to local struggles is crucial. This is obvious in Indigenous people's critiques of activists who focus on faraway rather than local (and, particularly, urban) struggles (see Amadahy, 2008; Barker, 2010; Corntassel, 2006: 29). Foley has harshly critiqued the phenomenon of 'running off to the Northern Territory' to work in a remote Aboriginal community (see also Bell, 2003). Foley argues that this action is misguided because it is based on four false assumptions: (1) that Aboriginal people are to be helped; (2) that intervention will help (see also Lea, 2008: 3); (3) that 'real' Aborigines are elsewhere; (4) that there is no issue in one's own backyard. Further, he argues that it indicates to him a lack of self-reflection (why does one think like that?) and suspect motivations:

> That's not a sign of people who genuinely want to be allies in the quest for justice. That's all about people who've got some sort of serious, inner, psychological problem of their own who are

looking for something for themselves, not for anyone else. (cited
in Land, 2011a: 55)

Adam Barker (2010), referring to Native critiques of the 'Free
Tibet syndrome' in the North American context, suggests a
similar explanation for this impulse on the part of 'would-be
allies' to 'cast their decolonizing gaze to faraway places while
ignoring local indigenous struggles' (Corntassel, 2006: 36).
Barker maintains that this displays a wish to 'restore comfort'
in the face of feelings of 'guilt or shame' that can attend a
growing consciousness of colonialism's injustices (Barker, 2010:
321). Focusing on 'faraway places' avoids a confrontation with
more direct complicity. In a further critique, Foley notes that
this action tends to result in a flow of benefits not to the people
in the Northern Territory but to the person who went there.
One of the benefits is an enhanced 'reputation and image'
(Foley, in Land, 2011a: 55) for the 'BINT', the person who has
Been in the Northern Territory (Bell, 2003).

It is important to note points of both similarity and contrast
between the phenomenon of running off to the Northern Territory, as Foley describes it, and other reasons for going there.
For instance, the act of answering a national call-out to activists
to support a faraway cause such as the Irati Wanti campaign
against the proposed National Radioactive Waste Repository
in northern South Australia (Crombie et al., 1998; Kupa Piti
Kungka Tjuta, 2003), or the blockade against a uranium mine at
Jabiluka near Jabiru, Northern Territory, initiated by the Mirrar
people, is a response to a clear invitation for allies to support an
Indigenous-led, collectively organized political initiative. This
contrasts with the normally self-generated impetus to go and
help out in a sometimes volunteer but usually, or eventually, a

paid role (such as a teacher or community development worker). In many such settings, non-Indigenous people at a pervasive day-to-day level, if not at a 'governance' level, control the work done (see Jordan, 2005). As for similarities, a participant in the Jabiluka campaign has identified the expectation of non-Indigenous Jabiluka campaign participants of receiving 'specific "soft" or "solidary" incentives' such as 'access to Aboriginal knowledge, and recognition and trust from Aboriginal traditional owners' in exchange for their political support (Paasonen, 2007: 90). Ali, a Victoria-born and educated participant in the Melbourne Kungkas collective which supported the Irati Wanti campaign, discussed her knowledge of the contentious nature of focusing on 'something so far away', and noted how the campaign gained from outsiders' attraction to its 'novel and exotic' character. I interviewed Ali as part of a group interview with two other members of the Melbourne Kungkas, Belinda and Cath. Belinda also talked about her awareness of the problematic desire to 'seek out the exotic':

> I really remember lots of lessons in the Kungkas resisting, or just disrupting, any attempt by us to seek out the exotic and the culture and all that. The first time I was at 10 Mile, Naomi was camped up there and she had this fuckin' mangy camp-dog and she wanted Mrs Smith, who is this full-on culture woman, to name it. [Cath sniggers] And, um, Mrs Smith named it Lassie. And [all laughing] Naomi was really upset and she was like, 'No, I really want a Yankunjatjara name, you know, proper name.' And Mrs Smith was like, 'Lassie-yah, Lassie-yah!' (Melbourne Kungkas, group interview)

Ali also pointed out that there were 'obvious reasons' why the KPKT sought to draw strategically on faraway support, including Melbourne: 'there's resources here, there's people here' (Melbourne Kungkas, group interview). There are important

nuances to the criticism of running off to the Northern
Territory.

As an alternative to 'running off to the Northern Territory',
Foley advocates engaging with local issues.

> How many people here now know *who* the Koori mob was who
> lived in the land that they are now, where you live? And it's not
> just a question of knowing, 'OK the Wurundjeri' or somebody,
> it's not just a question of knowing who they *were*, it's a question
> of, what happened to them? What do you know about what
> happened to the people who lived on the place that you live
> on now? And, you know, as you gain a sense of that, you gain
> a sense of just how enormous your own personal ignorance is.
> (Foley, cited in Land, 2011a: 52)

Foley framed these questions by saying that people needed
to grapple with how Australia's embedded racism 'relates
to them, personally', engaging them with questions about
complicity. Again, this found resonance with Cherokee scholar
Jeff Corntassel's strategies for dealing with complicity rather
than avoiding its discomforts: 'settler populations can begin by
decolonizing their thinking, engaging in insurgent education,
making amends to local indigenous peoples and seeking out
indigenous-led alliances' (Corntassel, 2006: 37). This kind of
focus on the local is something that resonates strongly with
Indigenous epistemologies, and with the work of Indigenous
and other educators who challenge conventional education
(Butler, 2009; Gruenewald, 2003: 3). David Gruenewald,
arguing for a 'critical pedagogy of place' that would ground
education in local social experience and ecological concerns,
makes explicit the question which follows from the one Foley
raised. Gruenewald asks, 'What happened here? What will
happen here?' (2003: 11). Thus, for Foley and Gruenewald,

such local knowing leads to acting: the first question leads inevitably, in the critical tradition, to the second question about possible transformation.

Cam Walker makes a similar argument about the importance of place, and of the 'truths' that emerge through a reckoning with place. Cam says a cognizance of living on someone's land is fundamental to the analysis that guides his activism:

> So there's the fact you live on Aboriginal land and that brings a whole bunch of truths with it ... I think we live in a generic culture where place doesn't matter. So I think once you understand that place actually matters, it has to take you to the door of, you know, Indigenous rights and sovereignty. Cos place and people have been so connected here for so long. (interview)

Supporting local struggles is key to the politics of solidarity. It is a decolonizing move and ethic because it resists the colonialist notion that land is an unknown wilderness and that its people are undifferentiated (this is suggested by using the homogenizing term 'Aboriginal', rather than the name of each polity). It is interlinked with the projects of developing self-understanding and reckoning with complicity, as well as with self-education and sharing what you've learned with others.

Pay the Rent

The concept of 'paying the rent' is simple and powerful, but in some areas there are practical difficulties for people who want to do this. Pay the Rent is based on the conviction that Aboriginal people own the land, and non-Aboriginal people (including Aboriginal people from other areas) who live on it should pay rent to them in recognition of this. More details are included in a Pay the Rent flyer and the conceptually linked non-Indigenous 'Request for Permission to Live on Country as an Interim Permanent Resident' (see Appendix IV). Despite the endorsement of the concept nationally through NAIHO, its uptake by local mobs has not been universal. For one thing, it is hard work to convince non-Indigenous people to pay the rent. Another barrier to establishing Pay the Rent more widely could be Indigenous peoples' lack of resources to organize as a polity which could receive and manage payments. It is worth noting how Robbie Thorpe and Denis Walker address this barrier. For Robbie Thorpe, Pay the Rent offers non-Indigenous people a chance to 'justify their occupation' of Aboriginal land as well as providing support to un-resourced sovereign Aboriginal polities and initiatives. Denis Walker connects paying the rent with treaty-making, such that his model treaty takes the form of recognition of Aboriginal land ownership and violent and illegal dispossession, and sets out the terms of a lease in which payments can support a polity or campaign. One such campaign is Walker's Sacred Treaty Circles; in this case, paying the rent resources Aboriginal people to re/organize as polities (see Appendix IV for a link to Walker's model treaty).

Paying the rent is linked to the project of finding out what happened to the local mob, in that it is to the local mob that rent should be paid in the first instance. Tony Birch (2007) advocates the project, as did Helen, Barry Mitchell, Robbie Thorpe and Gary Murray in my interviews. Gary Murray's mention of it was as part of a discussion about recent agreements between the state government and traditional owners under Native Title legislation in Victoria in which he critiqued a lack of ongoing guaranteed funding to traditional owner groups. As Gary observed: 'What flows from that is land rights compensation, reparation – ongoing compensation. So you take our land forever, you have to pay us forever.' Barry Mitchell, a member of AWD, described his involvement with Pay the Rent:

> The concept of paying the rent was put to [AWD] by local Kooris, and we started to develop the programme in close consultation with them. That involved explaining the concept to other non-Indigenous people and encouraging them to participate, and setting up a banking system to facilitate direct deposits into a Koori-controlled bank account. As far as we know, we were the first to put the Pay the Rent concept into practice in Australia.

The spirit of Pay the Rent can also be honoured in other forms. Helen described how organizations within the radical lesbian political scene go about it:

> We have a 10 per cent policy whenever we have a camp or conference ... Everyone pays a rego fee and then 10 per cent of that is either donated to an Aboriginal organization (which the organizers choose) or alternatively it goes to cover free entry for any Aboriginal woman who wants to come ... It's basically handed over to Aboriginal women or lesbians to decide where it should be distributed to.

Helen points out that this commitment is not trivial: 'The radical lesbian cultural thing is mostly populated by women with not much money, so it is sort of quite a big thing.'

There are many strengths to the Pay the Rent concept, and it certainly provides an opportunity for non-Indigenous people to 'put your money where your mouth is'.

Supporting Indigenous-led alliances

Another strategy for settler populations looking for ways to act politically is to seek out Indigenous-led alliances (as Corntassel,

2006, has suggested). However, there are a number of issues to be attentive to. Indigenous people may have different ideas about *how* to address *which particular* problems, raising questions about which Indigenous people and which issues get support. Further, within a given Indigenous community there may be differing views on prevailing issues (Cam Walker, interview). Within the collectivity I am concerned with, Indigenous people are working on a range of different levels, directing their activist work at a range of targets. Who, then, decides what issues non-Indigenous people will lend their support to?

Several Indigenous people I interviewed talked about the question of what issues gain committed support. For instance, Gary Murray talked about his view of the factors at play in both 'black and white' people's decisions about what issues to support, which fights to commit to. I had asked Gary about whether he'd had a relationship of genuine dialogue, or a good connection with any non-Indigenous people in particular, and he answered by talking about his sense that there is a cycle of mostly ineffectual, relatively short-lived struggle, before moving on 'to the next issue':

> Gary: I think wherever you go, whatever the issue is … you always find goodwill, to start off with. And that's what you've got to build on. And you've got to maintain it. You know, sometimes you do, sometimes you don't …
>
> Clare: Do you feel like those issues are getting resolved or they're just falling away or the energy around them is falling away … ?
>
> Gary: Some do. Some do, some don't. Depends on whether they're resourced, and whether people are wholly committed to it, and how serious the issue is. You know, like a fight over a burial ground will be a lot tougher and stronger and people will stay for the long haul, than say, I dunno, a fight over the old Health Service in Gertrude St is an example.

Clare: Do you mean Aboriginal people will fight that harder?
Gary: Yeah. Both. Bit of both I think. Both black and white.

Gary indicates that there are so many issues cropping up all the time, mostly caused by decisions by government, that people's focus, both 'black and white', is scattered. Yet other factors are 'how serious the issue is', whether people are 'wholly committed to it', and whether campaign organizers are able to maintain and build on the support base.

Robbie Thorpe has also raised the question of what issues get support. He has asked 'whether people see their way to supporting what we're doing here'. Robbie regards the issues of the Black GST (genocide, sovereignty, treaty) as fundamental, and says he would like to see people support this agenda: 'You don't need to bring your own ideas.' I read these statements as being based on prior experiences of supporters who want 'to pursue their own ideas, and even enrol Indigenous people in their own initiatives and projects, rather than throw their support behind what Aboriginal people had been saying over and over again were their priorities' (Land, 2011a).

As I have written, this raises questions about 'how and why supporters of Indigenous struggles decide what to support. Is it based more on the personal preference, interests and agendas of non-Indigenous people than it is on those of Indigenous people? Is this something that needs to be interrogated?' (Land, 2011a). One factor that might be turning non-Indigenous people off issues like genocide, sovereignty and treaty is a sense of powerlessness to address such fundamental issues, including a lack of knowledge of how issues such as genocide, sovereignty and treaty could be addressed strategically and practically, beyond just demanding that the government address them somehow. There are in fact practical steps one can take, such as supporting projects like Pay the Rent (see Appendix IV), and finding out what genocide, sovereignty and treaty mean for Aboriginal agendas. Further, there could be deep, perhaps unacknowledged, fear and reluctance to face these problems. While seeking out Indigenous-led alliances is a direct way of providing support, Tom Keefer cautions non-Native people to be sensitive to the issue of whether their support for a particular Indigenous person or group could be experienced as divisive within that Indigenous community. (However, note that Keefer, 2007, writes in a Canadian context and cautions against mechanically extending his claims to other contexts where they may not be applicable.)

Directly assisting an Indigenous person

Despite the importance of contributing to the enormous task of self-education and educating the majority of the population, some Indigenous people I interviewed felt that there was also a role for non-Indigenous people to directly assist individual Indigenous people in their activist work. Robbie Thorpe proposed that

> Non-Aboriginal people should attach themselves to Aboriginal people who are, you know, particularly promoting issues of sovereignty and things like that, the real justice issues, and support them. Whatever support they need. (Robbie Thorpe, interview)

Even Foley seems to allow for a role for highly knowledgeable non-Indigenous people to directly support and engage with Indigenous people where needed (Land, 2011a). This kind of support relationship tends to be established serendipitously. However, some communities have at times formalized a process for establishing such relationships; one model that operated in Big Mountain in Arizona involved 'appointing people to elders'. Cam Walker has observed that 'if you could manage to do that you'd take a lot of the hit and missed-ness out of the relationship … and make sure it was good for both parties' (interview). Cam Walker and another non-Indigenous person, Ali (Melbourne Kungkas, group interview), have engaged in such support relationships, describing them as formative. Cam Walker reflected:

> Earlier on in my activist life – I can't find a nice way to put it – I was slave for various people. You know, the driving, the kind of, the looking after individual people. I probably did about two years of that. And 'apprenticeship' is probably a nice kind of way of putting it, where you just had a really intense relationship with someone; they were clearly the boss, you were the youngster who was learning, and you were kind of the gofer. And that was a fantastic experience to have and – especially as a young activist from the realm where effectively we're anarchists in our philosophy and we're all equal, and we all should have equal say in our decision-making, and consensus rules – to be in a classic, age-old, you know, mentor–disciple kind of relationship where they're the boss and you're not the boss. I think that was a fantastic experience. (Cam Walker, interview)

Cam talked about the many things he had learned from this experience. First, as stated in the quotation above, he learnt to be comfortable with putting aside his political philosophy of 'equal say' and accepting an Indigenous person having 'some sort of power over me' (Cam Walker, interview). Further, it gave Cam insight into his 'role in the universe', and specifically his role in a relationship whose terms were set by the culture of the person he worked with, in which young men are valued differently from the way young men are valued in white society (this speaks to the importance of an intersectional approach to oppression and how cross-cultural contexts complicate it). It also provided an opportunity for 'understanding the reality of living life as an Aboriginal person'. Another important insight that came through spending so much time together was:

> You get to the point of going: we're all people, after all, with all our beauty and our failures, and then that allows you to go to the next stage which is much more real relationships, rather than a relationship with an image, you know, a romantic image. (Cam Walker, interview)

Rather than be disillusioned by this realization that anyone can be fallible (as he has observed in the response of some non-Indigenous people in the same situation), Cam saw it as enabling a 'more real' relationship. Cam also talked about the difference that spending this time as an 'apprentice' made to the quality of his understanding of what the wars and the invasion in Australia have meant for Aboriginal people:

> You know, you can read about oppression and the wars and the invasion. But when you hang out with people, as you know, the past keeps splashing over into the present, and, instead of understanding that intellectually, you kind of get it more a sense in your bones. So I just think it's a really useful thing to do. (Cam Walker, interview)

In this and the previous quotation from the interview with Cam it can be seen that public political action and self-understanding work are inextricable – or, rather, that each feeds the other. Cam's apprentice work changed him personally, changed his ways of relating (giving him insights that enabled 'more real' relationships), and deepened his understanding of the relationship of the past to the present reality of Aboriginal people's lives: the sense he felt in his bones. However, Cam did make sure to point out that he was 'not saying every relationship like that's going to be healthy'.

This potential for a relationship to be unhealthy was reflected in Ali's experience. She talked about 'the ridiculous kind of demands that can be put on white supporters and that is not healthy, in terms of becoming, like, servants because you feel you have to, or that otherwise you're not doing it properly' (Melbourne Kungkas, group interview).

Another interviewee, Jane Belfrage, registered that she had an ambivalent understanding of an experience of work that she described as a form of 'service':

> When I was involved in helping [two Aboriginal women] set up the Health Service I just did whatever they asked me to do. And I did small things. Like, I was there for tea and coffee. And I listened to them. They debriefed with me ... I participated in very humble ways. But it was like I was a servant or something like that. Well, that's probably because I'm a Catholic, you know, because I was brought up in – and there's a role for service. So I think basically service is essential. Ah. This might sound contradictory. But I would never do anything that made me feel humiliated.

Jane could to some extent make sense of the servant-like role she played because her family upbringing as a Catholic had made acts of 'service' acceptable. However, she seems to suggest that doing servant-like work could also be understood as humiliating. Jane then went on to talk about the discomfort of working in roles that approached a threshold between self-respect and humiliation:

> I just think you have to be able to endure the contradictions. I
> don't think there's answers. I think an attitude of acceptance of
> complexity, contradiction, discomfort, and all of those things,
> um, is the path, and you can't escape it ... Basically you have to
> be able to maintain your self-respect. That might be a measure
> you can use – can I still respect myself and do this, or act in this
> way, or hold my tongue, or continue to listen, or continue to
> reflect, or even just continue to feel this discomfort?

This extract from Jane's interview points to the work of active
reflection that is necessary in order to hold in productive
tension the competing principles of serving, on the one hand,
and maintaining self-respect, on the other.

Members of the Melbourne Kungkas also felt some tension
over the service roles (driving, cooking, making cups of tea)
they performed for the KPKT. They found themselves wanting
something out of it; yet they asked themselves, is it OK to want
something out of it? Such as recognition? One of the KPKT
knowing your name? (Melbourne Kungkas, group interview).
Does this feeling of wanting recognition arise from the possibility that for them the servant-like work was not satisfying?

Jane Belfrage and the Melbourne Kungkas seemed to struggle more with the politics of the servant-like role than Cam
Walker did, probably because of the issue of gender. Cam talked
about how his experience of a servant-like role was radicalizing
because it cut across the male privilege he was accorded in white
culture. By contrast, for Jane and the Melbourne Kungkas – all
women – the servant-like role was congruent with the servile
role accorded to young women in white culture.

Servant-like support for Aboriginal people was understood
differently among non-Indigenous people I interviewed.
Generally, an experience of sustained, intimate work directly

supporting one or more Indigenous people was valued by non-Indigenous people as an opportunity for deep learning. However, the benefits that Cam identified for the person positioned as an 'apprentice' must be read alongside an attentiveness to questions about how benefit (or detriment) flowed to Indigenous people. Was there direct benefit? Was the service valuable? What is the impact of an apprentice quitting? What about the Indigenous people who didn't get an apprentice? Did the presence of the apprentice have a negative impact in the Indigenous community?

Support for Indigenous-led alliances and direct support for Indigenous people promoting issues of sovereignty are two important forms of public political action, both of which have their own complexities.

Dilemmas surrounding public political action

The suggestions for public political action just outlined included both broadly and more narrowly endorsed ideas, and included some cautions as to the complexities that can arise. The potential complexities in the servant-like work described above point both to the existence of significant dilemmas and tensions faced by 'allies' in their political work and to the active, internal, reflective work some non-Indigenous people are undertaking as they do that political work.

The practices and qualities of humility and an equivocal relationship with the practice of self-effacement are a great preoccupation for reflective allies. Humility underlies many of the behaviours of allies: not saying anything, listening, believing, doubting one's own paradigm/relearning other ways, not thinking of oneself as 'good' and 'benevolent'. It is also connected to important issues such as realizing that many allies have come (and gone) before, realizing how much Aboriginal people know about white culture, and how prevalent racism is. Margaret identifies it as one of the 'key qualities for being an ally'. 'Humility' and 'letting go of knowing' are linked. On these qualities, Margaret says:

> Humility – being passionately aware that you could be completely wrong. Letting go of knowing, of being right, of having the answers – always being aware of how much you do not know. (Margaret, 2010)

Holding your tongue can be an appropriate way for a prospective ally to start out. It can be a strategy for limiting the harm that can be done by speaking from a place of ignorance and/or limiting the expression of ingrained habits of white privilege such as taking up too much speaking time or space. Given the importance of humility, it is worth exploring various views on the advisability of practising self-effacement and holding back one's opinions versus the value of 'talking straight' and being honest about what you think. I will explore the tensions, or balances to be struck, between questioning oneself and talking straight, between being self-conscious and careful and being able to relate relaxedly and organically (Bobiwash and Butler, n.d., 1999–2000).

Humility is associated with some of the qualities of being a guest. Cam Walker's view of the 'rules' in 'the realm of directly relating to Indigenous people' includes 'asking whose land you're on'; 'asking permission to settle, to do stuff, to enter and leave'; and 'you've got to go in with a sense of humbleness and desire not to be upsetting people, and an ability to grovel when you need to and apologize' (interview).

These 'rules' for behaviour are a courteous way of behaving towards the owners of the land. However, there is a balance to be struck between the humility that is proper for a guest and an unhealthy subservience that stems from never disagreeing, even when key principles seem to be at stake. Whitefella dentist Bill Roberts manifested a necessary humility when he worked under the direction of the Victorian Aboriginal Health Service in the context of genuine community control. In that case, Bill saw Aboriginal people exemplifying the principles of community control and other principles Bill held dear. Humility and valuing others' expertise can translate as unhealthy subservience when key principles are at stake (principles such as community control, and notions of what is good and right). I have previously written about this with Eve Vincent, suggesting that non-Indigenous people seeking to 'mitigate their privileged position through an uncritical acceptance of Aboriginal people's ideas and deference to their leadership ... absolve themselves of any responsibility to think for themselves...' Also, 'we cannot continue to agree with all Aboriginal people, given their contrasting views on the best way forward' (Land and Vincent, 2005; see also Maddison, 2009).

Helen sees the problem of 'not criticizing at all' as an imbalance. Helen sees attempts to 'step back a bit' as necessary, but says sometimes this is taken 'too far':

> To me, when you don't see people as fully human and therefore, you know, you can't criticize them and you idolize them, that's not a beneficial relationship ... You *do* have to step back a bit, and allow Aboriginal people to make decisions for themselves, and not rush in and, you know, offer solutions and patronize ... But sometimes you go too far, and you start that sort of not criticizing at all and not offering an opinion at all ... It's counterproductive. (Helen, interview)

Helen has also noticed how white people's worries or anxieties about doing or saying something wrong can impact on our/their very ability to relate to Aboriginal people, saying: 'they become paralysed in their relationship with Aboriginal people'. This worry about doing something wrong can also be seen as reflecting a position of privilege in that white people don't act or say anything because this leaves them vulnerable to criticism. Helen identified submissive, obsequious behaviour towards Aboriginal people as a kind of dishonesty, because it is as if the Aboriginal person is 'scary', as if they have power that – Helen argues – in a white dominant culture they do not have:

> You're basically doing this role reversal of treating the Aboriginal person as the scary person, instead of the white person ... you know, because the person with power is the scary person. So you're putting the Aboriginal person in the position of power, because that's what you're used to. ... But by creating another power relationship, you're actually not ... creating an equality, you know, that's not equality, that's power again. But it's a false power 'cos it's not true, because a white person still, in a white dominant culture, has the power, even if they're pretending that they haven't. And that's where things get really messy because the person who's pretending that they're not, but still has the power, then creates these psychologically dodgy situations. (Helen, interview)

If it is dishonest to act scared of Aboriginal people, then how do Aboriginal people and supporters deal with power? Helen says it is dishonest to be frightened to criticize Aboriginal people, but putting Aboriginal people on top creates another power relationship, which doesn't reflect an ethic of 'being the change we seek'. Riggs and Augoustinos (2004) would perhaps offer the psychoanalytic interpretation of the phenomenon

Helen describes as a projection of our scariness onto Aboriginal people. To me Helen's reflection only builds the argument for accountability constructs to be put in place.

The paradox of non-Indigenous people being so careful that we/they can't relate to Indigenous people was illustrated in a light-hearted way in an anecdote offered by Belinda, a member of the Melbourne Kungkas:

> I mean, it was always noticeable to me that, like I was very shy [with the KPKT] and pretty self conscious and ... the kind of paradox of trying so hard to be the good anti-racist, and being quite deferring always ... and then noticing that they loved people who were not self-conscious. ... and there was this girl out at 10 Mile ... she was American and, basically, she didn't have Australian white colonial angst, and she got on really well with them, 'cos she was just really natural, and she asked all the questions that you would be like, 'I can't ask that, I wouldn't want to insult or patronise' ... And you know, in the end, they are human relationships, where ... both sides wanted to enjoy each other, really. (Melbourne Kungkas, group interview)

So, ironically, the attempt to 'be the good anti-racist' by questioning oneself and curtailing one's own culturally specific and white-privileged conditioning was seen as a disadvantage in relating to Aboriginal people in that instance. Psychological research into a similar question (how the interpersonal behaviour of white Canadians interacting with First Nations Canadians is impacted by their concern not to manifest prejudice) is also suggestive of this effect (Vorauer and Turpie, 2004). Cath, another member of the Melbourne Kungkas, reflected that over time her debilitating self-consciousness waned: '[T]he thing that changed for me was just about ... feeling more – comfortable's the wrong word ... being able to be more cheeky or ... less uptight and concerned about the implications of everything I did' (interview). This relates to Lugones's discussion of '"world"-travelling': Lugones (1987) noticed she was not 'playful' in the white world, as she was in her own Latina world. While Cath's experience was not analogous to Lugones's in that it was a journey *out* of the world of white culture, it speaks to the strategic importance of members of dominant groups experiencing discomfort.

Anti-racist organizer Frances Kendall (2006) says – and Bill Roberts and Helen have said in interviews – that vigilance is important, that it is important to listen to what Aboriginal people say and to interrogate one's own initial response as potentially coming from a 'white' habit of mind. However, some Aboriginal people have talked about their desire for non-Indigenous people to 'talk straight' (Gary Murray, interview; Robbie Thorpe, interview). Gary Murray observed:

> I think a lot of white people tend to be overawed by it now, right? And they do tread maybe too carefully. So that's another issue that's probably cropped up in the last few years. ... So you will get the condescending stuff but you'll also get: 'I'm going to tread real careful here. So careful that I'm not going to do *nothing*.' Ha ha. (Gary Murray, interview)

What I think is happening here is that a non-Indigenous person is in a position of some power, knows enough to be aware of the possibility of getting into a political mess, yet does not know enough to navigate the situation, or is too scared to criticize an Indigenous person, or to ask more questions, or to take a risk. Instead, the strategy is to stall, to end up doing 'nothing', which is essentially a form of passive aggression.

Robbie Thorpe's approach has been to dispel the idea of non-Indigenous people being too cautious about saying the right thing. He says, 'I'd rather you say what you think, exactly how you think it. Because that gives me something to work with ... So it's better to be honest about how you feel.' Further, he takes the approach of trying to empower and energize non-Indigenous people (see below). This is congruent with his impatience with genocide, his belief in the urgency to act, and his approach to identity politics – his bringing people into a shared subjectivity around opposition to genocide. On the question of deference:

> Robbie: The people that I've been around, I think I've empowered them to some degree, given them confidence. And shown that we're equal to you, we're not better than you, we're equal to you, and hopefully that's come across, and hopefully that gives them some... – energizes them.
>
> Clare: Yeah, and you do, really – you give people – you encourage people to speak and to act, you know, as a first step. You know, obviously you want people to be informed, but you do give – in a sense, you give a wide-ranging permission for people to speak their minds and to, yeah, and not to be too cautious, I suppose.
>
> Robbie: That's right.

Key points in Robbie's approach are that he attempts to empower people to speak and act against genocide rather than arrogate to himself the speaker's role; and that he would rather non-Indigenous people be honest than to 'think they've got to say things a certain way'. At one point in the interview I asked Robbie what it's like for him to work with non-Aboriginal people: 'Is it stressful? Does it take a toll on you?'

> No, it doesn't stress me. I'm just resigned to the fact that people have been denied truth, been misinformed, indoctrinated, all those things. And you've got to wade through that a bit and give

people who don't know nothing, really. They might think they
do, but you just sit them down and start talking: they don't know
nothing, really. And you know, it's refreshing to have people
who do know. (Robbie Thorpe, interview)

The excerpts discussed above serve as an exploration of the
many instances in which it seems necessary for non-Indigenous
people to manifest some kind of humility or self-effacement,
and times when it seems necessary or possible to let go of self-
consciousness, or to talk straight and be honest. This shows that
everything is context-dependent, and that it is not possible to
lay out rules to be followed universally. Instead, it is necessary
to maintain a practice of critical self-reflection which enables
competing priorities to be balanced, and to be brave about
thinking for oneself when key principles seem to be at stake.

Conclusion

One of the three key issues in the politics of solidarity is the
need for non-Indigenous people to act politically with self-
understanding. This means conducting critical self-reflection
and committing to public political action. Both of these projects
should be informed by a decolonizing ethic of attentiveness to
place and local struggles.

Critical self-reflection by non-Indigenous people is directed
to knowing ourselves, understanding ourselves, interrogating
where our focus should be, and developing cognizance of the
workings of race and privilege. Public political action can take a
variety of forms, and these may have some attendant challenges
and dilemmas. It is the ability to apply and prioritize a range
of sometimes contradictory principles in a particular context
that is the mark of a sophisticated ally.

Along with all the critical self-reflection, it is important to retain a sense of humour. Laughing at oneself may even be useful as a way of avoiding unproductive gestures of self-abasement that say 'I am White and ineradicably guilty; I need all the help and understanding I can get' (da Silva, 2008: 9). To laugh at oneself as a non-Indigenous person is to eschew the pride of being ashamed (see Ahmed, 2004), to acknowledge an uncomfortable truth, and to know that one has to get over it under one's own steam. Another way in which this can work politically is that it does not demand an Indigenous person to help, forgive, approve of or make non-Indigenous people feel better.

SIX

A moral and political framework for non-Indigenous people's solidarity

It is important for non-Indigenous people to develop their understanding of Indigenous struggles before they rush in, on an impulse, to fulfil their desires to 'help' Indigenous people. Indigenous people, scholars and activists are clearly working to shift would-be allies' understandings of what the 'problem' is and of the broader context of social change. This underscores the importance of non-Indigenous people developing a moral and political framework through which to be supportive of Indigenous people. Strategically, reconstruction of interests is seen to create a healthier, less paternalistic basis on which to build solidarity. It is also seen to lead to a greater determination by non-Indigenous people to fight for social justice.

Indigenous people have challenged non-Indigenous people about how we/they conceptualize our/their support for Indigenous people in particular by invoking notions of what is in non-Indigenous peoples' interests. Why have Indigenous people done this and what is its political and strategic importance?

Questioning non-Indigenous people's motivations

Asking non-Indigenous people about their motivations to get involved in Indigenous struggles was put on my agenda by Tony Birch, a member of my critical reference group, very early on in the research that led to this book. After I showed him my proposed interview questions, he suggested I include others about non-Indigenous people's motivations for wanting to get involved in Indigenous struggles. This input from Tony Birch was something I ran with. As I have come to appreciate it more fully and to see it as related to questions of interests, it has become part of what I now understand as a key issue in the project of decolonizing solidarity.

Tony Birch suggested that he would like to see non-Indigenous people understanding their engagement with Indigenous people within a broad moral and political framework. Without this, he would be suspicious that people were in it for reasons such as gaining a personal sense of redemption. This resonated with Gooder and Jacobs's (2000) exploration of the phenomenon of the 'sorry people' of Australia's reconciliation era and their motivations. Frank Hytten, with whom I worked at ANTaR Victoria in 2004–06, suggested that, if we're honest, a lot of our activism is for 'our salvation'. Frank suggested that people like he and I share an obsession with the quality of our relationships with Indigenous people:

> We notice it with Indigenous people, people like you and me maybe, because we're desperate to get good relationships with them for whatever reason, ha, right? For *our* satisfaction or *our* salvation really, I think a lot of this stuff we're doing is sort of for our salvation in a way. (Frank Hytten, interview)

Once I started my interviews, I found Tony Birch's concern with what prompted non-Indigenous people to get involved in Indigenous issues echoed by Yorta Yorta man bryan Andy. bryan said he would have loved to put a question to participants in the popular bridge walks that the government-appointed

Council on Aboriginal Reconciliation sponsored in Australia at the end of the decade of reconciliation:

> I just would have loved to have, say, done a vox pop on people at the reconciliation walk, for example, and actually just sort of say, 'Well, why are you here? Is it because your friends are here, or is it because...?' And I know people who didn't give a shit about Indigenous people prior to this whole movement, and wouldn't know whose land they're on, kind of thing, but yet they participate in those things because they were seen as the thing to do at the time, or as something that was trendy ... You can know a difference between people that are actually engaged and switched on and meaningful and sincere, as opposed to those who might be a bit more, yeah, you know, just setting a trend or followers. I don't know if I'm being a bit harsh. But yep. (bryan Andy, interview)

So bryan's sense was that many of those who participated in the bridge walks were doing it for superficial reasons: because it was trendy. Wayne Atkinson talked about whether non-Indigenous supporters have got 'ulterior motives to use this as a stepping stone' into employment in the Aboriginal 'industry', becoming 'senior bureaucrats or whatever within the system' saying 'this creates a tension'. That said, for Wayne Atkinson,

> A lot of people, non-Indigenous supporters, were aware of these issues. They learned the ropes, from being out there, they played that supportive role, step up, become a spokesperson ... and that's a fine line, I believe, that many people walk, they choose to walk, and some do it pretty well. (Wayne Atkinson, interview)

Some uninterrogated, suspect motivations for getting involved in pro-Aboriginal politics include: dealing with some deep personal psychological problem (Foley, cited in Land, 2011a); finding working with black people exciting (Keefer, 2007); and wanting to make friends with or even have children with Aboriginal people (Kendall, 2006; Marjorie Thorpe, CRG meeting). In some cases, allies are operating on assumptions about receiving 'incentives' such as access to Aboriginal knowledge and recognition from Aboriginal people (Paasonen, 2007). The main characteristics that make these motivations or assumptions 'suspect' are their seemingly unconscious nature (people don't seem to be aware of them, show no 'self-insight', and may see themselves as virtuous).

Critique of the impulse to 'help' Indigenous people

There is a broad consensus that 'helping' is not a good basis for ally work. The idea of helping is connected to the widespread Australian settler practice of feeling distressed and worrying about Aboriginal people (Cowlishaw, 2003; Maddison, 2009). Worrying itself is seen as 'enmeshed in an individual's sense of social and cultural identity, self, and power' (Green et al., 2007: 407). This is a dominant culture discourse that needs to be recognized as such and interrogated. As Fiona Nicoll has written:

> I found that whenever I spoke publicly about Indigenous issues,
> I would be approached by other white people as a 'good woman',
> or 'a woman who cares'. This was pretty disconcerting … It
> was also in contrast to the response of Indigenous people who, I
> have subsequently been told, were probably trying to figure out
> whether I was a missionary, a mercenary, a misfit, a moron or a
> strange hybrid of all of the above. (Nicoll, 2000: 376)

Nicoll later goes on to say that the 'good woman' attribution 'not only tells me that what I have said has been misunderstood. It shows me that these people see Indigenous people as those for whom "good white people" should be doing – or

saying – something' (Nicoll, 2000: 379). Cath, a member of
the Melbourne Kungkas, talked about her family's comfort
with the erroneous idea that she was '*helping* the Aborigines ...
And I was just like, "Oh my God ... how do you even start to
explain what it actually means, what I was doing?"' (Melbourne
Kungkas, group interview). As Gary Foley observes:

> It's not just a question of 'Oh I'll go and help the poor little
> blackfellas.' Don't come and help us, we don't need you. But if
> you're fair dinkum about achieving social change, your agenda is
> much bigger than us. (Foley, cited in Land, 2011a: 52)

For Foley, wanting to 'help' usually indicates that the would-
be helper has an under-articulated political analysis, and a lack
of insight about their underlying desires and, probably, narcis-
sism (see also Kowal, 2015). It is important for non-Indigenous
people to be clear about their reasons for wanting to be an ally
(Kendall, 2006). For Kendall, an ally is a 'change agent', not
a 'helper'. Further, she says: 'You have to be absolutely clear
that you are doing this because it is in your interest or for the
greater good' (Kendall, 2006: 140). Importantly, a would-be
ally's sense of whether he or she is acting in his or her own or
in others' interests can be seen to speak to how reliable that
person might be as an ally. As Darlene Johnston has said, in
the particular context of a fishing rights struggle by the people
of Anishnabee, Cape Croker in Ontario, Canada:

> I don't rely on them [external allies]. If I had money to put into
> research or alliance-building, I would put it into research. I
> would make a priority of community education to make sure
> that our members know what happened and what we are going
> to do, because that is where there is determination. And I feel
> way more confident in the determination and stubbornness of
> our community. (Wallace et al., 2010: 99)

Shifting would-be allies' understandings of the problem

It is possible to shift non-Indigenous people's sense of the issue, and to shift problematic modes of addressing it. An enabling experience of discomfort may well be part of bringing about this shift. Non-Indigenous people's critical self-reflection and self-education work can be directed to interrogating their view of themselves and of Indigenous people, and developing their understanding of what sort of actions – by whom – would redress the problem.

Non-Indigenous people who display an understanding of a broad agenda for social change, not just a focus on Indigenous people, are regarded as having a sound basis for supporting Indigenous struggles. Gunditjmara elder Alma Thorpe, one of the founders of the Victorian Aboriginal Health Service, indicated this when talking about Janet Bacon, one of the doctors she worked with. Janet's devotion to a range of causes was evidently a factor in the high regard in which Alma held her:

> There was Dr Janet Bacon, who was a wonderful woman. She was our first doctor ... She was the most beautiful woman, and gave her life to *causes*: it wasn't just the black cause; she was radical. (Alma Thorpe, interview)

Gunditjmara and Gunai woman Glenda Thorpe, former CEO of Melbourne Aboriginal Youth Sport and Recreation (MAYSAR), posed a question for non-Indigenous people about how they identify their/our interests: 'Can I just say I think it's as fundamental as asking yourself: are you happy in this society?' (Glenda Thorpe, cited in Land, 2011a: 51).

Glenda has also argued that, rather than an engagement with Indigenous people being about 'helping' or 'do-gooder things', 'it's about saying "I don't want my children and my grandchildren and my generations to come to live in this horrible world that we currently live in". We have the power as a small group of people to make that change.' Notably, Glenda spoke as 'we', in an inclusive way, suggesting that everybody who questions how society is going shares in the project of making change collectively.

Gary Foley has made a similar point, for 'People who are committed to bringing about some sort of meaningful change in society – not just for us, for everybody', there's an enormous task that 'confronts us all' (Foley, cited in Land, 2011a: 51). This reference to a shared task, and the aside 'not just for us, for everybody', does similar work to Glenda's statement, asking non-Indigenous people to see their own interests reflected in a struggle that is much broader than seeking justice for Indigenous people. Likewise, Robbie Thorpe mounts an anticapitalist critique of society that benefits a small minority: 'I'm sure there's other people out there who want to look for another system that's workable, not for the greedy 5 per cent' (interview).

Relationships with Indigenous struggles: inheritance or choice?

It is important to be conscious of the ways in which a sense of commitment to Indigenous struggles can vary between people. Indigenous people often describe their relationship with Indigenous struggles as one of inheritance. For Gary Murray, to be who he is, is to have a duty to pursue his people's rights:

> Through my father, I'm a Wamba Wamba person. That is, we're from the Gumjanjuk people, black cockatoo with the red crescent

– that's our totem. I'm from the Baraparapa people, both though my father and mother, and they're the platypus people. And through my father and mother again I'm Yorta Yorta. Through my father I'm Dhudhuroa. Through my mother I'm Dja Dja Wurrung, from the crow people. And also Japajulk and Wergaia, which is pelican people. So we have a number of nations that we are distinctly part of, both biologically and culturally, and politically and legally and everything else. And what flows from that is we have this baggage, this cultural duty, this obligation to pursue our rights on behalf of our ancestors and on behalf of our families today and on behalf of future generations.

It's drilled into us ... that we have an inheritance of issues as well as what's out there in terms of our culture, our tradition, our customs, our land rights and all that sort of stuff. And we have to *work* to restore our ancestors and our descendants their rightful place back in their country. (Gary Murray, interview)

Wayne Atkinson, Yorta Yorta, spoke in terms similar to Gary Murray concerning the question, 'How do you see the cause that you're involved in?'

One is born into this rather daunting reality of belonging to a community that seems to be in constant struggle. And one also needs to look at that in terms of our history, in that it wasn't always like that. But as a result of British colonization and the treatment of our people, marginalization, and denial of land justice, and those issues, they're all the factors that contribute to the issue of Indigenous people constantly being in a state of struggle, in terms of trying to unleash themselves from all of those created circumstances, and achieve greater equality or recognition, as themselves: Indigenous people, First Nations, First People of this land. (Wayne Atkinson, interview)

And Robbie Thorpe on his commitment:

I'm just one of the last people standing, who has to do this job because there's no one else to do it. I'm not a spokesperson; I'm a sportsperson at heart. I never wanted to do all this mental anguish stuff all the time, it's horrible. I don't want to be talking about genocide all the time. But if someone's not gonna say something about it, I will.

> I got taught by a lot of good, educated people like the late Dr Bruce McGuinness, and the Foleys and my mother. They were the real intellectuals who taught me. I had great elders around me, I lived in a great community, I had a great family. Very unique situation for an Aboriginal person in this country. So I was created out of those circumstances, so if I've got the capabilities of doing something I'm going to do it. Whatever way I can do it I'll be doing it. (Robbie Thorpe, interview)

Chris Twining articulated her awareness of a distinction between the level of choice she had to contribute to Indigenous struggles and that of Indigenous people such as Lisa Thorpe, with whom she has co-facilitated 'Without Prejudice' workshops over many years:

> I realize … I lead a very comfortable life, I can travel any time I like. [My husband] Laurie's retired, he's got a good pension, I really don't have to worry too much about life, I can just do this as a – like it's not a hobby – I mean I do *believe* in it and all that sort of stuff – but I don't *have* to do it. Whereas for Lisa or for Aboriginal people that's their life, they've got to keep on doing this sort of stuff. Does that make sense? They haven't got a lot of choice in it really. (Chris Twining, interview)

Helen talked about having had a 'passionate interest in Indigenous issues', even when she was a 'little kid'. For Helen, 'the question of, you know, Indigenous–non-Indigenous relationships … is a fairly central theme in my life.' When I asked whether she could see foresee any benefits or satisfaction coming to her from all the activist work she does, or any other motivations, Helen said, 'Yes. If I felt that I was living in a more just society I would feel happier.' Helen then situated her sense of her own motivations as a lifelong activist on a range of issues in the context of her perception of slightly pathological motivations in certain others:

It can be a kind of addiction, political activism. I've seen that in activists … and then I think especially on this Aboriginal issue, it can come from a feeling of white guilt that drives you. You know, you want to assuage the guilt. And I've come to learn that's a really bad motivation, and can have really, uh, damaging sort of effects on both the person and the Aboriginal people that they're working with. (Helen, interview)

Frank Hytten has spent much of his working life trying to advocate for people who are oppressed. He light-heartedly described himself as maybe a little addicted to activism:

In one sense … all my activism is self-indulgent. I'm doing it as much for meaning for me as I'm doing it for any other person, you know? … I can always stop … Apart from my addiction to it, you know, which might be a different issue. (Frank Hytten, interview)

Frank spoke about deriving satisfaction in his activism from making even 'small', 'pathetic'-sounding little things happen in his roles over the years in social service and social movement organizations: 'I'll find a way of making something happen. It's not the thing that everybody wants, because that's not possible, but I get satisfaction from saying "I can make it happen".' One example was drawing together enough seed money to print several hundred T-shirts for the day of the Federal Parliament's 2008 'Apology to Australia's Indigenous Peoples': 'It's so pathetic that it sort of almost beggars belief on one level, but it's really exciting on a day-to-day basis' (Frank Hytten, interview).

Experienced and reflective non-Indigenous people are generally able to articulate their interests and their personal sense of a framework for their activism. This includes an awareness of the politics of the basis for their involvement and their relationship to Indigenous struggles.

What are interests – and why do they need to be reconstructed?

In general people are seen to act in accordance with their interests. Yet, as scholars have observed, any person's or people's sense of what constitutes their own interests is a political issue (Molyneux, 1985; Pease, 2002; Valiente, 2003). It is also historically constructed. David Roediger (1999: 13) demonstrates that sections of the working-class population in the USA whose economic interests were 'practically identical' to those of poor black people came to believe over time that their interests lay with more privileged whites. They were manipulated into racism, and their understanding of themselves as 'white' paid off with psychological and other wages. For Roediger, it is tragic that people in the USA see themselves through and function within racial categories (1999: 12, 186).

Reconstructing the interests of members of dominant groups is informed by strategies that have been used by members of subordinated groups to empower themselves. Such members reformulate their sense of what their interests are through a process of becoming politicized or conscientized. Part of the work of conscientization, a process described by Paolo Freire (1985), is to begin to analyse one's own oppression and to come to see ways in which it is experienced in common with other people. To undertake this is also to move from a practical sense of one's interests to a strategic sense, which then prompts questions about the need to pursue systemic change.

An example from feminist literature on women's gender interests helps make clear the distinction between 'practical' and 'strategic' interests (Molyneux, 1985). Valiente (2003: 241) shows how practical gender interests stem from women's usual (gendered) occupations, such as bringing up and educating children: women mobilize to enable themselves to undertake these occupations better or more easily (see also Molyneux, 1985). In this construction of interests, there is usually no questioning of the 'gender order' (Valiente, 2003: 242). Women tend to mobilize around their practical interests when they or their families are personally affected. Practical gender interests are contrasted with 'strategic gender interests' (reflective of a feminist, rather than a feminine, consciousness). Strategic gender interests are based on an analysis of women's status as a whole, on improving this, on reducing women's subordination. This is based on a questioning of the unequal position of women in society (Valiente, 2003: 241–2).

Giving members of dominant groups reasons to work for justice

Understanding this contrast between practical and strategic interests helps to open up other important ideas. People can be thought of as having 'natural' interests, 'material' interests and 'ideal' interests, as Pease (2002) discusses in his study of debates over men's interests within feminist and pro-feminist circles. From one viewpoint, men have too much to lose to be reliable allies with women in challenging patriarchy. However, this is only true if you see men as having objective interests determined by their social location as beneficiaries of patriarchy. Rejecting this notion, Pease argues that 'persons do not have objective interests as a result of their location; rather they "*formulate* a sense of having particular interests" … within the context of the available discourses in situations in which they are located and that they coproduce' (2002: 170). What, then, are some of the more wide-ranging interests that a person might have? Pease says these could range from 'doing something because it will make one feel better, to doing it because if one does not, it will be diminishing one's integrity as an ethical being' (Pease, 2002: 171). This view of the constructed – rather than the determined – nature of men's interests leaves open the possibility that interests can be reconstructed. They can be reconstructed towards 'enlightened self-interests' (Pease, 2002: 165, 166).

But how? In Pease's experience, men can find this process occurring through their own critical self-reflection and their public political action: these two practices inform each other, and *can result in reconstructed interests* (2002: 174). In the practice of pro-feminism, men may 'recreate themselves as subjects in their ethical activity and so reconstitute their interests ... [This] changes our sense of what constitutes our self-interest' (2002: 174).

This suggests that beyond the arguments outlined in the previous chapter about the importance of acting politically with self-understanding, there is another compelling reason for non-Indigenous people to do both kinds of work. Critical self-reflection and public political work have the potential to feed into a process of reconstructing the interests of members of dominant groups who are attempting to act as allies.

When the interests of Indigenous people and non-Indigenous people are understood as opposed, non-Indigenous people are understood as having 'too much to lose' to be reliable allies of Indigenous people. It is not difficult to imagine that many non-Indigenous people would perceive our/their interests in land as opposed to Indigenous people's interests in land, and conversely difficult to see those interests as congruent. For non-Indigenous people to support Indigenous interests (in land) would be to defy the central logic of the prevailing system, of which each of us is – individually – a constituent. 'Whitefellas' constitute the system in the way Monica Morgan has so clearly asserted:

> the fact is whitefellas have got their own power through the system and the structure and that. It doesn't matter if you are an individual whitefella and you say 'I'm not part of the system'. You *are* a part of the system. You are dead-set *part* of the system. You *are* the system. (Monica Morgan, interview)

We are part of the system, we are the system, we are colonialism. To be a reliable ally, then, is to critique the system, to attempt to change the system, to reduce our level of colonial involvement (Barker, 2010: 318), to undermine its logics, and to try to convince ourselves and others that the system – which does its most violent work on Indigenous people – is also not in our (enlightened) self-interest.

Working to support Indigenous struggles could serve non-Indigenous interests by:

- making us feel happier;
- increasing our sense of personal integrity as ethical beings;
- being congruent with 'abstract principles' such as 'justice', or more concrete beliefs such as the notion that 'exterminating people is wrong' (Lindqvist, 1997);
- helping to undermine a system that produces permanent change to the environment in an ecologically unsustainable fashion;
- trying to undo the system that does oppressive work on all/ most of us, but most particularly and obviously along the axis of Indigeneity.

The last point is perhaps the one through which non-Indigenous people might best come to see how our interests are served by our support of Indigenous struggles; that is, by being able to articulate a thorough critique of Western colonialism, and opposing the work of empire along all lines of oppression. Further, in relation to environmental sustainability, Robbie Thorpe sees the land as the great leveller. It is only when non-Indigenous people realize that our system, while bringing certain material benefits to us, is ultimately imperilling our survival because it is attended by 'ecocide' (destruction of the environment) that we will begin to act and to turn to Indigenous people as a resource to value and to learn something from (Robbie Thorpe, interview).

There are limited scenarios in which non-Indigenous people or institutions in settler-colonial contexts are motivated to engage with Indigenous people out of a concern for their own immediate material self-interests. This only occurs when settlers and governments see their interests threatened by Indigenous people (Neveu, 2010). One such rare scenario in the Australian context was the decision of the High Court in the *Mabo* case (1992), in which the common law of Australia belatedly recognized the existence of Aboriginal law, and, through that, a system of Aboriginal title over land. In the wake of that decision, many non-Indigenous landholders such as pastoralists and miners felt uncertain of their tenure and, it being in their business interests to operate on the basis of certainty, some entered negotiations with Indigenous people. A major flaw in the Native Title Act 1993, the legislative response to the *Mabo* decision, is that Aboriginal people who passed an initial hurdle of recognition as likely to be able to prove they were traditional owners only gained the right to negotiate and not to veto proposed developments, such as mining, on their ancestral lands. Given their disadvantageous bargaining position in native title and other negotiations, Aboriginal people have argued that there should be international scrutiny of agreements to ensure they are equitable.

Dilemmas in the project of encouraging members of dominant groups to interrogate interests

How can change committed to reconstructing the interests of members of dominant groups be achieved? This is one of the biggest questions of strategy in solidarity politics: both Indigenous people and experienced allies are engaged with it.

According to Pease, discomfort is necessary for men to reach a willingness to change. Linda Martín Alcoff suggests the same applies to non-Indigenous people: 'rational arguments against racism will not be sufficient to make a progressive move' (1998: 24). Sullivan (2006) concurs, asserting the need for multiple strategies, in particular those which could undermine 'unconscious habits of white privilege'. What is needed in addition to 'rational arguments' against the logic of racism? A strategy that recurs in various accounts hinges on notions of engagement with 'non-white spaces' (Sullivan, 2006), of 'boundary spanning' (Sacks and Lindholm, 2002), of '"world"-travelling' (Lugones, 1987). Each of these, it is important to note, articulates the project, the objectives and the dangers differently.

The shared vocabulary of space and movement is notable, and, as is clear to Sullivan (2006) and Lugones (1987), should be accompanied by a cognizance of the territorial expansiveness (colonizing habits) of white people, which entails the ever-present caution that attempts to disrupt white privilege can simultaneously work to enhance expansiveness. In Sullivan's view, 'white people tend to act and think as if all spaces – whether geographical, physical, linguistic, economic, spiritual, bodily, or otherwise – are or should be available for them to move in and out of as they wish' (2006: 10).

The practice of excursions out of white/Anglo 'worlds' into an engagement with non-white spaces is suggested in several important critical texts as a strategy for furthering anti-racist white projects. While 'relocating out of ... environments that encourage the white solipsism of living as if only white people existed or mattered can be a powerful way of disrupting and transforming unconscious habits of white privilege', such a practice can also work to reinforce them. For Sullivan, this is a paradox that 'cannot be completely eliminated'. But, 'rather than despairing or giving up, a person needs to engage in an ongoing struggle to find ways to use white privilege against itself. A significant part of that struggle involves trying to understand one's own complex relationship – and complicity – with white privilege, and this is true whatever one's race' (Sullivan, 2006: 11). Paulette Regan, writing as a Ph.D. student, attests that for her the discomfort of being in 'unfamiliar territory' has been transformative. She attributes to Mohawk scholar Taiaiake Alfred the notion that 'the process of being uncomfortable is essential for non-Indigenous people to move from being enemy to adversary to ally' (Regan, 2005: 3). Responding to this claim, Regan writes:

> I ... found myself thinking about my own experiences of being uncomfortable, working as a non-Indigenous woman within

indigenous contexts over the years. I realized that my own deepest learning has always come from those times when I was in unfamiliar territory – culturally, intellectually and emotionally. (Regan, 2005: 6)

Regan's words affirm the productive potential of discomfort, and again use the language of space and territory, which underscores the need for an embodied attention to boundaries. That is, attention to issues such as who is in what space, who is comfortable, when spaces need to be Indigenous-only, and, on a larger scale, dynamics of gentrification, is important.

What are the costs of privilege?

Another strategy for tackling the reluctance of members of dominant groups to undo their privilege is to highlight the costs of not doing so. It is disingenuous to suggest that non-Indigenous people do not have to 'give anything up' in order for justice to be done. Yet for strategic reasons this is often downplayed (as in Benjamin et al., 2010) in the hope that this will encourage more people to support measures of justice. Members of dominant groups have a tendency to make life choices which reflect and maintain the system rather than deliberately deciding not to benefit from all the extra opportunities that come the way of the privileged. If we agree that Indigenous lands are exploited for the benefit of non-Indigenous people and in the service of global capitalism, then surely the realization of Indigenous rights would come at some form of expense? Tom Keefer (2007) explains that it is corporations and the greedy few who would have to pay, as they have benefited the most. What members of dominant groups must give up is a key issue for non-Indigenous people to explore and to deal with, yet one that has not received much attention to date. It is an uncomfortable topic, which we will discuss in the next chapter.

Let us focus here on the costs of privilege. Lillian Holt has argued that all people in Australia are diminished by white racism: both its victims and white people, through our/their apparent tolerance of racism, are diminished as ethical beings. Helen echoed this point, which has also been invoked by major Australian political leaders. In his election campaign speech just prior to being elected prime minister in 1972, leader of the Australian Labor Party Gough Whitlam committed to 'legislate to give aborigines land rights – not just because their case is beyond argument, but because all of us as Australians are diminished while the aborigines are denied their rightful place in this nation'.

Robbie Thorpe tries to make 'Australians' see that they/we are soon to find ourselves – or, in fact, noting recent extreme natural disasters, that we may already be – directly affected by the same forces that are destroying Indigenous people as a people, and destroying their way of life. The increasing occurrence of natural disasters is explained not so much as a result of climate change but through a spiritual and legal framework:

> We know: you don't destroy these sacred places. And there's going to be a result; this is it coming now … If you remove the people whose job it is to be the custodians and the caretakers of this sacred garden, and go and rape it and pillage it and plunder it and create a big toxic pool, a toxic waste dump, well, you're going to have problems, obviously … That's what the land rights struggle was all about … We're talking about the land's right too. People have a right to that land, and the land's also got its own rights … That's the real law: the law of the land. You've got to respect the ancestor spirits. Don't make them angry. (Robbie Thorpe, interview)

While Indigenous people's situation can be generalized as one of immediate and direct crisis, in which morbidity and death are preponderant, many non-Indigenous people in Australia do not experience crises that threaten survival (Paasonen, 2007). One of Robbie's strategies for generating a stronger sense of non-Indigenous people's interests being at stake is to encourage Australians to see the imminence of our own direct material suffering.

Further, Robbie highlights the costs of colonialism for the colonists, in particular through his wordplay whereby 'Australian' becomes 'A-Stray-Alien'. This provides a concise expression of what critical whiteness scholars might call the 'costs' of whiteness for the settler colonial Australian context. Robbie alludes to what non-Indigenous people have lost by going to the country, and his view of the impoverishment of being white in Australia. To be an 'Australian' is to be 'A-Stray-Alien': wandering, lost, rootless, a stranger to this land, constituted by a spiritually and ethically bereft dominant culture. To be A-Stray-Alien is to be 'dehumanized, dispossessed'. The contrast between Aboriginal relationships to land and that of the dominant culture is key to Robbie's analysis: 'It's not just a lump of dirt sitting there; it's sacred. The dehumanized, dispossessed people who landed on our shores 200 years ago don't see this. Because they've lost their connection with earth, their mother' (Robbie Thorpe, interview). Robbie argues that in Australia, Westerners' spiritual disconnection from land guides an exploitative and unsustainable relationship which is leading inexorably towards environmental destruction: a problem for everybody. In this view, the interests and long-term survival of all in this land are intertwined with those of

Aboriginal people, their care and knowledge of the land and their philosophy of 'caring and sharing'.

On a similar note, Holt (1999) has spoken of the need for white people to heal themselves (rather than seek to heal/help Indigenous people); while Moreton-Robinson (2008: 93) argues that settler Americans in the USA are understood as 'disoriented, displaced and diasporic racialized subjects', made worse by ignoring Indigenous sovereignties.

These insights regarding the costs of settler colonialism for settlers resonate strongly with a significant literature on what whiteness 'costs', as well as strategies for redressing this. For Gary Howard, a white man and multicultural educator in the USA, what we could call the critical self-reflection part of his work is his continuing commitment to 'personal harmony, and ... a new way of being white', conducted through the project of finding a 'deep connection with personal culture that is indigenous to my own heritage ... authentically connected to my own history' (Howard, 1999: 222–3). Further to this, writer Mab Segrest (2001), a white 'race traitor', provides a polemical cost–benefit analysis of whiteness, including a discussion of how the inhuman acts of white imperialism have damaged white people individually and collectively. In Robbie Thorpe's insight regarding Australians being 'dehumanized', there is another link to Segrest's view of 'the profound damage racism has done to us if we as a people could participate in such an inhuman set of practices over five centuries of European hegemony' (2001: 44). Segrest argues that 'we whites' have given up our 'love of humanity' to a racist system (2001: 46).

Of course, highlighting the 'costs of whiteness' is aimed at encouraging white people to feel more 'personally invested' in challenging white racism. This is a challenging project. Anti-racist organizer William Aal has shared some of the challenges he has encountered and responses that he has developed in his work with NOAR, the National Organization for an American Revolution:

> What we have had to develop are some ways to help white people understand what a high price they pay for their privileged position – so that ultimately they can see that the reason to work for justice is also to free themselves. (Aal, 2001: 305)

As well as an inertia caused by guilt and the worry about doing something wrong, Aal and his colleagues have found inaction to be linked to 'defensiveness': 'most white people know very well their skin color is tied to social privileges – so they feel guilty and at the same time don't feel personally invested in change' (2001: 305). As a strategy for addressing this challenge NOAR asks white people to consider questions such as, 'What did you and/or your family have to give up to be white?' (2001: 306). Aal paraphrases James Baldwin to sum up what white people 'give up': 'The price of whiteness ... is the loss of community' (2001: 307). Aal's insights are generally salient in the Australian context, while those of Robbie Thorpe provide a local specificity and a necessary emphasis on settler colonialism.

'A point of no return for allies'

For some members of privileged groups, involvement in supporting struggles for justice begins to reconstruct their subjectivity. This can be permanent, such that a new sense of self makes it impossible not to remain committed to supporting struggles for justice.

Writing from a white non-Indigenous perspective, Nicoll describes her own discomfort at having confronted the problem of colonialism, her complicity and her attempt to resist this: 'since coming out as white and landing on the ground of Australian race relations, I periodically have panic attacks and think: "I've got to get out of here. Beam me back to *terra nullius*"' (Nicoll, 2000: 382). Something of what Nicoll describes as knowing she can't get back to that 'before' space is to be found in Pease's claim about a 'point of no return for allies' (Pease, 2010b: 184). Pease is aware of some criticism of his focus on considering the role of privileged groups in contributing to movements for social change, particularly the 'doubt that privileged groups will voluntarily commit themselves to challenge their own privilege' (Pease, 2010b: 184). However, Pease still holds out the possibility that the privileged can become long-term allies: 'my experience in campaigns tells me that there comes a point of no return for allies. Significant reconstruction of subjectivities can occur to the point where turning away from activist involvements is no longer viable' (Pease, 2010b: 184). A subjectivity structured around principles of justice and equality between fellow beings would mean it is hard to walk away from activist commitments.

I found this sense of a point of no return expressed by Frank Hytten, as well as Ali, in an answer to the question of whether she'd had experiences of 'finding this kind of work too difficult … like you don't want to continue':

> I kind of found by that stage, like, most of my friends or
> networks were involved in Indigenous issues or were Indigenous.
> … And it was – even though I sort of wanted to escape from it
> all, I found it was such a part of my life I couldn't really! … I

went [travelling] to try and, sort of, separate myself from people
or issues or something, but it didn't really work ... the formative
years of growing up were so preoccupied with those issues, so felt
quite hollow not being more active on it. (Melbourne Kungkas,
group interview)

Cautions in the project of reconstructing interests

There are politics around attending to the 'costs of whiteness'
and encouraging non-Indigenous people to see how colonialist
thought does its work on 'us too'. Essentially, this is because
such projects can feed into the tendency of white people and
members of other privileged groups to 'shift the focus back
to us' (Kendall, 2006: 72). Pease (2010b) has noted several controversies in the debate over reconstructing the interests of
the privileged. There is disagreement over Ann Bishop's view
that you have to have been oppressed and recognized your
oppression before you can become an ally (Pease, 2010b: 173).
Not all members of privileged groups are oppressed in some
other dimension, even if they experience costs associated with
their privilege. Others argue that encouraging the privileged
to come to see fighting oppression as in fact in their own
self-interests is suspect. Critical race scholars have critiqued the
phenomemon of 'ressentiment' (Probyn, 2004); while feminists
have critiqued the 'race to innocence' (Fellows and Razack,
1998). Others have critiqued the move to 'discount' our white
privilege by pointing out our other oppressions (Nicoll, 2000).

Altruism is seen as a more worthy, because generous, reason
for members of dominant groups to support social justice struggles than self-interest. On the other hand, with pragmatism
in mind, educators and community practitioners have found
that appealing to 'ethical and moral arguments on their own'

may not provide members of privileged groups with enough motivation to overcome material interests linked to privilege (Pease, 2010b: 175). Acting to serve someone else's interests does not seem to be enough to secure the commitment of a member of a privileged group to supporting the struggle of a dominated group. From an Indigenous perspective, reliable levels of 'determination and stubbornness' by allies are not assured if ally-work is based on altruism alone (Wallace et al., 2010: 99).

If we reconstruct our interests are we still 'allies', or something else?

To work as an ally is to undertake 'activism ... where those involved are not direct beneficiaries' (Pease, 2010b: 180, citing Borshuk). Yet, if members of dominant groups really see that we/they are working to change a society that, in its colonialism, does oppressive work on (all/most of) us, then we/they are, ultimately, beneficiaries of that activism.

To reconstruct one's interests, then, is to change the basis of the relationship with others who struggle. It would no longer be a relation based on 'us' and 'them' thought – a connotation of the term 'ally' (Margaret, 2010). Importantly, this change is not directed to denying differences which still divide those committed to achieving 'meaningful social change'; nor does it avoid the central issue of land. However, reconstructing the interests of members of dominant groups does bear the potential for different modes of relating: modes marked by a greater sense of mutuality. As Robbie Thorpe observes, 'We've got an issue here. What are we going to do? Worry about the blackness and whiteness? Or worry about where we're going to as a people in this country?' (interview; see also Targan, interview). To see ourselves, as Robbie does, as 'trying to get to the same destination' politically is to open up the potential for a different personal interaction. This might mean that some of the problematic dynamics of paternalism, racism and dominance are less intrusive on relationships across Indigenous–non-Indigenous difference in the activist context. That said, if non-Indigenous people and white people simply reclassified ourselves as victims we would be forgetting that we are socialized by and transacting with a racist world and that this has material and relational consequences which we need to struggle against.

So this is not about reclassifying ourselves at the level of discourse, but about redirecting our efforts and our energies towards serving reconstructed interests. Interests cannot be read objectively from structural location. It is germane to consider how a person's actions and the shape of a person's life serve the interests of the dominant group and whether this can be transformed. Albert Memmi described such transformation as a process of 'becoming a turncoat' (1965: 103). In the case of non-Indigenous people working in Indigenous people's interests (as part of a broader framework of serving their/our own emancipatory interests), it involves asking whether one's location in relation to colonialism can be read from whose interests one serves. Perhaps this is what is meant on the rare occasions that Indigenous people make remarks such as 'he was more of a Koori than a gub'[1] (Foley, cited in Land, 2011a: 56). The argument that social location should be ascribed on the basis of

---

1. 'Gub' is an abbreviation of 'gubbah', meaning whitefella, or non-Koori.

actions – not 'objective' notions like DNA – can be identified in Foley's writings on the poet and novelist Mudrooroo, who has had his identity as an Aboriginal person disputed. Foley regards Mudrooroo as an Aboriginal person for his work in the interests of Aboriginal people, and for having been there, in the streets, rallying and fighting alongside/with/as an Aboriginal person when times were tough (Foley, 1997b). Reconstructing interests can contribute to a practice that is based on a radicalized logic for relationships. This new logic is not based on 'us' and 'them', or on being 'allies' to 'others'.

There are legitimate concerns that the project of reconstructing interests could feed into a tendency by white people to 'shift the focus back to us'. However, there are strong arguments for the pragmatic utility of this project. Interrogating and reconstructing non-Indigenous people's interests emerge as key to decolonizing solidarity.

Indeed, the predominant impulses that drive middle-class settler activists to support Indigenous people cannot lead to successful and powerful alliances with Indigenous people and to meaningful social change unless they are significantly transformed through a process of reconstructing interests and undertaking both public political action and critical self-reflection.

SEVEN

Reckoning with complicity

A key element of the politics of solidarity is the necessity of reckoning with complicity. This cuts across the projects of acting politically with self-understanding and reconstructing interests.

Non-Indigenous people are challenged to confront our complicity with colonialism and dispossession. This begins with being aware of complicity and for many involves dealing with discomfort about that. The challenge is to admit it, to resist it, to undo it, yet also to see how it provides us with opportunities to resist the workings of colonialism (Keefer, 2007). These aspects of reckoning with complicity are nonetheless based on the realization that complicity is inescapable. This is a contradiction that must be factored in and reflected upon continuously.

The challenge around complicity is directly related to the need for non-Indigenous people to reconstruct their/our interests. It instigates a questioning of how non-Indigenous people are bound up in the system, what we would 'risk' or 'lose' if we were to abandon it, and, from another perspective, what we would 'gain'. It also involves interrogating the range of contrasting actions that discomfort about complicity can prompt (see Barker, 2010). It cuts across the agenda of acting politically with self-understanding, because if discomfort is felt, dealing with it becomes an element of the work of critical self-reflection. A suggested strategy for avoiding its sometimes debilitating effects is to engage in public political action. Issues around complicity also intersect with public political action because of the way public political action can feed into a new conception of interests. That is, becoming actively involved in political projects can itself result in a different perception of one's own self-interest, potentially generating new inspiration to confront complicity.

The hard work of reckoning with complicity springs from the recognition by non-Indigenous people that Australia is Aboriginal land. For non-Indigenous people, this recognition should not only inform our public political action – so that, for example, Cam Walker undertakes collectivist environmental activism on a pro-sovereignty basis – but should also be reflected in the shape of our lives. For Cam, the 'hard work for us' non-Indigenous people is to grapple with the question, 'how can you be non-Indigenous but live here and love this continent, and plan to live here forever and plan to have your kids here forever, in an honourable way?'

Interrogating and reconstructing the shape of one's life represent a project of reckoning with privilege, reckoning with being on the land of certain Aboriginal people. It is about reckoning with knowing that being there was enabled by their dispossession and displacement – or even extermination – and is enabled still by everything that keeps things that way.

To settle as colonists on Aboriginal land involves that land being vacated. In Australia, this was achieved by such methods as killing Aboriginal people, displacing them from their land

and containing them in reserves. Scholars of comparative genocide have argued that a corollary of settler colonialism is a particular kind of genocide. In order to accept this, it helps to understand settler colonization as a process rather than an event (Short, 2010). By extension, settler-colonial genocide is a process rather than an event like the emblematic genocides of Nazi Germany and Rwanda. Most Aboriginal people recognize themselves as having suffered and continuing to suffer genocide (Behrendt, 2001). However, non-Indigenous people have found it harder to recognize Australia's genocide (Barta, 2008). Most non-Indigenous historians have shrunk from this term (Barta, 2008; and see Curthoys and Docker, 2001). Nevertheless, in 1998 a Supreme Court judge in the Australian Capital Territory found 'ample evidence to satisfy me that acts of genocide were committed during the colonization of Australia' (Curthoys et al., 2008: 125). Some events in Australia's history – massacres, taking children away – are more readily recognizable in the UN definition of genocide (Barta, 2008). However, there is very little knowledge or acceptance of the notion that to undermine the culture of a people – to destroy a people as a people – is to bring about genocide (Short, 2010). This notion makes it clear that government policies of removing Aboriginal people from their land, preventing people from speaking their language and assimilation are aimed at destroying Aboriginal peoples as peoples. Aboriginal spokespeople are clear about their struggle being one of survival, and survival as distinct peoples in the face of an amorphous but omnipresent process of settler-colonial genocide. Wider recognition of the ongoing process of genocide in Australia is a long way off. A key barrier for the state and dominant culture is that there has never been a 'point of rupture' or 'point of conclusion' to the process of settler colonialism (Balint and Evans, 2011). To fully admit the gravity of the injustice is bound to making a complete break with the regime that sustains it and a full process of restitution (Barkan, 2000; Maddison, 2011). This echoes Robbie Thorpe's rhetorical question: When did the war end? (Land, 2001).

Is there a way to interrupt this process of genocide? Socio-legal scholars Jennifer Balint and Julie Evans (2011) find possibilities for the pursuit of just outcomes in settler-colonial states in the strategies for transitional justice that have been employed in contemporary regime change and post-conflict political transition. There are possibilities for interrupting the process of genocide in the political and legal arena, as well as in that multitude of ways in which our lives are implicated in holding up the colonialist system. As Keefer (2007) says, the social location of non-natives implicates us in colonialism, providing us with 'opportunities to disrupt it'.

Living on Aboriginal land is enabled by genocide, and genocide is recognized as ongoing, a process inextricable from the settler-colonial logic of Australia. A politics of solidarity in this context must recognize that Indigenous people 'live among' settlers whose colonization has brought genocide (Thornton, 2002). Non-Indigenous people might ask, in reckoning with complicity, how does the shape of my life keep the system intact? How does the shape of my life reflect the acknowledgement of sovereignty and/or the dismantling of privilege? Note that this goes further than the critical self-reflection work (of raising one's own consciousness about one's privilege and complicity, and identifying habits of white privilege) and the public political work (of trying to undo racism in family, friends and institutions). It goes to *actual material sacrifice*, to questioning *everything* about our lifestyles (Barker, 2010). And it also goes to being – and being regarded as – a genuine ally.

Goenpul woman and academic Aileen Moreton-Robinson (2000, xvii) has posed a question with the potential to bring the shape and detail of colonial complicities to the fore. It arose during an interaction Moreton-Robinson had with a white feminist professor who seemed intent on offering 'unsolicited advice about what we should do [about the denial of Indigenous rights in this country] and wanted us to advise her about what we might want her to do'. Moreton-Robinson's response was to ask the white feminist herself to 'tell us what the limits were to what she would do'. Non-Indigenous people could consider this question in order to uncover in themselves/ourselves sites of complicity and potential resistance.

So now we have three key sites for non-Indigenous people's work. Non-Indigenous people are challenged to undertake critical self-reflection, to commit to public political action, and to do personal-material work: to change the shape of our lives.

Changing the system, living with contradictions or blending in

In long-term relationships between non-Indigenous supporters of and Indigenous instigators of Indigenous struggles, politically salient differences in the shapes of their/our lives become more obvious. For example, lives are shaped by unequal distribution of morbidity and mortality, and in the unequal accumulation of wealth. As critical race theorist Cheryl Harris (1993) has shown, wealth disparities track race in post-civil rights USA. This poses a challenge for non-Indigenous people; our agency in relation to privilege and life choices becomes a site of interrogation.

During our interview, Monica Morgan reflected on her life's struggle to date with some frustration: the underlying issue at stake seemed to be her view of people's complicity with 'the system' that is structured colonially. I had asked Monica to describe her Indigenous rights 'work'. Monica talked about several eras in her work, 'Like, '70s I was an activist, and '80s I was mum and I was more in community development ... More of my collaborative work with whitefellas and activists have commenced in the '90s ... and this first part of this century.' This led to a reflection on her work with non-Indigenous people, and its value:

> Monica: I've been doing things with unionists, and environmentalists, and even politicians, like, you know, the Greens. But I think they're caught in their own system too, you know.
>
> Clare: So that holds people back or limits what they can actually do, or...?
>
> Monica: Your expectations need to be guided by ... them too. They're a part of the system. You know, they have to work, and live and evolve within that system.

And later:

> Monica: To me the whole thing has to change ... I know the system has to change, and I haven't found enough people who are working towards that end ... But in the end I'm just thinking – I don't know what I think. Are they caught up in the system too? And they don't know how to get out of – maybe it's all too big sometimes.

I read in these and other excerpts Monica's expression of frustration that 'everyone', even 'the ones that were supposed to be the most, you know, proactive on Indigenous rights', was still prejudiced; 'they're also wedded to the system because that's their existence' (interview). I interpret Monica as saying that being 'wedded to the system' both culturally and economically is what produces a fundamental reluctance among non-Indigenous people to change the system. Monica is frustrated by this but also suggests, generously, that it is understandable; that 'for them to abandon their system, they're abandoning themselves. Maybe it's hard for them … Yeah, I think so' (interview).

Is it enough to criticize 'the system'? Does the state not exist within the self (Lea, 2008: 235)? Will non-Indigenous people abandon our own system? Do we want to? On what level will we abandon it? Is it possible to abandon its economic logics (such as owning property and 'paying taxes to an illegal regime', as Robbie says), or to stop voting in elections (that is, cease reiterating, at regular intervals, our consent to being governed by an illegitimate sovereign)? Would these actions be politically effective? This is the crux of the challenge made by Monica Morgan and Robbie Thorpe to non-Indigenous people to reckon with their complicity. (Both also concern themselves with Indigenous people's complicity.) Yet there is a diversity of opinion regarding this. Marxist theorist Gerry Cohen (2000) deals with the question of what duty those who subscribe to egalitarian ideals have to actually realize egalitarianism in their own behaviour and economic status. Should one change oneself, or is this pointless? Cohen finds this issue a deep political and moral/theological question. The answer partly depends on whether you have faith in the 'obstetric' view of history (that the revolution is inevitable and that activists work as midwives), or whether you believe personal moral transformation is integral to the possibility of realizing socialism, in which case changing people one by one brings socialism closer (Cohen, 2000).

This issue of the contradiction between living comfortably in the system and being an agent for changing it was touched on by Jon Hawkes, someone I interviewed in his capacity as a reflective non-Indigenous person and close friend of Gary Foley. Jon identified his attentiveness to contradictions as key to Maoist theory, with which he is conversant (it is also key to Marxist theory more generally). Jon described the contradiction as 'riding the cusp between being able to survive in a contemporary reality, and creating the conditions in which that reality might change':

> Jon: And those things are in a sense *eternally* in contradiction. That on the one hand, one *has* to find a way to be able to provide for your family, [and] to reach the next generation … to teach, [to] disseminate … On the other hand all of the agencies through which one might do all those things are effectively papering over the contradictions inherent in a society based on greed and profit. And when you're conscious of that it's really quite – well, it's not actually quite difficult, but it's sort of – it's interesting to have to ride that wave.

Some people address this contradiction by seeking to live outside the system, as an expression of their allegiance to Indigenous people. But is this politically useful? One of the strategies is to utilize allies' privilege to subversive ends. As Frank Hytten says, 'If you've got privilege, use it. There are ways to use it self-indulgently and there are ways to use it in the service of other human beings' (interview). This approach to privilege applies to deploying access and resources as well as to ways of being: 'go in with some strength, some spine', rather than as a 'passive, unthinking servant'; focus on challenging the status quo rather than on 'shrinking' or taking up less space, although that can be appropriate and beneficial sometimes (Howard and Gell in Margaret, 2013: 91). There is a balancing act between rejecting the system and its privileges and taking this 'too far', resulting in self-marginalization and losing the ability to deploy the privilege one does have for progressive ends. Monica made an observation about how non-Indigenous people who can see the problems with the system deal with it. The options for non-Indigenous people seemed to be to either 'blend in' or to break down:

> Only white people can change the system but I don't see it's gonna happen. A small handful of non-Indigenous people that see that, but their impact is gonna be – you know, they probably get frustrated and go off and live in the world themselves and, you know, *blend in*. Or they become like them poor *darlings* that used to hang around the Tent Embassy, you seen them *broken* white kids? So, so disillusioned with their own society, they're just feeling so lost, because they can't come into – they can't be blackfellas and they can't be whitefellas. Yeah. You know, [a sister from the Embassy] used to tell me that she spends most of her time counselling poor white kids … Well, they come from really *rich* families, she said! But they're broken – like, she spends a lot of her time counselling broken white kids, yeah.

This contradiction (between surviving within the system but being an agent seeking to change it) is one of the things, then, that might be reflected on or negotiated by non-Indigenous people cognizant of the politics of solidarity.

'Restoring comfort' and other choices

The contradiction between developing a critical analysis of a system that oppresses Indigenous people and recognizing one's involvement in maintaining that system certainly raises questions for some non-Indigenous people. Coming to realize that unearned privileges accrue to white people reveals that as racism puts some at a disadvantage, its corollary is to put white people at an advantage (McIntosh, 2006). For Peggy McIntosh, some of the privileges enjoyed by white people 'are only what one would want for everyone in a just society'; these should be distributed equally. Other privileges that 'give license to be ignorant, oblivious, arrogant and destructive' need to be undone (2006: 76). White people's inaction in the face of this enables the system to be maintained. Ahmed (2004) is helpful in showing how institutionalized racism is created and maintained by actions not recognized by white people as racist. She says institutions, if they admit their bad behaviour, tend to frame their racism in terms of what they have failed to do – that is, failed '"to provide" for non-white others "because" of a difference that is somehow "theirs"' (Ahmed, 2004: 1). Ahmed is suggesting that racism should be more usefully understood as 'an ongoing series of actions that shape institutions, in the sense of the norms that get reproduced or "posited" over time', evident not 'in what "we" fail to do, but what "we" have already done, whereby the "we" is an effect of the doing' (Ahmed, 2004: 2). In this view, institutionalized racism is understood as the manifestation of an array of exclusionary actions.

The question, 'What should we do?', as political theorist and social organizer Adam Barker notes, is asked frequently. When it is an 'honest, engaged question', he says, there is 'nothing wrong with it'. Yet he discerns that it is, problematically at times,

> motivated by feelings of guilt or shame, generated when Settler people encounter the undeniable consequences of their lifestyles

in the oppression of Indigenous peoples. This indicates a concern
for the problems evident in Settler society as a whole, but often
a lack of willingness to sacrifice personally in order to solve
the problems that have been presented. Here, the more direct
question is actually, 'How do I restore comfort to myself?'
(Barker, 2010: 321)

Biko has written about the same question, as asked by white
liberals in South Africa:

> The question often comes up 'What can I do?' If you ask [a
> white liberal] to do something like stopping to use segregated
> facilities or dropping out of varsity to work at menial jobs like
> all blacks or defying and denouncing all provisions that make
> him privileged, you always get the answer 'but that's unrealistic!'
> While this may be true, it only serves to illustrate the fact that
> no matter what a white man does, the colour of his skin – his
> passport to privilege – will always put him miles ahead of the
> black man. Thus in the ultimate analysis no white person can
> escape being part of the oppressor camp. (Biko, 1988: 37)

Barker claims there are two typical strategies employed by
settler people to 'restore comfort' without having to sacrifice
personally: first, 'empty apologizing', and second, limiting an
engagement with injustices to those occurring 'somewhere else'.
In the North American context this response is dubbed the
'Free Tibet Syndrome'; this finds its exact Australian parallel
in the phenomenon of 'running off to the Northern Territory'.
Restoring comfort to oneself via the Free Tibet Syndrome
involves fighting injustices:

> but only with those clearly perpetuated somewhere else, by
> someone else. This allows the release of pent-up guilt over
> opulent and privileged lifestyles through the contribution to
> 'some good end', without actual personal sacrifice or discomfort
> … Meanwhile, practical actions that could be taken in the
> immediate social and political context of the colonial settler's
> own life and location are ignored. (Barker, 2010: 322)

Further settler responses to discomfort about complicity are: searching for a black ancestor – Jane Belfrage admitted fantasizing about this (interview); and appealing to government to fix the situation rather than realizing that 'we will all need to change' and beginning that work in our own lives (Maddison, 2011: 9).

A positive example of practical action that could be taken, and that contrasts with the responses critiqued above, is the work of whitefella dentist Bill Roberts, whom I was advised to interview. As Foley indicates,

> Bill Roberts was a legend in this community. He was a Collins St specialist and he walked away from that at the peak of his career. … He could have been an incredibly wealthy man. Instead … he walked away from Collins St and all the wealth and all the privilege, and he came down here to the end of Gertrude St. And he was our first dentist in the Victorian Aboriginal Health Service. (Foley, cited in Land, 2011a: 56)

Bill worked with VAHS and NAIHO for the rest of his life, over twenty-five years, becoming 'loved and revered'. The fact that he 'left his Collins St practice' echoes in the stories told of Bill. Bill *gave something up*. 'Collins St' is code for the scale of Bill's renounced wealth: it is the most prestigious address in the central business district of Melbourne. Yet it is also important to note the way Bill talked about this material sacrifice: he talked about having gained a great deal working with Aboriginal people, saying it was probably more than he gave.

Strategies white people use to avoid personal sacrifice

The strategy of 'empty apologizing' can be observed in the Australian context (see Atkinson, 2006; Foley and McKinnon, 2008). Watson has made similar observations about non-Indigenous people's reactions to assertions regarding the ongoing nature of colonization; regarding the continuance of a colonizing relationship between non-Indigenous and Indigenous people. Watson says that such assertions 'lead to "white discomfort and unsettling conversations"; they create a desire for the appeasement of white guilt in high places within the nation-state. Why have those conversations? Can we hear them?' (Watson, 2005: 47). Ahmed (2004), writing about what she calls the non-performativity of anti-racism, is intrigued by genealogies of anti-racist utterances in a racist country: where do they go and what do they 'do', if anything? Aal (2001: 305) has noted that in his organization's anti-racist work 'We have seen how white people, especially those who are better educated, are very good at using antiracist language to allow themselves to feel good about themselves without actually having to change.' This may or may not be a conscious strategy to avoid reckoning with complicity.

Ahmed identifies the irony that feeling bad about being racist can be converted into a good feeling – this is resonant with Barker's view of restoring comfort through 'empty apologizing'. She asks us to consider what happens when admitting one's racism and declaring one's bad feeling about it. Ahmed (2004: 2–3) uses the phenomenon of 'shame for being or having been implicated in racism' and, specifically in the Australian context, the demand for the nation to recognize racism towards Aboriginal people and to 'express its shame'. She says that 'in allowing us to feel bad, shame also allows the nation to feel better or even to feel good … if we recognise the brutality of that history through shame, then we can be proud' – the 'we' here being the ideal Australian (white) – an image upheld by the shame–pride conversion. Ahmed (2004: 4) argues that 'the presumption that saying is doing – that being sorry means that we have overcome the very thing we are sorry about – hence works to support racism in the present'. What is achieved is the repositioning of the white subject as the 'social ideal'. For a white subject to feel proud about its shame involves a 'self-perception of "being good". Anti-racism may even provide the conditions for a new discourse of white pride' (Ahmed, 2004: 4). So the 'goal of whiteness studies' – as articulated by some scholars – of 'creating a positive, proud, attractive antiracist white identity' is problematized. On the other hand, 'negative' identity formation is called into question because of the likelihood this will be co-present with a sense of alienation which might undermine motivation to contribute to social change (Pease, 2010b: 175). While in some circles whiteness entails stigma (Kowal, 2010), this 'stigma' must be accepted by the white person through a process of radicalization. It is not a message given to white people by dominant-culture discourse. This discussion points to questions regarding strategies for achieving social change.

Honestly, what should we do?

Affluent Westerners confronted by problems with settler society often feel discomfort. Strategically, generating discomfort and distress among members of dominant groups can function to shift people out of their complacency and encourage a confrontation with complicity or privilege (Pease, 2012). Discomfort is often the result of a 'transformation experience' (Pease 2002: 173) that has made us 'question literally everything that we do' (Barker, 2010: 321). Barker exhorts settler people to engage honestly in considering 'what should we do?' He goes on to discuss *actual personal sacrifice*, as Sarah Maddison (2011) discusses 'adaptive change' and 'real and sustained loss', which are more honest ways of speaking about redistribution than I have seen in most academic works on privilege. Pease, in *Undoing Privilege*, notes that,

> While some aspects of privilege cannot be renounced or given up because they are structurally conferred, a socially just society would restructure so that this no longer occurred. Privileged groups will experience this as a loss. (Pease, 2010b: 185)

In my view it is important to wind back immoral levels of consumption (Jensen, 2003) and to reject wealth and status accumulation as the guiding logic for life. Yet, as suggested in the following excerpt from the interview with Cam Walker, even to change the shape of one's life voluntarily so as to live relatively modestly is to remain 'fabulously wealthy' compared to most Indigenous people in Australia. Cam was reflecting on how he feels the material inequality of unearned privilege sits with people:

> I am fabulously wealthy compared to a lot of my Aboriginal friends. I have a regular job, I have income, I have a roof over my head and all that type of stuff. So I think that's a hidden power dynamic that no one ever really acknowledges, and that can be quite hard to deal with. ... I think all the adventures I've had with my work and stuff like that, that friends my age who are Aboriginal haven't had. ... We like to think we're all mates or we've stepped into, you know, a situation where we acknowledge the elders. But it's kind of missing that whole elephant in the room – of difference of opportunity, resources, access to money, that type of thing. ... How you deal with that in a kind of real way is sometimes a little bit fraught.

What shape would dealing with it in a 'real way' take? Does it mean wealth disparity would be spoken about rather than not among friends? Does it mean giving money to people? Should one refuse to buy property? Try to match the wealth of people one has a relationship with? Is there even any point (in strategic terms) in reshaping our lives on an individual basis, if there is not a critical mass of people doing so? Is developing personal integrity an unwise priority in the face of the argument that privilege can be used strategically for progressive ends? I have found Robert Jensen's (2003) sketch of an answer to the question 'What is a moral level of consumption?' helpful for its proposal that people limit themselves to a level of consumption and wealth that is globally attainable according to the limits of the Earth's resources. For instance, Jensen points out that there is not enough metal on Earth for everyone to personally own a car, suggesting therefore that doing so is immoral; instead, cars could be shared. From a different angle, Pease (2010b) discusses Eurocentrism, consumerism and the direct link to poverty else-where in the world. Clearly individual decisions must connect with work to generate collective action. This underlines the importance of critical self-reflection, public political action and personal-material work, and their interrelatedness.

Attending to the flow of benefits: ethical solidarity

Even non-Indigenous people's active political solidarity work may produce new complicities. They may benefit from their activism in support of Indigenous struggles in a variety of ways, while Indigenous people may remain no better off. Once involved in anti-racism, white people gain the oppor-tunity to 'identify themselves as "good whites"', or indeed to accept this attribution by others, both Indigenous and non-Indigenous (Green et al., 2007: 407). 'Kudos' and 'add-on value' are distributed to non-Indigenous people on account of their association with Indigenous people (Lampert, 2003: 23). For white people to highlight their/our 'relationships with people of colour' and give the impression of 'insider status' is sometimes a strategy to distance our/themselves from racism (Green et al., 2007: 407). Non-Indigenous activists can find themselves being ascribed expert status or having their reputation enhanced as a result of activism (Chris Twining, interview; Melbourne Kungkas, group interview; see also Foley, cited in Land, 2011a).

In academic settings, in particular, I find problematic the element of 'display' entailed in my or any other non-Indigenous person discussing an Indigenous person with whom I have worked or interacted. Displaying relationships with Aboriginal people may function as a crafty appropriation to bolster one's own authority to speak and, especially, as a strategy for evading criticism. Benefiting from this kind of 'display' relies on the fact that in a racist world, in which there are so many complexities in the valuing and devaluing of Aboriginal people, white liberals will accord moral authority to Indigenous people (especially old, 'authentic'-looking ones) and, by extension, non-Indigenous people who appear to have some direct connection with Indigenous people. Robbie Thorpe questioned this, however, when I raised it with him (interview). He gave me permission to 'display' our long-standing collaboration, saying I should make use of the authority this would lend me, if it was for the purpose of convincing people to support Indigenous struggles. This shows how relationships between Indigenous people and non-Indigenous activists can be valuable to both parties if non-Indigenous people are using them in the *right way*, rather than to enhance our own privilege.

Tangible benefits that may flow from solidarity work can include non-Indigenous people moving into employment opportunities for which their voluntary work or activism gives them relevant experience (Nina Collins, interview). Such benefits can be disavowed by not applying for or staying in jobs that an Aboriginal person ought to be employed to do, especially if Aboriginal people have applied (see Margaret, 2013: 76). On the other hand, being an ally can be 'to the detriment of careers' (Margaret, 2013: 80). A proposed Code of Ethics for Antiracist White Allies suggests donating a portion of any salary, speaker fee or other income received for challenging racism (Calderón and Wise, 2012). These considerations point to the importance of non-Indigenous people being attentive to the ways in which privilege might be reinscribed through the very process of trying to bring about the societal change that would undo it.

Finally, even those who are deeply committed to and informed about anti-racism and decolonizing solidarity might find themselves/ourselves 'ambushed' by racist thoughts and responses to everyday mundane situations, despite what they/we know to be true: 'Whiteness ensnares even as one strives to fight against white racism' (Yancy, 2012: 169). As well as demonstrating that habits of white privilege are both urgent and difficult to change, this observation further suggests that a sense of arrival at some place of anti-racist mastery is illusory; there may be no clear exit (Sullivan, 2006; Yancy, 2012: 169, 175).

Conclusion

Reckoning with complicity is multifaceted, involving admitting one's embroilment in a society that provides unearned dividends to certain groups of people, and admitting that one operates from within the structures that one critiques. It involves confronting the fact that colonialism creates local problems, not just faraway problems. This more directly implicates the self, begging more urgent questions about what actual personal sacrifice might be needed to address such problems and injustice.

CONCLUSION

Solidarity with other struggles

Prospective or existing supporters of Indigenous people in settler nations – whether they be independent activists or workers in the community, public or private sectors – will find this book helpful in order to initiate or extend their work in support of Indigenous struggles for social change.

The politics laid out, while specific to supporting Indigenous struggles in south-east Australia, are also informative for other solidarity projects. It is clear that there are numerous parallels between the solidarity politics that apply in south-east and other parts of Australia and those in like settler nations: Aotearoa/New Zealand, Canada and the USA. Further, non-Anglo and non-Western imperial nations or states such as France, Spain, Portugal, Germany and Indonesia/Java have created colonial legacies in relation to which the politics laid out in this book will resonate. The unfolding settler/occupation situation in Israel and Palestine is another case in point.

More broadly, this book has implications for anyone with a commitment to 'others': the non-poor working to end poverty; people from affluent countries who are involved as expatriate aid workers or volunteers in international community development projects; citizens supporting the stateless and refugees; cisgender and heterosexual-identified parents, friends and allies of people who identify as LGBTQI (lesbian, gay, bisexual, transgender, queer, intersex). Many people in these fields want an answer to the questions, 'What can I do to help you people?' 'Why is this so hard?'

The contrasts and nuances in solidarity politics relating to Indigenous struggles in settler nations other than Australia help to reveal and affirm why certain practices are important in Australia. They may also call into question existing habits of solidarity or claims about the nature of support wanted and suggest new directions.

Key dilemmas negotiated by social justice supporters primarily concerned with supporting the agendas of marginalized groups and polities other than Indigenous peoples are also instructive for those supporting Indigenous struggles in south-east Australia.

By way of conclusion, this chapter describes some key tenets of expressing solidarity with other struggles, and considers important debates that have unfolded within them. In doing so, it addresses a number of important issues. First, it explains how the book is relevant to more or less parallel struggles and endeavours. Second, it shows the key ways in which the politics differ in different contexts. By discussing the politics of solidarity in other struggles, the importance of those particular to south-east Australia are brought more clearly into view. Finally, a reflection on experiences of intersections between oppression and privilege in the lives of supporters of Indigenous struggles in south-east Australia reveals how the politics of solidarity are lived out within and between social justice struggles.

As in the south-east Australian scene, the practice of solidarity in other contexts is an active one: a practice of knowing the principles that apply and actively negotiating and balancing them when circumstances and questions of strategy throw them into conflict.

International community development

Reflective, critically informed international community development workers involved in aid projects are occupied by many of the same dilemmas as settler supporters of Indigenous struggles (Kowal, 2015: 13–15). Indeed, international NGO workers would probably be well placed to identify the power dynamics and problematics involved in addressing conditions in Fourth World Aboriginal communities and in negotiating relations with well-meaning outsiders.

Aid workers and settler supporters of Aboriginal struggles require markedly similar background understandings when preparing to work with communities or campaigners. This must include political and historical analysis, not just cultural information. They need to 'Read traditional stories and historical analysis related to the country [they] are working in, to understand how meanings have developed about ideas such as leadership, respect, reactions to foreigners, communities, aid, introduction of new ideas, development and change' and 'Seek to understand [their] own cultural values' (Rhodes, 2014: 213–14). Aid workers with a sense of history are also aware of the importance of humility, expressed by seeking out more experienced expatriates and going on to share insights with others who are on a similar journey (Rhodes, 2014: 213).

One of the differences between international aid work and support for local Indigenous struggles is the less direct complicity with the domination of the communities with which they are working. In an immediate sense, this can create a less uneasy working relationship.

Israeli solidarity with Palestinians

In Israel and Palestine, the search for ways to resist and undo ongoing settlement and eviction has thrown up ideas such as non-normalization, which attempts to problematize activities that create the impression that harmony exists or that it can be created without attention to the return of land and refugees. While its parameters can sometimes be interpreted differently, non-normalization is at root a stance that insists that any activity that aims to 'bring Palestinians (and/or Arabs) and Israelis (people or institutions) together without having as its goal resistance to and exposure of the Israeli occupation and all forms of discrimination' must be boycotted (PACBI, 2011).

The idea of non-normalization has important implications for those seeking to express solidarity with Palestinian struggles from within as well as outside of Israel and Palestine. Instigated by the Palestinian Campaign for the Academic and Cultural Boycott of Israel (PACBI) and a key tenet of the broader Boycott, Divestment and Sanctions movement (see www.bdsmovement. net), non-normalization guides boycott activity against Israel until it complies with international law and Palestinian rights. It is also a stance that asks Palestinian citizens of Israel to discern between forms of normalization presented by everyday life that are necessary for survival and those that are not and should be eschewed. It encourages resistance to those forms of participation that contribute to 'a deceptive appearance of tolerance, democracy and normal life in Israel for an international audience who may not know better' (PACBI, 2011).

Strategic issues addressed by Palestinian proponents of non-normalization and anti-Zionist Israelis include the means by which those working towards the return of land and refugees, such as the organization Zochrot (http://zochrot.org/en), can maintain accountability to Palestinians in the absence of dialogue; and the notion that the experience of participating in joint action can produce positive political transformation in some Israelis (Sheizaf, 2012).

For Israelis, in particular, non-normalization poses a challenge: to consider complicity in ongoing injustice and notions of being a beneficiary, albeit a reluctant one, of the expulsion of Palestinians in the 1948 Nakba/catastrophe (Sheizaf, 2012). Non-normalization asks sympathetic Israelis to identify the ways in which they make demands of Palestinians to 'be nice', and forces a focus on an honest reckoning with 'the issues on the ground – the occupation, the refugee problem' and the urgency of realizing real steps to redress these (Sheizaf, 2012). There are clear parallels here with the function of the government-sponsored Reconciliation process in Australia and its largely successful deferral of the national land rights and compensation agenda. As Robbie Thorpe has said, 'Let's reconcile the *accounts*.'

Non-normalization might be counterposed with the Maori cultural ethic of *aroha*/love, seen as a prerequisite to any productive political alliance (Hoskins, 2012). Yet this would be to uproot an ethic from its political and historical context: rhetoric and ideologies that frame relationships across difference change according to political and material realities.

The Israel–Palestine conflict is another case in which a structural view appropriately distinguishes between the colonizer/settler and the colonized, yet where lived experience means some settlers are both oppressor and oppressed: consider the experiences of Yemenite and Iraqi Jewish settlers who were subject to assimilatory processes, including the separation of children from their families, being renamed with Hebrew names or being prevented from speaking Arabic (L'Hirondelle et al., 2011). Under the colonizer/colonized binary, what is the status of pre-twentieth-century Jewish immigrants to Palestine (Sheizaf, 2012)?

Solidarity work can contribute usefully to remembering, combating attempts to erase and reframe the existence, experiences and claims of Palestinians. In a politics that echoes the notion of a subjectivity based on a shared critique and commitment to a shared goal, solidarity work can also be directed to creating a 'common Israeli–Palestinian discourse among those who object to the current regime' (Miller, 2012).

Refugee solidarity

In 1992 Australia introduced into its Migration Act a policy of mandatory detention, resulting in the incarceration of refugees arriving by boat and, in theory, any visitor to Australia who breaches a visa condition or stays longer than allowed.

The policy has been actively resisted from within Australia's numerous detention camps, and supported by ex-detainees and other residents and citizens. The supporter constituency has become increasingly more organized. Networks of people providing homestay (accommodation for asylum-seekers in private homes) and NGOs have grown in scope in an attempt to provide for the urgent welfare needs of refugees or those on restrictive humanitarian visas, and to advocate for an end to mandatory detention. Over time this has thrown up questions about voice, representation and the economy of solidarity. Organizations that are intended to support refugees have been challenged to pay attention to the flow benefits in terms of waged work, status and voice, and whether those most directly affected are positioned to determine the demands or directions of campaigns.

There are debates over what demands people mobilize around: 'Not in our name!' (a slogan favoured by some Australian citizens holding rallies) or 'Help us get out of here!' (a persistent demand of refugees in detention, hunger strikers, those who have broken out of camps) (Thompson, 2014). The issue of who speaks and who sets the political strategy has been debated (O'Shea, 2014). Two insights from the politics of solidarity with Indigenous struggles may apply. First, the notion that those with access to multiple privileges have a greater responsibility to undo their privilege could help guide the question of who should step back and make space for others to speak. Second, of relevance is the principle that those most directly affected should be the ones leading a struggle and setting the strategy. This is not just important in principle, but also because it may well determine the practical reality of whose political agenda and interests get advanced by the struggle.

A number of issues quickly become apparent to privilege-cognizant people wanting to support refugees and asylum-seekers, especially those who are in detention. In practical terms, how can would-be supporters find out about the experiences and agendas of those who have been isolated by government in offshore, remote or urban detention centres, or indeed dispersed around the country in community detention, often occupied with conditions of acute financial stress? Can detainees speak

on behalf of themselves from within detention? Without repri-
mand? If not, should someone speak on their behalf? In whose
name? Is it possible for those in detention to speak from a position of collective strength? In forging personal support relationships with people in detention, supporters might be confronted
by questions such as: 'Are all refugees left-wing progressives?'
'Are refugees all religiously pluralistic?' And in organizing for
other supporters to be politically transformed and come to
oppose mandatory detention, activists will realize that not all
people who have survived detention will want to speak about
the conditions or be involved in pro-refugee campaigns. Who
bears the emotional cost of recounting stories of experiences
in detention? And, further, does the strategic value of activist
work directed to providing a platform for stories to be aired
need to be revised, since this strategy has not yet succeeded in
getting people out of camps or ending mandatory detention?

Trans* solidarity

Contemporary solidarity and allyship politics in relation to
people who identify as LGBTQI and associated justice struggles
have as an important antecedent the organization Parent and
Friends of Lesbians and Gays (PFLAG), which was founded in
the USA in 1972–73. PFLAG's project Straights for Equality,
instigated in 2007, has been influential in a reinvigorated push
to encourage support, allyship and justice. Yet being an ally of
people who identify as lesbian or gay does not automatically
confer knowledge of trans* allyship (or bi or intersex allyship
for that matter). Projects such as Transfamily and Transgender
Victoria's 'What makes an Ally?' represent the development of
a more structured ally community and politics in Australia.

As in any justice struggle, those who believe they are supporters need to take the time to learn and educate themselves about the experiences and collective histories of people most directly affected by the particular injustice. This should be done in a way that seeks out the voices of and learns from, but does not unduly burden, people most affected by it.

Issues around outing and visibility are important among the many elements of allyship with people identifying as LGBTQI. At times it may be affirming to have one's gender or sexual self-identity announced and emphasized as a point of pride and strength; at other times it may not. Considerations specific to trans* identification include it being inappropriate, and possibly dangerous in terms of the extent of violent transphobia, to 'out' a trans* person. Further, to out someone as trans* may function to invalidate a person's identification.

It is instructive to note that outing and visibility in relation to trans* identity at times play out differently than for Aboriginal identity, and this needs to be taken into account in ally work. In some contexts it is supportive and safe to proactively affirm a person's Aboriginality, especially when a stereotypical view that correlates Aboriginality and skin colour can make an Aboriginal person invisible in ways that undermine self-identification.

In trans* ally politics there is a call for heterosexual-identified people to bring their own assumed normality into view (UC Davis LGBTQIA Resource Center, 2014). A person who is not transgender can undo their assumed normality by using the term 'cis' – 'cisgender' designates a person who identifies with their birth-assigned sex (Transgender Victoria, 2013a). A similar politics applies in ally education and solidarity across a range of struggles, where issues of being a beneficiary, having unearned privilege and a 'default' identity are confronted.

In and between struggles: personal experiences of intersections between privilege and oppression

In several interviews conducted for this book, people reflected on intersections between privilege and oppression in their own experience. Specifically, notions of intersectionality connect to the importance of identifying a broader agenda for social change in which many non-Indigenous people's interests are reflected; to questions about the way in which this research invokes a binary distinction between 'Indigenous' and 'non-Indigenous'; and to the politics of how people may at times problematically call on or disavow their experience of oppression and privilege. Importantly, this complicates the way people reflect on and live out their struggles and their solidarity, and provides another perspective on the applicability of solidarity politics in and between Indigenous struggles in the south-east of Australia and elsewhere. Non-Indigenous people may also be working class; Indigenous people may also be gay.

Discussions among highly reflective people regarding a range of experiences of oppression and privilege in the colonial setting provide new perspectives on intersectionality. An intersectional view is enriched by considering how oppression and privilege might play out in even more complex, contingent and shifting ways within and between distinct social worlds. Key to this enriched understanding of intersectionality is the sense that aspects of identity may be valued differently in (and among) some Aboriginal social worlds from how they are valued in dominant culture.

Key examples of intersectionality from my interviews include a discussion of Indigeneity with Sina Ana Brown-Davis, an Indigenous activist and mother from Ngati Whatua ki Kaipara in Aotearoa/New Zealand. Sina is Indigenous, yet not in south-east Australia: 'I'm Indigenous back home.' Sina talks about how Indigeneity is not determinative of active solidarity with Indigenous people; Maori in Australia, to her shame, largely do not support Indigenous people politically in Australia: 'A lot of Maori come here 'cos they're not living the racism back home and economically life is a lot easier for them. But I just see their support of Aboriginal struggle to be sort of pretty thin on the ground. That's a huge disappointment.'

Sina held many things in common with Indigenous people. However, being Indigenous but non-Indigenous, Sina is clear about rejecting appropriative gestures:

> I love hanging out with the mob! But one really good example was at Camp Sovereignty [2006]. They had Indigenous Solidarity Day. All the Aboriginal people and stuff all went around the fire. I got invited. And I said, 'No! It's really nice just to see you mob do that.' So I think non-Indigenous people have got to come to that realization: no, we don't have to rush in and grab and be a part of it. (Sina Brown-Davis, interview)

For Helen, cognizance of her white privilege was cut across by her class and her identity as a lesbian. In Helen's words: 'I'd say my father was basically a peasant. My mother came from what you'd call a working-class German family.' Helen has experienced times when being a working-class person has made it harder 'to take on people from more middle-class, high status', in the context of wanting to challenge other white people about their dominant behaviour towards Aboriginal people.

Helen also talked about how she mediates her lesbian identity for heterosexual people by trying to let them get to know her before she tells them that she is a lesbian, 'Because as a lesbian you know that it's best that people get to know you, because that way the stereotypes don't immediately pop up, which separates them from you.' While Helen knows many Aboriginal lesbians – from outback communities as well as cities – she is also aware that 'for any heterosexual person it can be a problematic identity to relate to, and I know for people in communities, especially if they're Christian, it can be a problematic one.' Helen and I met for two interviews on subsequent days. In between the interviews, Helen had to come out to Lynette, her 'friend from Yuendumu, who's lived quite a traditional life' (and who Helen knows 'feels quite close to me and quite dependent on me as a friend in this strange place', Melbourne). Helen's coming out to Lynette was precipitated by a conversation following a women-only event to which Helen took her friend:

> One reason I took her to a women's event is because my experience of women from communities is [that] they relate in fairly gender-separated spheres, they feel much more comfortable in women-only spaces. And she said to me she really enjoyed the women-only space and she told me she finds it difficult to socialize in male–female mixed groups in Melbourne, because it's not really normal for her and it makes her uncomfortable. And she said she was really happy in that situation. But one of my lesbian friends was there, so we sat with her and, you know, and they were getting along really well and chatting…

When Lynette worked out that the person she'd been talking to was a lesbian, she wanted to talk to Helen about her shock, and indicate how it was 'not acceptable' in her culture. Helen felt she had both to acknowledge that she knew many Aboriginal lesbians, and to come out to Lynette:

> I said, 'Look I really need to tell you that I'm a lesbian' ...
> and she was really shocked about that ... then she started
> talking about how there were a couple of young women in her
> community who'd got together...

Lynette described a forced marriage and violence towards the women involved. In Helen's words: 'And she's telling me this and that's really painful to me, you know, like ... she experiences racism, but I experience that as really quite painful. But she didn't realize what she was doing to me...' Nevertheless, Helen said: 'I didn't feel her sort of shut off from me.' This offered the promise that Lynette might come to accept Helen's sexuality as a kind of 'stranger sociality' (Povinelli, 2006: 231), although Helen suspected that Lynette was less open to the idea of Aboriginal people being homosexual. For me, this shows how the context of place, culture and religion intersects with the way the meanings of issues like sexuality, gendered lives and women-only space are made and/or challenged.

In another interview, Jon Hawkes talked about reckoning with his physical largeness, understood as a form of embodied privilege. I had asked Jon about whether he has felt the need to dismantle privilege in relation to Aboriginal people, along colonizer–colonizer lines, in the same way that he had talked in the interview about confronting male privilege. There was a pause of almost a minute.

> Jon: The advantage, the *primal* advantage, that I've always felt
> of myself is that I am large. Not that I am white, or that I have
> privilege; it's that I can walk down a street, in the dark, and not
> feel threatened.

Clare: Because you have a certain physicality?

Jon: Yeah, 'cos I am large. And that largeness is psychic as well as physical ... So, there's a largeness to me that I'm comfortable with and that I attempt not to use to my own personal advantage. And occasionally – so this is *really* personal – so occasionally people will point out that I am, and when they do I attempt to rein it in. That level of advantage is not an advantage I can *do* anything about, other than attempt to use it for socially useful ends. You know, I can't not be large.

The fact that Jon's embodied advantage cannot be fully undone helps to illuminate the ways in which other privileges are at once tenacious but possible to diminish or partly compensate for. As I believe Jon's reflections show, the extent to which this is possible is linked to how self-consciously that privilege is known: if Jon was unaware of how his body gave him largeness in a 'psychic' sense he would not attempt to mediate how it functions for 'socially useful ends', or to lessen its effect by trying to 'rein it in'.

Questions of age came up in two of my interviews (Jane Belfrage; Melbourne Kungkas). The Melbourne Kungkas, in particular, talked about the complexities of 'difference' in their work to support the aspirations of the Kupa Piti Kungka Tjuta. Important instances of difference were not only or always Indigenous–non-Indigenous difference, but were just as much about class, education, consumption of different media and diets, age, and status across distinct worlds. These factors cut across each other in complex and contradictory directions. The question of how age functions across Indigenous–non-Indigenous difference is a difficult one to unravel, because under colonialism age has a different salience in colonizing culture than it does in colonized culture. Povinelli (2006) points out how age is involved in the conditions placed on 'recognition' of Indigenous people. Further, in Western culture age is given contradictory values. In the colonizing situation of Australia, morbidity and mortality are unevenly distributed so that the age and population profiles of the colonized population are completely distinct from those of the colonizer population.

Cam Walker's description of coming to sense the different cultural valuings of his status in Western as opposed to Gungallida culture was very thought-provoking for me. Cam discussed his experiences as a young man working very closely with Wadjularbinna Nulyarimma, a Gungallida woman from the 'Gulf country of Queensland', in about 1992 or 1993, 'in the early stages of the campaign against Century Zinc'. He talked about the significant insights that his experience of working with and for Wadjularbinna and others gave him:

> [I]t gives you insights into, well, your role in the universe, and often that's a gendered thing of, you know, where men and women work, and young men versus old men, and, you know, women with kids as opposed to women without kids in traditional culture. And ... we all have our different values and our roles, if that makes sense. So it was just interesting – 'cos we don't have that in our society, of you know, 'I'm just a bloke', sort of thing. Whereas, you know, a young man fulfils a particular role often in a traditional culture. And in many ways they're one of the more expendable kind of parts of that society. So it's just kind of good, I think, in this society, which is so patriarchal, to be in that relationship.

For Cam, getting a sense of his role in terms of Gungallida culture in contrast to his role in 'our society' fundamentally influenced his sense of himself, his 'role in the universe'. The idea of the young man as an expendable category, and of the differing places of women with without children, helped to complicate, for me, the idea of intersectionality. An intersectional approach must take into account place, colonialism and culture in its understanding of the workings of privilege and oppression in relationships and negotiations between people contributing to Indigenous struggles. This discussion of reflections on Indigeneity, class, sexuality, embodied privilege, gender and age which arose in my interviews shows how an intersectional approach – complicated through place, colonialism and culture – is an important part of a critical engagement relating under settler colonialism.

Those involved in and/or supporting Indigenous struggles bring their own multifaceted identities and knowledge of a range of struggles to bear on their political relationships.

Conclusion

Recently, as I emerged from the process of researching and writing this book, I sought to become more informed about Australia's treatment of refugees. The first step I took – apart from reading, with my stepdaughter, David Nyuol Vincent's autobiography about escaping from Sudan and settling in Australia – was to attend a two-day anti-racism workshop conducted by RISE, a Melbourne-based organization controlled and run by refugees, ex-detainees and survivors. In my determination to be a long-term ally of a long-term struggle, to avoid being a typical, transient supporter, I had confined my social justice commitments almost exclusively to pro-Aboriginal struggles. It was seeing Gary Foley on the video ad for the RISE anti-racism workshops that embarrassed me into realizing that I was lagging way behind Aboriginal activists in sustaining a commitment to other justice struggles. It led me to recall Robbie Thorpe's work to support refugee-background volunteers to become broadcasters at 3CR community radio and his provision, together with Wiradjuri elder Ray Jackson, of Aboriginal passports to Tamil asylum-seekers in 2012 (Georgatos, 2012). Presenters at the RISE workshop urged the adoption of a political framework that made links between the racialized regimes that oppress both Aboriginal people and a range of people of colour in Australia and oppression along other axes such as gender, sexuality and ability. They also stated very clearly that it was not enough to hear about racialized discrimination at the workshop. Knowing had to be honoured by acting. People with access to multiple privileges have the greatest responsibility to contribute to social justice struggles. As Pru Gell, a long-time supporter of Indigenous peoples' rights, has said (in Margaret, 2013: 94), being busy is 'not a justification for not doing something ... If being an ally is really important to me, what other responsibilities and commitments need to be let go so that there's actually the room to do that?'

This book has been inspired by questions generated through my personal experiences of attempting solidarity with south-east Indigenous struggles, and an awareness of the frustration experienced by Indigenous people who contest with each new generation of supporters the mode of their solidarity (Foley, 1999). It has considered some key dilemmas inherent in Indigenous–non-Indigenous relationships in a context in which these structural categories are the focus of critical attention both at the level of the state and between individuals. By discerning and engaging with the politics of solidarity with south-east Indigenous struggles, this book is both a response to Indigenous people's challenges and an attempt to draw non-Indigenous people into further conversations about the nature of such engagement.

APPENDIX I

Acronyms

AAF	Australian–Aboriginal Fellowship
AAL	Australian Aborigines League
AAPA	Australian Aborigines Progressive Association
AAU	Alliance Against Uranium
AAV	Aboriginal Affairs Victoria
ACCHO	Aboriginal Community Controlled Health Organisation
ACF	Australian Conservation Foundation
ACFOA	Australian Council for Overseas Aid
ACR	Australian Catholic Relief
ACTU	Australian Council of Trade Unions
AHSHL	AIDS, Hepatitis and Sexual Health Line Inc.
ALP	Australian Labor Party
ALS	Aboriginal Legal Service
ANFA	Australian Nuclear Free Alliance
ANTaR	Australians for Native Title and Reconciliation (national body)
ANTaR Victoria	ANTaR Victoria – Working for Land Justice and Reconciliation; formerly Australians for Native Title and Reconciliation Victoria (2000); formerly Defenders of Native Title (1997) (state body)
APA	Aborigines Progressive Association
APG	Aboriginal Provisional Government
ASIO	Australian Security Intelligence Organisation
ATSIC	Aboriginal and Torres Strait Islander Commission

AWD	Action for World Development
Black GST	Black GST (Genocide, Sovereignty, Treaty)
CAAMA	Central Australian Aboriginal Media Association
CAR	Council for Aboriginal Reconciliation
Comintern	Communist International
CPA	Communist Party of Australia
CRA	Conzinc Riotinto of Australia; became Rio Tinto Limited (part of Rio Tinto Group)
CRG	Critical reference group
DHS	Department of Human Services
ECNT	Environment Centre Northern Territory
EIS	Environmental Impact Statement
FAA	Foundation for Aboriginal Affairs
FAIRA	Foundation for Aboriginal and Islander Research Action
FCAA	Federal Council for Aboriginal Advancement; renamed FCAATSI in 1964
FCAATSI	Federal Council for the Advancement of Aborigines and Torres Strait Islanders; formerly the Federal Council for Aboriginal Advancement
FoE	Friends of the Earth
FTC	Family Therapy Centre
GFFTL	Grupo Feto Foinsa'e Timor Lorosa'e/East Timor Young Women's Association
GVEG	Goulburn Valley Environment Group
HCCV	Hepatitis C Council Victoria Inc.
HSC	Higher School Certificate (completion of Year 12)
ILC	Indigenous Land Corporation
ITAS	Indigenous Tutorial Assistance Scheme
JAG	Jabiluka Action Group
KPKT	Kupa Piti Kungka Tjuta
KSUTL	Konsellu Solidariedade Universitariu Timor Lorosa'e/East Timor Student Solidarity Council
LGBTQI	Lesbian, gay, bisexual, transgender, queer, intersex

MAYSAR	Melbourne Aboriginal Youth Sport and Recreation
MLDRIN	Murray and Lower Darling Rivers Indigenous Nations
MOU	Memorandum of Understanding
NAIDOC	National Aboriginal and Islander Day Observance Committee
NAIHO	National Aboriginal and Islander Health Organisation
NAILSS	National Aboriginal and Islander Legal Service Secretariat
NSWBLF	New South Wales Builders Labourers Federation
NTC	National Tribal Council
NTLRA	Northern Territory Land Rights Act
PACBI	Palestinian Campaign for the Academic and Cultural Boycott of Israel
PFLAG	Parents and Friends of Lesbians and Gays
Rio Tinto	Multinational mining and resources group headquartered in London and Melbourne; comprises Rio Tinto Ltd (formerly CRA) and Rio Tinto PLC
SAFA	Student Action for Aborigines
SLJR	Students for Land Justice and Reconciliation
SNAICC	Secretariat of National Aboriginal and Islander Child Care
SOS	Students of Sustainability
TWS	The Wilderness Society
UNIA	Universal Negro Improvement Association
USET	University Students for East Timor
VAAL	Victorian Aborigines Advancement League
VACCHO	Victorian Aboriginal Community Controlled Health Organisation
VAHS	Victorian Aboriginal Health Service (Fitzroy)
WCC	World Council of Churches
WWF	World Wide Fund for Nature; formerly known as World Wildlife Fund
WWF	Waterside Workers' Federation

Key events and organizations in south-east Indigenous struggles

This timeline highlights key moments, people and organizations in south-east Indigenous struggles and their broader context. In particular I have sought to include campaigns in which people I interviewed were involved. While not exhaustive, the timeline is included in order to demonstrate the character of Indigenous struggles, as well as solidarity by Indigenous and non-Indigenous people. It includes details which show some of the lineages and links that exist between events and people.

The timeline draws on many sources, in particular *The Encyclopaedia of Aboriginal Australia*; Attwood and Markus, *The Struggle for Aboriginal Rights: A Documentary History*; the Australasian Legal Information Institute website (AustLII); and Foley's 'Timeline of Significant Moments in the Indigenous Struggle in South-east Australia' (published on the Koori History Website).

1846	Residents of Flinders Island, off the mainland of Van Diemen's Land/Tasmania, petition Queen Victoria (Attwood and Markus, 1999: 38).
1860	Six members of the Moira tribe (Yorta Yorta) propose a tax on steamer boats using the Murray River to fund compensation for damage caused to their fisheries (Barwick, 1972: 47).
1863–86	Deputation of residents from Coranderrk walk to Melbourne to convey a message to the Queen and later to meet with the chief secretary (Attwood and Markus, 1999: 43–9).
1881–90	Moira and Ulupna tribes (Yorta Yorta) of the Murray River, later residents of Maloga Mission and

Cummeragunja, write petitions (1881 and 1887) and a deputation of reverends convey another petition to the premier (1890) (Attwood and Markus, 1999: 51–4).

1899   Twenty-five Framlingham residents resist closure of the station and refuse eviction to Lake Tyers, Victoria (Chesterman and Galligan, 1997: 27).

1907–08 Fred Maynard and Tom Lacey are associated with two visits that world-renowned black American boxer Jack Johnson made to Sydney (Foley, 2006).

1920s   Universal Negro Improvement Association (Sydney chapter) includes Fred Maynard and Tom Lacey, who would later found the AAPA (1925–27) (Foley, 2006).

1925–27 Australian Aborigines Progressive Association (AAPA), the 'first Aboriginal political organization to create formal links between communities over a wide area', officially launched. Founding leaders are Fred Maynard and Tom Lacey (Foley, 2006).

1926   Native Union formed by William Harris in Western Australia (Haebich, 1992: 269).

1926–35 Salt Pan Creek, an Aboriginal squatters' camp south-west of Sydney containing refugee families of the dispossessed and people seeking to escape the harsh and brutal policies of the Aborigines Protection Board, becomes a focal point of intensifying Aboriginal resistance in NSW. Significant alliances, strategies and future leaders are developed. People such as Jack Campbell, George and Jack Patten, Pearl Gibbs and Bill Onus all spend time in the camp. In 1933 Joe Anderson is filmed at Salt Pan Creek by cinesound news making a strong statement in support of Indigenous Rights (Foley, 2006). Salt Pan Creek had been a site of Indigenous resistance from as early as 1809, when Tedbury (son of Pemulwuy) was involved in a skirmish with a white settler (Foley, 2006).

1933   Australian Aborigines League (AAL) established in Melbourne, led by William Cooper, and including Doug Nicholls, Shadrach James and Marge Tucker. Non-Indigenous supporters include trade unionists, Christians and members of the Communist Party of Australia (CPA) (Foley, 2006).

AAL's first campaign is to collect signatures for a petition to King George (Foley, 2006).

1937   Aborigines Progressive Association (APA) founded. Leaders include Bill Fergusson, Pearl Gibbs and Jack Patten, all of whom cultivate significant non-Indigenous support, including from trade unionists (Foley, 2006).

1937–62   Jackson's Track, near Drouin in Victoria, is for this period a haven for Aboriginal people who live there, out of reach of the Aborigines Protection/Welfare Board.

1938   Day of Mourning and all-Aboriginal conference convened by AAL and APA on the occasion of the national Sesquicentennial Celebrations of invasion.

1938   William Cooper leads a deputation from the AAL to the German Consulate in Melbourne on 6 December. They present a resolution 'condemning the persecution of Jews and Christians in Germany'. The consul-general refuses them admittance (Foley, 2006).

1939   200 Cumeragunja residents decide to 'walk off' the reserve in protest at Aborigines Protection Board policies. They cross the Murray River into Victoria and set up camp at Barmah. The walk-off is the culmination of years of unrest and protests against discrimination, 'intimidation, starvation and victimization' at the hands of reserve management. Jack Patten and his brother George are arrested for 'incitement' (Foley, 2006).

1946–   Strike by Aboriginal stockworkers in the Pilbara area of Western Australia, where most of the Indigenous workers are receiving no cash wages at all. Strikers are seized by police at gunpoint and put in chains. The Pilbara strike is supported by 19 unions in Western Australia, 7 federal unions and 4 trades and labour councils. In the east, Bill Onus is involved in organizing support for the strikers. The Western Australian branch of the Seamen's Union places a ban on the transport of wool from stations affected by the strike, winning almost immediate concessions from the pastoralists. A white Communist unionist,

Don McLeod, is arrested during the Pilbara strike for 'inciting Aborigines to leave their place of lawful employment'; the Aboriginal strikers march on the jail and McLeod is freed (Foley, 2006).

1951   Mary Clarke, a resident of Framlingham, calls for white people to pay the rent (Attwood and Markus, 1999: 166–7).

1956   Australian-Aboriginal Fellowship (AAF) is co-founded in Sydney by Pearl Gibbs, former secretary of the Aborigines Progressive Association (Foley, 2006).

1957   Victorian Aborigines Advancement League (VAAL) established. Passes an 'Aboriginalization' motion in 1969.

1958   Federal Council for Aboriginal Advancement (FCAA), the first national Aboriginal organization, formed at a meeting in Adelaide. Twenty-five people representing eight organizations attend; only three (Bert Groves, Doug Nicholls and Jeff Barnes) are Aboriginal (Foley, 2006). FCAA renamed FCAATSI in 1964.

1962–70 Campaign to save Lake Tyers following a government decision to abolish this last remaining Victorian reserve. Land rights eventually secured in 1970, under the Aboriginal Lands Act. The Victorian government hands back 4,000 acres at Lake Tyers and 583 acres at Framlingham to two Aboriginal trusts, although criteria for trust membership are problematic (Taffe, 2008).

1965   Charles Perkins, one of the first Aboriginal people to enrol at an Australian university, and Reverend Ted Noffs of the Wayside Chapel, organize a 'Freedom Ride' with thirty white Sydney University students from the group Student Action for Aborigines (SAFA). This bus ride into regional NSW is an attempt to expose racism and desegregate communities. It is a dangerous but ultimately 'highly effective' 'consciousness-raising exercise' (Foley, 2006).

1966   Gurindji walk-off begins. In 1975 prime minister Gough Whitlam grants leasehold rights. After a twenty-year struggle the Gurindji obtain freehold title to Daguragu (1986) (Foley, 2006).

1967	Referendum, in which nearly 91 per cent of voters agree to remove clauses from the constitution which had prevented the Commonwealth from making laws for Aboriginal people, and had excluded Aboriginal people from being reckoned in the numbers of the people in the Commonwealth (Horton, 1994, vol. 2: 933–4; Taffe, 2008).
1967	Aborigines Advancement League, Melbourne, elects veteran activist Bill Onus as chairman. In that position, which he holds until his death in 1968, he becomes a significant mentor to his nephew Bruce McGuinness, who goes on to become one of the most important activists of his era (Foley, 2006).
1969	Brisbane Tribal Council established, including Denis Walker, son of Oodgeroo (Taffe, 2008).
1970	National Tribal Council established following a split within FCAATSI. Founding members include Doug Nichols and Oodgeroo Noonuccal (Kath Walker).
1970	Protests against the bicentenary of Captain Cook's landing; memorial celebrations and re-enactment are held at Kurnell, Botany Bay, 29 April, initiated by Chicka Dixon.

  Protests at Cook's Cottage in Melbourne (Foley, 2006; Horner, 2004: 157–8). |
1970	Rally convened by the Save the Gurindji Committee in Sydney, near the offices of Vestey's, led by Paul Coe and addressed by Frank Hardy, 31 July. Many people are arrested; Coe the first to be arrested 'as soon as he spoke' (Horner, 2004: 161).
1970	Aboriginal Legal Service (ALS) established: its first council is elected at the end of a public meeting in October. ALS opens for business on 27 August (Horner, 2004: 162).
1970	Land Rights Act 1970 grants former reserve land to Framlingham and Lake Tyers Aboriginal Trusts, Victoria.
1970	Black Power Conference in Atlanta, Georgia, in the USA, attended by Melbourne and Sydney-based Bruce McGuinness, Sol Bellear, Bob Maza, Patsy Kruger and Jack Davis, of Perth (Foley, n.d.).

1971	Action for World Development established by the Australian Council of Churches (ACC) with the aim of running a national campaign against racism. Frank Engel elected general secretary of ACC in January 1971.
1971	Anti-apartheid protests against the South African Rugby Springbok tour.

Members of the New South Wales Builders Labourers Federation (NSWBLF) arrested while attempting to cut down goal posts.

Gary Foley, Billie Craigie and Bindi Williams go to Aotearoa in solidarity with Springbok tour protests there – the only protest that succeeds in stopping a game.

1971   Bunnerong Land Claim in Sherbrooke Forest in the Dandenong ranges in eastern Melbourne led by Lin Onus, who establishes an occupation in February. Protesters forced out when their hut is set on fire in April (Koori History Website).

1971   Friends of the Earth established in Australia (Burgmann, 2003b: 193).

1971   Gove/Yirrkala case (*Milirrpum* v. *Nabalco Pty Ltd*) that had been launched by the Yolgnu people against the Nabalco mining company and the federal government rejected. It is an attempt to assert sovereign rights to halt a bauxite mine on the Gove peninsula. The Yolgnu are represented in the case by Justice Woodward, who goes on to head the Land Rights Commission, which leads to the Northern Territory Land Rights Act, 1976.

1972   Aboriginal Medical Service established, Redfern.

1972   Aboriginal Embassy established on the lawns of Parliament House, Canberra, on 26 January (Australia Day/Invasion Day), the morning after Prime Minister McMahon's 'provocative' announcement on land rights, and in recent memory of the Gove case of 1971 case, which went against the Yolgnu people.

The Aboriginal Embassy elevates Aboriginal political agendas to the national and international stage; impacts on the historic election result in 1972;

and leads to land rights legislation in the Northern Territory.

The Embassy is re-established in Canberra many times between 1972 and 1992 and has a permanent presence there from 1992 onwards. Offshoots of the Embassy are established in other parts of Australia at other times (Sydney Olympics 2000, Stolenwealth Games 2006). Other communities and campaigns are inspired by the Aboriginal Embassy to set up political encampments on the lawns of Parliament (Robinson, 1994: 63; Conway, 2010).

1972	Moratorium for land rights held in cities and regional centres across Australia.
1972	World Council of Churches conducts a twelve-month campaign against racism.
1972	Black Panther Party formed, with Denis Walker and Sam Watson as founding members.
1972, 1974	Two Aboriginal delegations tour the People's Republic of China. Chicka Dixon leads the first; Gary Foley and Evelyn Scott lead the second (Koori History Website).
1972–73	Union and ACTU boycott campaigns against French nuclear testing in the Pacific (Burgmann, 2003b: 176).
1973	Victorian Aboriginal Health Service established.
1973	National Aboriginal and Islander Health Organisation established.
1973	First urban land rights achieved in Redfern with the help of the NSWBLF. Aboriginal Housing Company established.
1975–	Mass movements against uranium mining under the National Uranium Moratorium Campaign, including Australian Railways Union strike in 1976, achieve an Australian Labor Party (ALP) moratorium (1977). Once elected, the ALP reneges, first adopting a 'one mine' (1982) and then a 'three mines' policy (1984), enabling Roxby Downs, Narbalek and Ranger mines to continue (Burgmann, 2003b: 172–4, 184).
1975–90	Koori Kollij Health Worker Education begins as a community-based education programme at Swinburne University (Victorian Aboriginal Education

Association Inc. timeline), led by Bruce McGuinness and Gary Foley. Later gains philanthropic and some government funding and operates from its own premises in Collingwood (1982).

1976   Northern Territory Land Rights Act (NTLRA) passed in federal parliament.

1976–79   *Coe* v. *Commonwealth* case mounted; dismissed on appeal. Redfern-based Paul Coe mounts a High Court case against the Commonwealth of Australia and the UK government, arguing that British sovereignty was declared wrongfully, that Aboriginal people are a sovereign nation, and that the doctrine of *terra nullius* is false (Horton, 1994, vol. 1: 206).

1976–87   Framlingham community in south-west Victoria begins a campaign to regain rights to the Framlingham Forest, which had been excised from the original 1861 reserve in 1894. In 1979 the community blockades the road to the forest picnic ground. Finally in 1987 the Framlingham Aboriginal Trust gains part of the forest through legislation in the Commonwealth Parliament (Wikipedia).

1979   Aboriginal Information Centre in London and connections with the German 'Greens' movement established following a visit by Gary Foley in 1978 to the Cannes Film Festival for the film *Backroads* (Koori History Website).

1979   Logging ceases on Mumbulla Mountain, near Wallaga Lake in NSW, following a campaign led by Guboo Ted Thomas of the Yuin nation.

1980   Foundation for Aboriginal and Islander Research Action (FAIRA) established, Brisbane. One of its core activities is to research and campaign for the repatriation of ancestral remains (Horton, 1994, vol. 2: 1167–8).

1980s   Portland community struggle against the destruction of almost 200 Aboriginal sites by Alcoa to build an aluminium smelter. Sandra Onus and Christina Isabel, members of the Gunditjmara community, launch legal action, which has a win in the High Court; yet by this time most of the sites have been destroyed. There is a settlement and some lands are returned to the community as a result (Message Stick, 2008; *Onus v. Alcoa of Australia Ltd* (1981) HCA 50).

1982   Major Aboriginal-led camp and protests on the occasion of the Commonwealth Games, Musgrave Park, Brisbane, Queensland.

1982   Koori Information Centre established in Fitzroy; publishes *Koorier*. Works to build the media component of the struggle. Among those involved are Robbie Thorpe, Wayne Atkinson, Jacqui Katona, Lin Onus.

1983–86   The ALP wins the federal election in 1983; Bob Hawke becomes prime minister. The new minister for Aboriginal affairs, Clyde Holding, sets up a National Land Rights Working Party to develop national land rights legislation. Over the next three years the ALP waters down its own policy and eventually abandons its own national land rights legislation. It also passes amendments to the NTLRA, watering it down (Foley, 2006).

1984   Mr Charles Perkins becomes secretary of the Department of Aboriginal Affairs (Foley, 2006).

1987–88   Michael Mansell of Tasmania (then Aborigine of the Year) and other delegates attend a World Conference on Zionism, Racism and Imperialism in Libya. A further delegation the following year secures support for Aboriginal causes, including the Aboriginal passport, from Colonel Gaddafi (Horton, 1994, vol. 2: 654–5; Wikipedia).

1988   Protests against the Bicentennial Celebrations.

     'March for Hope and Justice', Sydney: an estimated 20,000 Aboriginal people join their supporters from the trade unions, the churches, ethnic groups and the wider community, in a demonstration of survival. A joint statement signed by the heads of fourteen churches calls for Aboriginal rights, including a secure land base (Foley, 2006).

     Burnum Burnum plants the Aboriginal flag on the white cliffs of Dover on British soil on 26 January, and issues a declaration 'offering the British a kompartoo or fresh start' (Horton, 1994, vol. 1: 168–9).

Bob Weatherall 'buys back' all Aboriginal land from the Queensland government, paying with beads, blankets and a bag of flour (Horton, 1994, vol. 2: 1167–8).

The Central, Northern and Tiwi Land Councils and Pitjantjatjara Council had decided in November 1987 to boycott the Bicentennial Celebrations (Foley, 2006).

1989   Aboriginal and Torres Strait Islanders Commission (ATSIC) Act establishes a national elected representative structure for Commonwealth Aboriginal Affairs (Foley, 2006).

1990   Aboriginal Provisional Government (APG) formed by delegates to the National Federation of Land Councils meeting in Kakadu National Park. Founding office bearers are Bob Weatherall, Michael Mansell, Geoff Clarke, Robbie Thorpe and Lyall Munro (all of south-east Australia). Regional committees are established in each state following a national tour in 1992, and APG boasts the largest membership of any national Aboriginal group in Australia (Horton, 1994, vol. 1: 23).

1991   Council for Aboriginal Reconciliation Bill is passed to establish a mechanism for discussion of the reconciliation of Aboriginal and non-Aboriginal Australians. The reconciliation process is envisaged as a ten-year project. Former Central Land Council director Pat Dodson is appointed Council chairman (Foley, 2006; Horton, 1994, vol. 2: 931–2).

1991   After two years of intensive hearings and investigations, the Royal Commission into Aboriginal Deaths in Custody releases its National Report (Foley, 2006).

1991   Protest in Melbourne addressed by Robbie Thorpe and Gary Foley serves an eviction notice on the Supreme Court, claiming that the Court has wrongfully asserted jurisdiction and sovereignty. Thorpe theatrically places on trial for war crimes a statue of John Batman – colonizer in Van Diemen's Land (later Tasmania) and the Port Phillip district (later Melbourne) (Black GST site on Kooriweb).

1992	High Court overturns the doctrine of *terra nullius* and recognizes the existence of native title in the case of *Eddie Mabo and Others* v. *State of Queensland*, on 3 June (Foley, 2006).
1992	Prime Minister Paul Keating speaks at Redfern Park, Sydney, to mark the start of the Year of Indigenous People (Foley, 2006). In this now famous speech he declares that to find 'just solutions to the problems which beset the first Australians ... starting point might be to recognize that the problem starts with us non-Aboriginal Australians ... It was we who did the dispossessing ... We took the traditional lands and smashed the traditional way of life. We brought the diseases. The alcohol. We committed the murders. We took the children from their mothers. With some noble exceptions, we failed to make the most basic human response and enter into their hearts and minds. We failed to ask – how would I feel if this were done to me?'
1992	Twenty years after the first Aboriginal Embassy, another is set up and Old Parliament House occupied 'to draw attention to Aboriginal claims for sovereignty' (Horton, 1994, vol. 2: 1063).
1992–	Campaign against the Century Zinc mine in the Gulf country of Queensland, in which Wadjularbinna Nulyarimma from Gungallida Country is a key leader. The mine owner is CRA, one of the biggest mining companies in the world; it later morphs into Rio Tinto.
1992–95	Campaign against the closure of Northland Secondary College lasts three years and succeeds in reopening the school; Gary Foley elected to lead the parent and community campaign and is involved in the operation of a Rebel School (Koori History Website).
1993	Native Title Act passed in the federal parliament.
1994	Yorta Yorta request meeting with Goulburn Valley Environment Group (GVEG, formed in 1990) and the beginnings of an alliance emerge (La Nauze, 2009).
1994–2002	Yorta Yorta Native Title Claim, in which Wayne Atkinson is a principal claimant, runs for several

years, from lodgement through hearings and appeals. High Court appeal dismissed, upholding Federal Court finding against the Yorta Yorta claim.

*c.*1995   Koori–Gubbah Club established at Monash University, taking the name from a club at La Trobe University. bryan Andy is the club's first convener.

1996   *Wik* case determines that native title and pastoral leases can coexist.

1996–2009 Goolengook anti-logging protests in East Gippsland gain a moratorium on logging after a thirteen-year campaign, during which significant tracts were logged (www.vicrainforest.org/Gook/VEACgoolengook.php).

1997   *Bringing Them Home: Report of the National Inquiry into the Separation of Aboriginal and Torres Strait Islander Children from Their Families* is tabled in federal parliament on 26 May.

1997   Prime Minister John Howard opens the Australian Reconciliation Convention in Melbourne (26–28 May); he is judged to have 'hectored' the audience, many of whom turned their backs on him. The number of reconciliation groups jumps from 20 to 'more than 260' as an apparent consequence (Burgmann, 2003b: 91).

1997   *Thorpe* v. *Commonwealth* case mounted and lost. Robbie Thorpe alleges that the 'government has admitted the genocide' and seeks 'that the government justify its position to the international community and the world court' (*Thorpe* v. *The Commonwealth of Australia* (No. 3) (1997)).

1997   Defenders of Native Title established in Victoria; Australians for Native Title and Reconciliation established nationally.

1997, 1998 Indigenous Solidarity Group at Friends of the Earth organizes two conferences, at which the Irati Wanti campaign, among others, garners support (Friends of the Earth website).

1997–2000 Mirrar campaign against the Jabiluka uranium mine. The contested Jabiluka mine site is located within the internationally famous and nationally iconic Kakadu National Park in the Northern Territory.

1997–2002	Students for Land Justice and Reconciliation established at University of Melbourne under the original name of Defenders of Native Title. The name and agenda of the group are quickly changed when the group enters into dialogue with Gary Foley, who explains his critique of the Native Title Act (1993) and works with the group throughout its duration.
1998	*Native Title Act* amendments (the Ten Point Plan) proposed as a backlash to the *Wik* case. They are eventually passed in the federal parliament. The amendments water down the Native Title Act 1993.
1998–	Various genocide litigation cases mounted by members of Aboriginal nations from many parts of Australia, including Robbie Thorpe, Wadjularbinna Nulyarimma, Isabel Coe, Billy Craigie, Tom Trevorrow, Irene Watson, Kevin Buzzacott and Michael J. Anderson (AustLII). In response to this a Democrats senator introduces the Anti-Genocide Bill 1999 into the Australian Senate, but this never enters Australian law (Black GST site on Kooriweb).
1998–2004	Kupa Piti Kungka Tjuta, the senior Aboriginal women of Coober Pedy, including Antikarinya, Yankunytjatjara and Kokatha women, initiate the Irati Wanti ('The poison, leave it') campaign against the proposed national radioactive waste repository in northern South Australia. They secure the support of Greenies and win this struggle in 2004.
2000	The ten-year term of the Council on Aboriginal Reconciliation ends with thousands of Australians participating in celebratory marches, including across Sydney Harbour Bridge. The recommendations in the Council's Final Report include negotiating a process for agreement or treaty-making, and changing the constitution to remove race clauses and recognize Aboriginal and Torres Strait Islander peoples as first peoples.
2000	Protests on the occasion of the Olympic Games, including a camp, Embassy and Sacred Fire at Victoria Park, Sydney, NSW. Isabel Coe and senior elder Guboo Ted Thomas anchor the occupation.

2000	Arabunna man Kevin Buzzacott holds a ceremony at Kurnell, where Captain Cook first set foot on Australia, after a peace march from his homeland in South Australia (Begg, 2000).
2000	Yorta Yorta, FoE and GVEG agree on Barmah–Millewa campaign protocol (Friends of the Earth website).
2004	Jaara Bringing them Home Camp, an occupation of Franklinford, Victoria, part of the original Aboriginal Protectorate of the mid-1800s, established on 26 May (Sorry Day). It aims to highlight issues of sovereignty and genocide, the 'unfinished business' between the Australian government and Aboriginal people.
2004	Members of the Dja Dja Wurrung, led by Gary Murray, gain an emergency cultural heritage declaration on three bark etchings being exhibited at Museum Victoria, on loan from the British Museum. The declaration temporarily prevents their return. However, the Victorian minister for Aboriginal affairs declines to grant permanent protection.
2006	Black GST (Genocide, Sovereignty, Treaty) protests against the Commonwealth Games ('Stolenwealth Games'), King's Domain, Melbourne, Victoria. Centred around Camp Sovereignty and the Sacred Fire. Sacred Fire forcibly extinguished and Camp Sovereignty evicted after sixty days.
2007	Protests about the future of the old Health Service in Gertrude St Fitzroy, which had lain empty for years before being sublet to Mission Australia as a silver-service restaurant in which Aboriginal trainees would work.
2007	Seven environment groups sign a Cooperation Agreement with Murray and Lower Darling Rivers Indigenous Nations (MLDRIN), forming an alliance for the protection of the ecological and cultural integrity of these river systems (Friends of the Earth website).
2008	Prime Minister Kevin Rudd delivers an Apology to the Stolen Generations on behalf of the federal parliament, 13 February.

2011	Occupy Melbourne protesters, including Aboriginal people, centre issues of sovereignty in their protest and call for the Australian government to enter into treaties with first nations (Occupy Melbourne, 2011).
2012	Commemoration of the fortieth anniversary of the establishment of the Aboriginal Embassy held at the Embassy in Canberra (26–28 January). In the days and weeks after this, Embassies are established at Portland (Vic), Perth and Broome (WA), Musgrave Park in Brisbane (Qld), Sandon Point and Moree (NSW), as part of a Sovereign Union–National Unity government network.
2014	Tent Embassy established in Redfern in protest against Aboriginal Housing Company plan to redevelop housing stock with no guarantee of affordable Aboriginal housing being included.
2014	APG proposes Aboriginal-owned lands throughout Australia be declared the nation's seventh state, with rights to make laws.
2014	Warriors of the Aboriginal Resistance (WAR), a collective of young Aboriginal people, is officially launched in Brisbane on 12 November with Bogaine Skuthorpe-Spearim, Callum Clayton-Dixon, Jade Slockee, Meriki Onus and Pekeri Ruska as the founding members (Warriors of the Aboriginal Resistance, 2014). The launch is part of the First Nations response to the G20 Summit of 15–16 November 2014 (Brisbane Blacks, 2014). The WAR collective is committed to the cause of decolonization and the philosophy of Aboriginal Nationalism, and publishes the magazine *Black Nations Rising*.

Biographies of people involved in the book

This appendix provides brief biographies of people I interviewed, members of the reference group, my research supervisor and myself. In the case of people I interviewed, I have drawn from people's own words to construct a biography, having asked them during interviews how they see or describe themselves.

Where people I interviewed expressed the wish, I have used their real names in the research. Some people have chosen to remain anonymous; in these cases I have provided a changed first name and omitted the last name. All those involved in the project were based in Melbourne at the time of the interview, with the exception of Chicka Dixon (Sydney) and Monica Morgan (Echuca). Marjorie Thorpe, a member of the critical reference group, was based in East Gippsland; my research supervisor, Bob Pease, was based in Geelong.

People interviewed

BRYAN ANDY

'I'm Yorta Yorta. I come from Cummeragunja, which is in New South Wales on the New South Wales–Victorian border. I've worked in Indigenous affairs all of my working life since I was 18. That's ranged from working with ATSIC as a policy officer, and with Aboriginal Affairs Victoria at state level. I've had a lot to do with Stolen Generations and Sorry Day activities around Melbourne and within Victoria. I'm just a member of the community that does what they do to either achieve some kind of goal, or further a cause, or highlight a situation.'

bryan once worked for ANTaR Victoria. He co-founded the reconciliation-based student group the Koori–Gubbah Club at

Monash University. bryan has been involved in the arts, including numerous acting roles. During our interview bryan spoke at times of elements of his experiences as a gay man.

WAYNE ATKINSON

Wayne Atkinson is an elder of the Yorta Yorta and the Dja Dja Whurrung people of central and north-eastern Victoria. He has worked with his people on their epic struggle for land justice, including researching and preparing a claim in 1984, and as a principal claimant in the Yorta Yorta native title claim (1994–2002). Dr Atkinson has served as an elected representative of his ancestral lineage of some 1,200 kinfolk, as well as serving on the Yorta Yorta Elders Council.

Wayne Atkinson has gained extensive knowledge from cultural exchanges with Indigenous groups in the United States, Canada, New Zealand and the South Pacific Region. He studied Archaeology, History and Legal Studies at La Trobe University. He was awarded a B.A. with Honours in 1996, and was selected as the 1996 NAIDOC Indigenous scholar of the year. He completed his Ph.D. thesis, *Not One Iota: The Yorta Yorta Struggle for Land Justice*, in July 2001. He has lectured in History and Politics at the University of Melbourne, where he was a senior lecturer at the time of the interview, and where he was appointed a senior fellow. Wayne Atkinson has hosted many student and community groups on his Yorta Yorta homelands, and has worked closely with groups such as the Dharnya Action Group.

JANE BELFRAGE

'I'm an Australian of Anglo-Irish descent. I'm 50 years old. I was born in 1958 in Melbourne. I'm a middle-class woman, a single parent, tertiary educated with a Master's degree, and I'm a practising musician. I travelled around Australia as a child in 1968 visiting missions. My interest in Indigenous land rights and human rights started from when I was about 16. I became active in 1975 in the movement against uranium mining, which brought an awareness of the land rights movement, and was involved in land rights struggles at Framlingham and Portland in 1979 and 1980. I was active until the mid-1990s, round about twenty years ... People would perceive me as being an artist and a member of my family, a teacher, a very creative person. And someone who has also struggled with depression.'

SINA ANA BROWN-DAVIS

'I'm a descendent of the Teroho Tearoa Aho Napui peoples, Indigenous people of Aotearoa. I also descend from Samoan and Tongan peoples from my mother. I would describe myself as an Indigenous activist, primarily in the area of anti-globalization, and a mother.'

NINA COLLINS

Nina is a young, non-Indigenous, educated woman who at the time of the interview was working on a government-funded programme that offered 'remote' Indigenous students opportunities to study at boarding schools or universities in capital cities. Her voluntary commitments have included involvement in the philanthropic body EastWeb, which makes grants to young refugee and Indigenous people's projects.

Nina explained during our interview: 'My name is actually Kalinikos and we Anglicized it when our family came here. I'm half-Greek, and half-Polish Jewish on the other side ... But, at the same time, I have the privilege of whiteness ... I can totally fit in, and in that sense it doesn't really matter what my ethnic background is, because I am white and I have the benefits of being white.' Having one parent who was born in Australia and one who is an immigrant, Nina talked about how she doesn't view herself as *'Australian* Australian'.

While studying Arts at the University of Melbourne, Nina was a member of Students for Land Justice and Reconciliation.

Nina participated in a group interview with Cam McDonald. Cam met Gary Foley through Nina and they both count him as influential.

CHICKA DIXON (1928–2010)

'I come from Wallaga Lake mission on the South Coast of New South Wales. I am a proud Yuin warrior. You're put on the earth for a purpose. Mine was to fight for justice for Aboriginal people. I *know* it was. I'm a political animal. I support *all* oppressed people, throughout the world.'

Once a wharfie, Chicka was involved in the birthing of the Aboriginal Medical Service and the Aboriginal Legal Service in Redfern, Sydney. He represented his people on numerous delegations and study tours, including to China, Canada, the USA, Tahiti and Nigeria. He was the first chairman of the Aboriginal Arts Board and the first Aboriginal councillor on the Australia Council. In 2008 he was awarded three honorary doctorates: from the University of New South Wales, Macquarie University and the University of Technology Sydney. Until his death from asbestosis, a disease caused by asbestos exposure in his working life, Chicka wrote a regular column for the *Koori Mail*.

JON HAWKES

Jon Hawkes has lived and worked in radical political and cultural milieux, particularly through theatre and music. Jon was born in Wales. He spent formative early childhood years in Trinidad, West Indies, before emigrating to Australia. Jon maintains an indirect connection to Indigenous rights activism through his close friendship with activist and political historian Gary Foley. Jon has worked as director of the Community Arts Board at the Australia Council and at Community Music Victoria.

FRANK HYTTEN

'I'm one of the people who arrived here uninvited and stays here more or less uninvited. Being brought up in that subculture of the British military, Raj Indian, my culture is some kind of mixture of Indian, English and, obviously, Australian. Within that, I belong to the group of people who have a university education, who are all teachers or social workers, who talk to Ph.D. students. I'm someone who has lived outside the system, on the activist end, but enjoys all the benefits and privileges of the system. I'm not a millionaire, but I have a reasonably nice house, I drive a car and can do all the things that middle-class kind of Aussies can do.

'Most of my work life has been trying to "right injustices", trying to advocate for people who are otherwise oppressed. Fundamental to my work is the community development framework. I'm conscious that I've made a fairly nice living out of it, advocating on behalf of people who've got nothing. Most recently I've been working in relation to Indigenous people, with a focus on educating and changing the views of non-Indigenous people.'

At the time of the interview, Frank was CEO of Reconciliation Victoria, and a member of the ANTaR Victoria Committee of Management.

CAM MCDONALD

'I'm half-Iranian, half-Scottish Australian. So, I feel that within my family history I know what it's like to be colonized. It's an exploration of that which has drawn me to the same processes happening in Australia.

'When I think about it, I don't really look like a Cameron Mc-Donald, but because I have a name like that I think I get treated like a white person. Coming from a culture where men are quite soft in a lot of ways, and quite touchy and feely, I didn't realize to what extent I didn't fit in, and how the culture at the boys' school I attended, where it was very masculine, very macho, was jarring to me because of my ethnic background. But, then, at the same time I'm really Australian as well and do fit into the dominant social class really, in a lot of other ways.'

At the time of the interview Cam was working a couple of days a week as a tutor/integration aide at Northland Secondary College and studying for a Master's degree in Social Work, which involved a placement with an Indigenous community-controlled sport and recreation service.

Cam described himself as 'one of Gary Foley's little devotees'. He participated in a group interview with Nina Collins.

MELBOURNE KUNGKAS GROUP INTERVIEW

I interviewed Ali, Belinda and Cath (see separate biographies), three women who worked together as members of the Melbourne Kungkas. This was a Melbourne-based support group for the Kupa Piti Kungka Tjuta, who, as senior Aboriginal women of Kupa Piti (Coober Pedy), were leaders of the Irati Wanti campaign to stop the national nuclear waste dump near Coober Pedy in northern South Australia. Belinda and Cath had also been involved in the campaign against the Jabiluka uranium mine.

BARRY MITCHELL

'I have had a long-term interest in Indigenous issues, nurtured by my involvement in Christian education programmes run by the Presbyterian Church (later the Uniting Church) in the 1960s, and by the large-scale ecumenical programme Action for World Development (AWD) in the 1970s and later.

'My interest in development issues, and the causes of underdevelopment, became so strong that, in 1977, at the age of 40, I left my first vocation as an engineer with Telecom Australia and started working full-time with AWD Victoria as a development education officer. This in turn opened up a completely new set of experiences and a new understanding of how the world works. My later work in community health and social welfare in the western suburbs of Melbourne has been greatly influenced by the AWD experience with Aboriginal people.

'I am often conscious of the fact that I have grown up in a middle-class family with many privileges, and I have received a comprehensive education right through to tertiary level. My life experience has been very different from those of most Indigenous people I have met. When I reflect on (and occasionally write about) important events in my life, they invariably include people whose lives have been shaped by discrimination or struggle.'

MONICA MORGAN

Monica is a Yorta Yorta woman, a mother and grandmother. In the 1970s she was an activist; in the 1980s she was in community development. Her collaborative work with whitefellas and activists commenced in the 1990s.

WYRKER-MILLOO (MURRAY RIVER MESSENGER)
GARY MURRAY

Gary Murray is a multi-clanned Aboriginal person and Traditional Owner from Victoria and New South Wales. Through his father and his mother, he is from the Wamba Wamba, Baraparapa, Yorta Yorta, Dhudhuroa, Dja Dja Wurrung, Djupagulk, Wiradjeri, and Wergaia peoples. Since the age of 15 Gary has worked in innumerable capacities on land rights, native title, cultural heritage, repatriation, human rights and building community organizations and projects. He is chair of the Victorian Alps Traditional Owner Group in Eastern Victoria, an active member of the Victorian Traditional Owner Land Justice Group and of the Murray and Lower Darling Rivers Indigenous Nations.

BILL ROBERTS (1928–2009)

A whitefella activist with Action for World Development and the Australia East Timor Association, Bill quit his private practice to become the dentist at the Victorian Aboriginal Health Service in 1974. Bill took on additional duties, working with NAIHO, helping other Aboriginal communities to get health facilities started, and eventually serving as director of medical services at the health service prior to his retirement in 1999.

TARGAN (JOHNNIE TARGAN) (1955–2014)

'I'm a social equalizer, I believe in equality: for men, women, regardless of race, colour or creed. I believe everyone is created equal, and should be treated as such. In the narrower sense, I'm a black activist – a black, *Aboriginal* activist, which is narrower still.'

Targan was active in the student union at the Victorian College of the Arts, where he studied painting, and was instrumental in establishing the Wilin Centre for Indigenous Arts. In 2005–06 Targan was a member of the Black GST (Genocide, Sovereignty, Treaty) collective.

Targan was an artist and an actor, a cook and a Vietnam War veteran. Born at Camp Pell in Melbourne's Royal Park and raised in Collingwood, on his mother's side Targan's Aboriginal – and Afghan – roots lay in Western Australia. His father, a white man, was secretary of the Communist Party for fifteen years in Victoria.

ALMA THORPE

Alma is a Gunditjmara elder. She grew up in the Aboriginal community of Fitzroy, Melbourne. Alma was integrally involved in the development of the Aboriginal community-controlled health movement in Australia through the National Aboriginal and Islander Health Organization (NAIHO). She was the founding administrator/

director of the Victorian Aboriginal Health Service (VAHS), where she served as a director for a further thirty years. Alma left school before she turned 13 and worked for twelve years as a shoe machinist. She also worked as a barmaid before she became involved with the Health Service. Alma is a mother of seven.

LISA THORPE

Lisa is a Gunai and Gunditjmara woman. The youngest of Alma Thorpe's children, Lisa grew up around VAHS and has worked most of her life for Aboriginal community organizations, including VAHS, Yappera and the Victorian Aborigines Advancement League (VAAL). At the time of the interview Lisa was enrolled in a Master's programme in Public Health at the Institute for Koori Education at Deakin University, where she also coordinated the Bachelor of Early Childhood programme. Lisa has worked with Chris Twining conducting racism awareness workshops and consultancies.

Lisa participated in a paired interview with Chris Twining.

ROBBIE THORPE

Robbie Thorpe is from the Krauatungalung people of the Gunai Nation, the traditional owners of Lake Tyers, as well as the Gunditjmara Nation, whose homelands include Framlingham, Victoria. Robbie has been a strong advocate for 'Pay the Rent', an Aboriginal initiative which would provide an independent economic resource for Aboriginal peoples. Robbie has initiated a number of legal actions, where he has argued that crimes of genocide have been committed against Aboriginal peoples throughout the colonization of Australia. He was a founding office bearer of the Aboriginal Provisional Government in 1992. He has worked closely with anti-logging campaigners, Friends of the Earth and many others, building a strong network of allies and supporters. During 2005–06 Robbie was a member of the Black GST collective, and spokesperson for Camp Sovereignty. He has served as a director of Melbourne Aboriginal Youth Sport and Recreation (MAYSAR). He broadcasts two programmes on 3CR community radio. Robbie is the director of the Treaty Republic website (www.treatyrepublic.net).

Robbie participated in a paired interview with Clare Land.

CHRIS TWINING

Chris is a Celtic white Australian. She has worked in community education and community development for the past thirty years. Chris's engagement with colonization and community development in the pacific through Action for World Development (1988–95) developed into a lifelong focus on the impact of colonization in Australia. Chris has conducted racism-awareness education and consultancies in long-term collaborations with Aboriginal educators, since 2001 with Lisa Thorpe.

Chris participated in a paired interview with Lisa Thorpe.

CAM WALKER

Cam Walker is campaigns coordinator at Friends of the Earth (FoE) in Melbourne. FoE is a pro-sovereignty organization, which is unique among the bigger Green groups in Australia. In order to ensure that traditional owners have 'primacy of decision-making' over campaigns, FoE has created a 'relationship and a communication system' that allows it to hear from traditional owners what needs to be done, and let that guide what FoE does. Cam went into Indigenous solidarity fairly early on in his activism; the entry point each time was environmentalism. He worked for some two years in a 'slave' or 'apprentice' support role for senior Aboriginal campaigners, 'doing the driving, the looking after'.

Cam grew up in the eastern suburbs of Melbourne in the 1960s. At that time 'three-quarters of the place was bush and orchard'. So, for Cam, 'my childhood experience was seeing bush just constantly disappearing, under the burbs'. He says, 'once you understand that place actually matters, it *has* to take you to Indigenous rights and sovereignty.'

ALI/MELBOURNE KUNGKAS GROUP INTERVIEW

How would you identify yourself? 'Young, white, middle-class educated woman (on a working-class income) with left politics (but not clearly defined as socialist, anarchist etc.), family and life experiences outside mainstream Australia and an appreciation of the need for social change. A slowed down, burnt-out, somewhat recovering activist.'

What do you want to be seen as? 'Young white middle-class woman who loves the bush and culture and who uses her privileges to address issues of racism, genocide, historical injustice and environmental destruction. Someone who sees the need for and advocates for a diverse, just and sustainable future for all.'

How do you think others identify you? 'Depends who you ask. I have been called a "boong lover", "wannabe blackfella", "do-gooder", and conversely "inspirational", "kind-hearted", "committed" and so on.'

Ali has been involved in campaigns against nuclear testing in the Pacific and supporting individual activists working on genocide and/or sovereignty issues. She has also participated in physical conservation work. Ali is deeply concerned about corporate control of all our lives – including aspects such as food, medicine and intellectual property rights, and contemporary slavery – including sweatshops and the sex slave 'industry'.

Ali participated in the Melbourne Kungkas group interview with Cath and Belinda.

BELINDA/MELBOURNE KUNGKAS GROUP INTERVIEW

Belinda identifies herself as a white, middle-class, well-educated young mother who comes from a privileged background. Belinda is ambivalently city-based: she misses the bush, where she grew up. To that she adds that she was not culturally isolated; her father was part of the professional/political class and her extended family is 'involved in Australian public/political life at the highest levels'; she sees them as 'members of the liberal-left elite'. Belinda speaks of being attached to seeing herself as educated through the public school system. Of her politics, Belinda says: 'I have always been very committed to feminism ... I have never strongly lined up with a particular political philosophy, and I think this is actually because I have mostly been a solidarity activist.'

Belinda participated in the Melbourne Kungkas group interview with Cath and Ali.

Cath spoke about feelings of 'ambivalence' around identifying herself: 'There's the obvious stuff, once you're politicized, of identifying yourself in terms of your class background, and race, and gender, and sexuality.' Cath is a young, educated woman, with a middle-class white background, though her parents were both migrants. Her ambivalence about a privileged background was expressed by 'going through the period of wanting to pretend that you're not, and the great feral working-class pretence stages that I feel that heaps of people went through'. Cath speaks of another ambivalence: not ever having strongly identified with a particular kind of politics, but 'having gone into a range of stuff around feminism and environmentalism'. Cath grew up in inner-city Melbourne. She now knows this location as one in which 'I could have been exposed to Indigenous politics and Indigenous stuff quite early on but I don't feel like that at all from growing up there.' Rather, Cath was introduced to Indigenous politics through environmentalism.

Cath participated in the Melbourne Kungkas group interview with Belinda and Ali.

HELEN

Helen was born in Australia on Wathaurong land, from migrant (German and Polish) parents. She is a writer and a lesbian radical activist. She began attending anti-Vietnam War marches at the age of 13. Her lifelong radicalism has included women's liberation, lesbian politics and a passionate engagement with Aboriginal issues.

Members of the critical reference group

TONY BIRCH

Tony Birch is the inaugural Bruce McGuinness Research Fellow within the Moondani Balluk Academic Unit at Victoria University. Tony grew up in Fitzroy, Melbourne. He is a widely published writer of poetry, short fiction, and historical and cultural critique, whose oeuvre includes a book of short stories and four novels, *Shadowboxing* (2006), *Father's Day* (2009), *Blood* (2011) and *Ghost River* (2015). He holds a Ph.D. in urban history. He has taught creative writing at the

University of Melbourne, where he also taught Koori and non-Koori History. He has been a senior curator in the Indigenous Cultures Program, Museum Victoria. Tony Birch has collaborated with artists and photographers, and worked with community groups and schools in creative writing and history. His participation has included support for the East Timorese, strategic interventions in the 'history wars', and public discourse on Australia's policy on asylum-seekers.

GARY FOLEY

Gary Foley is a member of the Gumbaynggirr Nation and a well-known Koori activist, actor and academic historian. He maintains an archive of Koori political history, as well as an extensive website (www.kooriweb.org.au/foley). He moved from the semi-tropical paradise of Nambucca Heads in the north coast of New South Wales to Redfern in the late 1960s at the age of 17, becoming a participant in that era of growth and politicization of Sydney's Koori community. Gary contributed to the establishment of the Aboriginal Medical Service in 1972 and the Aboriginal Legal Service in 1971 (both in Redfern, Sydney), as well as to some of the biggest protest mobilizations of Aboriginal people, such as the Aboriginal Embassy (1972) and the protest against Australia's bicentennial celebrations (1988). He was the first Aboriginal director of the Aboriginal Arts Board in the 1980s and a curator at Melbourne Museum in the 2000s.

Gary moved to Melbourne, working closely with Bruce McGuinness, a beloved friend and mentor, at VAHS and Koori Kollij. Gary and his son Bruce Foley were key to overturning premier Jeff Kennett's decision to close Northlands Secondary College in East Preston, Melbourne, in an unrelenting three-year community campaign in the early 1990s. Gary gained his First Class Honours degree and his Ph.D. in history at the University of Melbourne as a mature student, and supported and mentored other students and activists in both the Indigenous Students Collective (ISC) and the non-Indigenous Students for Land Justice and Reconciliation (SLJR) at that university. During the campaign against the Jabiluka uranium mine he was invited by the Gundjehmi Aboriginal Corporation to serve as their Melbourne representative. Gary lectures at Victoria University.

MARJORIE THORPE

Marjorie is a member of the Gunai and Gunditjmara nations. She was born and raised in Yallourn and later Fitzroy, Victoria. She has worked as a director of the Victorian Aboriginal Child Care Agency (VACCA), coordinator of the Secretariat of National Aboriginal and Islander Child Care (SNAICC) and CEO of VAHS. Marjorie was Victorian co-commissioner for the Stolen Generations Inquiry and served as a member of the Council for Aboriginal Reconciliation for six years. During 2005–06 she was a member of the Black GST collective.

Research supervisor

PROFESSOR BOB PEASE

Bob Pease is chair of Social Work at Deakin University in Geelong, Australia. He supervised the research for the Ph.D. which forms the basis for this book. He has been involved in pro-feminist politics with men for many years and is a founding member of Men Against Sexual Assault in Melbourne and the organizer of the first White Ribbon Campaign against men's violence in Australia. He has published extensively on masculinity politics and critical social work practice. His most recent books include: *Migrant Men: Critical Studies of Masculinities and the Migration Experience* (Routledge 2009, co-editor); *Critical Social Work: Theories and Practices for a Socially Just World* (Allen & Unwin 2009, co-editor); *Undoing Privilege: Unearned Advantage in a Divided World* (Zed Books, 2010); *Men and Masculinities Around the World: Transforming Men's Practices* (Palgrave 2011, co-editor); and *The Politics of Recognition and Social Justice: Transforming Subjectivities and New Forms of Resistance* (Routledge 2014, co-editor).

The Author

CLARE LAND

I am an Anglo-identified Australian. All of my ancestors emigrated from the British Isles, although some had themselves only migrated to England in the 1780s. Most of them arrived in Australia in the 1890s. They have lived in Victoria, New South Wales and

Queensland. Raised in Canberra, I became involved in organized politics in 1994 when I was a first-year university student, first with the off-campus feminist collective which organized Reclaim the Night (an annual march against sexual violence), and later through The Bloody Feminists (1996–97) and other student clubs and projects affiliated with the Melbourne University Student Union (MUSU). I spent a year co-editing *Farrago*, the student newspaper, as one of MUSU's elected media officers in 1998. From then on, having met Gary Foley and Tony Birch that year, I focused my studies and my activism on colonial history and Indigenous struggles. This has included significant commitments to several collectives and campaigns, in particular Students for Land Justice and Reconciliation (SLJR, 1999–2002) and the Black GST/Camp Sovereignty (2005–06). I also contributed to the Mirrar-led campaign against the Jabiluka uranium mine (1998–99) and the Irati Wanti campaign against a nuclear waste dump near Kupa Piti/Coober Pedy as a member of the Melbourne Kungkas (2002). I joined a group of students from University Students for East Timor (USET) as a volunteer for a project instigated by East Timorese student activists (East Timor Student Solidarity Council/Konsellu Solidariedade Universitariu Timor Lorosa'e and the East Timor Young Women's Association/ Grupo Feto Foinsa'e Timor Lorosa'e) in East Timor for six months in 2000, and undertook paid community development work for ANTaR Victoria 2004–06. I am trained as a facilitator of Courageous Conversations About Race and was invited to join the facilitator team for the Anti-Racism Workshops run by RISE (Refugees, Survivors and Ex-Detainees) in 2013. I have been a volunteer broadcaster on 3CR community radio in Melbourne since 2001; since 2003 with Krauatungalung (Gunai)/Djapwurrung (Gunditjmara) man Robbie Thorpe on a programme titled *Fire First*, which we co-created at his instigation as an Indigenous–non-Indigenous collaboration. *Fire First* discusses colonialism in Australia from invasion to the present day.

I participated in a paired interview with Robbie Thorpe.

Links to original activist documents

'Pay the Rent' flyer by Robbie Thorpe
www.decolonizingsolidarity.org/pay-the-rent.pdf

Example of a Treaty and Lease by Denis Walker
www.decolonizingsolidarity.org/treaty.pdf

'Campaigning on Sovereign Aboriginal Lands' flyer
www.decolonizingsolidarity.org/campaigning-guide.pdf

'Request for Permission to Live on Country as an Interim Permanent Resident' by Jane Belfrage
www.decolonizingsolidarity.org/requesting-residency.pdf

'So, what DO Indigenous people want?! AND, what can I do about it?' by Frank Hytten
www.decolonizingsolidarity.org/what-can-i-do.pdf

A six-point program and practical ideas, including:
1. Acknowledge sovereignty;
2. Be honest about our history;
3. Safeguard Aboriginal cultural heritage;
4. Respect Aboriginal culture;
5. Ensure representation;
6. Pay reparations.

References

Aal, W. (2001) 'Moving from guilt to action: Antiracist organizing and the concept of "whiteness" for activism and the academy'. In B. Brander Rasmussen (ed.), *The Making and Unmaking of Whiteness*, pp. 294–310. Duke University Press, Durham NC.

Acker, M. (1996) 'The good guys'. *The IASOM Newsletter: The International Association for Studies of men*, 3(1): 12–19.

Ahmed, S. (2004) 'The non-performativity of anti-racism'. Paper presented at Text and Terrain: Legal Studies in Gender and Sexuality, a Centre LGS colloquium, University of Kent.

Alcoff, L.M. (1998) 'What should white people do?' *Hypatia*, 13(3): 6–26.

Alfred, T., and Coulthard, G. (2006) 'Wasáse movement: Indigenous radicalism today'. *New Socialist* 58: 2.

Amadahy, Z. (2008) '"Listen, take direction and stick around": A roundtable discussion of relationship building in Indigenous solidarity work'. *Briarpatch: Fighting the War on Error*, 37(4): 24–9.

Amadahy, Z., and Lawrence, B. (2009) 'Indigenous peoples and black people in Canada: Settlers or allies?' In A. Kempf (ed.), *Breaching the Colonial Contract: Anti-Colonialism in the US and Canada*, pp. 105–36. Springer, Dordrecht.

Amis, A. (n.d.) 'The Indigenous Solidarity Group (ISG) (1997–1999)'. www.foe. org.au/indigenous/learning-resources/foes-solidarity-work/the-indigenous-solidarity-group-isg-1997-1999; accessed 17 October 2011.

Anderson, T. (n.d.) 'Solidarity activism, identity politics and popular education'. www.kooriweb.org/foley/news/story18.html; accessed 23 April 2006.

Ang, I. (1995) 'I'm a feminist but... Other women and postnational feminism'. In B. Caine and R. Pringle (eds), *Transitions: New Australian Feminisms*, pp. 190–206. Allen & Unwin, St Leonards.

Atkinson, W.R. (1989) 'The Koori Oral History Programme', in M. Birtley and P. McQueen (eds), *New Responsibilities: Documenting Multicultural Australia: A Record of the Conference for Museums, Libraries, Archives and Historical Collections: Towards a National Agenda for a Multicultural Australia, 11-13 November 1988, Melbourne*, pp. 42–6. Museums Association of Australia, Victorian Branch/ Library Council of Victoria, Melbourne.

Atkinson, W.R. (2006) 'Fine words but few deeds'. *The Age*, 10 April.

Atkinson, W.R., Langton, M., Wanganeen, D., and Williams, M. (1985) 'Introduction – A celebration of resistance to colonisation', in M. Hill and A. Barlow (eds), *Black Australia 2: An Annotated Bibliography and Teachers' Guide to Resources on Aborigines and Torres Strait Islanders, 1977–82*, pp. 38–40. Australian Institute of Aboriginal Studies, Canberra.

Attwood, B., and Markus, A. (1999) *The Struggle for Aboriginal Rights: A Documentary History*. Allen & Unwin, St Leonards.

Augoustinos, M., and Riggs, D. (2007) 'Representing "us" and "them": Constructing white identities in everyday talk'. In G. Moloney and I. Walker (eds), *Social Representations and Identity: Content, Process, and Power*, pp. 109–30. Palgrave Macmillan, New York.

Australian Institute of Aboriginal and Torres Strait Islander Studies (2000) 'Guidelines for ethical research in Indigenous studies'. www.aiatsis.gov. au/_data/assets/pdf_file/2290/ethics_guidelines.pdf; accessed 6 August 2006.

Aveling, N. (2004) 'Being the descendant of colonialists: White identity in context'. *Race Ethnicity and Education*, 7(1), 57–71.

Awakening the Horse People (2014) 'Anti-colonial anarchism vs decolonization'. http://awakeningthehorse.wordpress.com/2014/04/14/anti-colonial-anarchism-vs-decolonization; accessed 27 April 2014.

Baier, A. (1986) 'Trust and antitrust'. *Ethics*, 96(2): 231–60.

Bailey, A. (1998) 'Locating traitorous identities: Toward a view of privilege-cognizant white character'. *Hypatia*, 13(3): 27–42.

Balint, J. (2014) 'Stating genocide in law: The Aboriginal Embassy and the ACT Supreme Court', in A. Schaap, G. Foley and E. Howell (eds), *The Aboriginal Tent Embassy: Sovereignty, Black Power, Land Rights and the State*, pp. 235–50. Routledge, Abingdon.

Balint, J., and Evans, J. (2011) 'Transitional justice and settler states', in M. Lee, G. Mason and S. Milivojevic (eds), *The Australian and New Zealand Critical Criminology Conference Proceedings*. Institute of Criminology, University of Sydney.

Barkan, E. (2000) *The Guilt of Nations: Restitution and Negotiating Historical Injustices*. Norton, New York.

Barker, A. (2010) 'From adversaries to allies: Forging respectful alliances between Indigenous and settler peoples'. In L. Davis (ed.), *Alliances: Re/envisioning Indigenous–non-Indigenous Relationships*, pp. 316–33. University of Toronto Press, Toronto.

Barta, T. (2008) 'Sorry, and not sorry, in Australia: How the apology to the stolen generations buried a history of genocide'. *Journal of Genocide Research*, 10(2): 201–14.

Barwick, D. (1963) *A Little More Than Kin: Regional Affiliation and Group Identity among Aboriginal Migrants in Melbourne*. Australian National University, Canberra.

Barwick, D. (1972) 'Coranderrk and Cummeragunja: Pioneers and policy'. In

T.S. Epstein and D.H. Penny (eds), *Opportunity and Response: Case Studies in Economic Development*, pp. 44–68. Hurst, London.

Barwick, D. (2005) *Rebellion at Coranderrk*. Aboriginal History, Canberra.

Batty, P. (2005) 'Private politics, public strategies: White advisers and their Aboriginal subjects'. *Oceania*, 75(3): 209–21.

Begg, Z. (2000) 'The whole world is watching Sydney'. *Green Left Weekly*, 13 September.

Behrendt, L. (2001) 'Genocide: The distance between law and life'. *Aboriginal History* 25: 132–47.

Bell, A. (2008) 'Recognition or ethics? De/centering and the legacy of settler colonialism'. *Cultural Studies*, 22(6): 850–69.

Bell, R. (2003) 'Bell's theorem: Aboriginal art: it's a white thing'. www.kooriweb.org/foley/great/art/bell.html; accessed 10 February 2004.

Bell, S., and Coleman, S. (eds) (1999) *The Anthropology of Friendship*. Berg, Oxford.

Benjamin, C., Preston, J., and Leger, M. (2010) 'The UN Declaration on the Rights of Indigenous Peoples: Partnerships to advance human rights'. In L. Davis (ed.), *Alliances: Re/envisioning Indigenous–non-Indigenous Relationships*, pp. 57–68. University of Toronto Press, Toronto.

Bhabha, H.K. (2004) *The Location of Culture*. Routledge, London and New York.

Biko, S. (ed.). (1988) *I Write What I Like*. Penguin, London.

Birch, T. (2007) '"The invisible fire": Indigenous sovereignty, history and responsibility'. In A. Moreton-Robinson (ed.), *Sovereign Subjects: Indigenous Sovereignty Matters*, pp. 105–17. Allen & Unwin, Crows Nest NSW.

Bishop, R. (1998) 'Freeing ourselves from neo-colonial domination in research: A Maori approach to creating knowledge'. *Qualitative Studies in Education*, 11(2): 199–219.

Black GST (2006) blackgst@riseup.net 'Newsletter, 3 April 2006'; accessed 15 August 2007.

Bobiwash, A.R., and Butler, P. (n.d. 1999–2000) 'Native people and environmental crusaders: Racism, re-colonization and do-gooders', interview with A. Rodney Bobiwash. *Aboriginal Rights Resource Tool Kit*, pp. 2.73–2.80. Canadian Labour Congress Anti-Racism and Human Rights Department, Ottawa.

Boughton, B. (2001) 'The Communist Party of Australia's involvement in the struggle for Aboriginal and Torres Strait Islander people's rights 1920–1970'. In R. Markey (ed.), *Labour and Community: Historical Essays*, pp. 263–94. University of Wollongong Press, Wollongong.

Boyce, J. (2011) *1835: The Founding of Melbourne & the Conquest of Australia*. Black, Collingwood, Victoria.

Bradley, J., and Seton, K. (2005) 'Self-determination or "Deep Colonising": land claims, colonial authority and indigenous representation'. In B. Hocking (ed.), *Unfinished Constitutional Business? Rethinking Indigenous Self-determination*, pp. 32–46. Aboriginal Studies Press, Canberra.

Brennan, S., Behrendt, L., Strelein, L., and Williams, G. (2005) *Treaty*. Federation Press, Annandale.

Brisbane Blacks (2014) 'Decolonisation Before Profit Program'. http://brisbane-blacks.com/g20/program; accessed 11 May 2015.

Briscoe, G. (2004) 'Afterword'. In J.C. Horner (ed.), *Seeking Racial Justice: An Insider's Memoir of the Movement for Aboriginal Advancement, 1938–1978*, pp. 192–8. Aboriginal Studies Press, Canberra.

Briscoe, G. (2010) *Racial Folly: A Twentieth-century Aboriginal Family*. ANU E Press, Canberra.

Broome, R. (2006) '"There were vegetables every year Mr Green was here": Right behaviour and the struggle for autonomy at Coranderrk Aboriginal reserve'. *History Australia*, 3(2): 43.1–43.16. DOI: 10.2104/ha060043.

Burbules, N.C., and Rice, S. (1991) 'Dialogue across differences: Continuing the conversation'. *Harvard Educational Review*, 61(4): 393–417.

Burghardt, S. (1982) *The Other Side of Organizing: Resolving the Personal Dilemmas and Political Demands of Daily Practice*. Schenkman Publishing, Cambridge MA.

Burgmann, M., and Burgmann, V. (1998) *Green Bans, Red Union: Environmental Activism and the New South Wales Builders Labourers' Federation*. UNSW Press, Sydney.

Burgmann, V. (2003a) 'The Aboriginal movement'. www.kooriweb.org/foley/resources/pdfs/13.pdf; accessed 20 July 2011.

Burgmann, V. (2003b) *Power, Profit and Protest: Australian Social Movements and Globalisation*. Allen & Unwin, Sydney.

Burgmann, V., and Burgmann, M. (1999) '"A rare shift in public thinking": Jack Mundey and the New South Wales Builders Labourers' Federation'. *Labour History* 77: 44–63.

Burgmann, V., and Milner, A. (1996) 'Intellectuals and the new social movements'. In T. O'Lincoln and R. Kuhn, *Class and Class Conflict in Australia*, pp. 114–30. Longman Australia, Melbourne.

Butler, K.J. (2009) *Teaching an Indigenous Sociology: A Response to Current Debate within Australian Sociology'*. Ph.D. thesis, University of Newcastle, NSW.

Bystydzienski, J., and Schacht, S. (eds) (2001) *Forging Radical Alliances across Difference: Coalition Politics for the New Millennium*. Rowman & Littlefield, London.

Calderón, JLove, and Wise, T. (2012) 'Code of ethics for antiracist white allies'. http://jlovecalderon.com/code-of-ethics-for-antiracist-white-allies; accessed 22 June 2014.

Castejon, V. (2002) 'Aboriginal affairs: Monologue or dialogue?' *Journal of Australian Studies*, 26(75): 27–31.

Cavadini, A. (dir.) (1972) *Ningla a-na: Hungry for Our Land*. Video documentary. Australian Film Institute, Melbourne.

Chesterman, J., and Galligan, B. (1997) *Citizens without Rights: Aborigines and Australian Citizenship*. Cambridge University Press, Cambridge and Melbourne.

Clark, T., and de Costa, R. (2011) 'Exploring non-Aboriginal attitudes towards reconciliation in Canada: The beginnings of targeted focus group research'. In A. Mathur, J. Dewar and M. DeGagné (eds), *Cultivating Canada:*

Reconciliation through the Lens of Cultural Diversity, pp. 329–39. Aboriginal Healing Foundation, Ottawa.

Cohen, G.A. (2000) *If You're an Egalitarian, How Come You're So Rich?* Harvard University Press, Cambridge MA.

Collins, P.H. (2004) 'Learning from the outsider within: The sociological significance of Black feminist thought'. In S.G. Harding (ed.), *The Feminist Standpoint Theory Reader: Intellectual and Political Controversies*, pp. 103–26. Routledge, New York and London.

Condon, B. (1993) 'John Batman's Statue Tried for War Crimes'. www.kooriweb. org/gst/genocide/batman.html; accessed 13 December 2011.

Conway, J. (ed.). (2010) *Step by Step: Women of East Timor, Stories of Resistance and Survival*. Charles Darwin University Press, Darwin.

Cook, K., and Goodall, H. (2013) *Making Change Happen: Black and White Activists Talk to Kevin Cook about Aboriginal, Union and Liberation Politics*. ACT ANU E Press, Canberra.

Corntassel, J. (2006) 'To be ungovernable'. *New Socialist* 58: 35–7.

Cowlishaw, G. (2000) 'Censoring race in 'post-colonial' anthropology'. *Critique of Anthropology*, 20(2): 101–23.

Cowlishaw, G. (2003) 'Disappointing Indigenous people: Violence and the refusal of help'. *Public Culture*, 15(1): 103–25.

Cowlishaw, G. (2004) *Blackfellas, Whitefellas, and the Hidden Injuries of Race*. Blackwell, Malden MA.

Crombie, E.U., Stewart, I.M., Wingfield, E.W., Brown, E.K., Wonga, A., Austin, E.M., and Muffler, B.N. (1998) 'First call out to the greenies'. 3 August. www.iratiwanti.org; accessed 15 August 2007.

Curthoys, A. (2002) *Freedom Ride: A Freedom Rider Remembers*. Allen & Unwin, Crows Nest NSW.

Curthoys, A., and Docker, J. (2001) 'Genocide? Australian Aboriginal history in international perspective'. *Aboriginal History* 25: 1–172.

Curthoys, A., Genovese, A., and Reilly, A. (2008) *Rights and Redemption: History, Law and Indigenous People*. University of New South Wales Press, Sydney.

da Silva, T.S. (2008) 'Redeeming self: The business of whiteness in post-Apartheid South African writing'. In A. Moreton-Robinson, M. Casey and F.J. Nicoll (eds), *Transnational Whiteness Matters*, pp. 3–17. Lexington Books, Lanham MD.

Davis, L. (ed.). (2010) *Alliances: Re/envisioning Indigenous–non-Indigenous Relationships*. University of Toronto Press, Toronto.

Dawson, M.S. (2007) 'Cast thy humble slough, and appeare fresh': Reappraising the advent of early modern English whiteness, *c.*1600–1750. In L. Boucher, J. Carey and K. Ellinghaus (eds), *Historicising Whiteness: Transnational Perspectives on the Construction of an Identity*, pp. 355–62. RMIT Publishing and School of Historical Studies, University of Melbourne, Melbourne.

Denzin, N.K. (2003) 'Performing (auto)ethnography politically'. *Review of Education, Pedagogy and Cultural Studies*, 25(3): 257–78.

Denzin, N.K., Lincoln, Y.S., and Smith, L.T. (eds) (2008) *Handbook of Critical and Indigenous Methodologies*. Sage, Los Angeles.

Docker, J. (2008) 'Are settler-colonies inherently genocidal? Re-reading Lemkin'. In A.D. Moses (ed.), *Empire, Colony, Genocide*, pp. 89–106. Berghahn Books, New York.

Ellis, C. (2004) *The Ethnographic I: A Methodological Novel about Autoethnography*. Alta Mira, Walnut Creek.

Etherington, K. (2004) *Becoming a Reflexive Researcher: Using Our Selves in Research*. Jessica Kingsley, London and Philadelphia PA.

Fanon, F. (1967) *The Wretched of the Earth*. Penguin, Harmondsworth.

Fanon, F. (1968) *Black Skin, White Masks*. Grove Press, New York.

Fellows, M.L., and Razack, S. (1998) 'The race to innocence: Confronting hierarchical relations among women'. *Journal of Gender, Race and Justice*, 1(2) (Spring): 335–52.

Foley, G. (1975) 'The history of the Aboriginal Medical Service: A study in bureaucratic obstruction'. *Identity*, 2(5): 38–40.

Foley, G. (1988) 'For Aboriginal sovereignty'. Paper given at the Rainbow Alliance conference, Melbourne, March 1988, *Arena* 83. www.kooriweb. org/foley/essays/speech1.html; accessed 25 August 2009.

Foley, G. (1997a) 'Australia and the Holocaust: A Koori perspective'. www. kooriweb.org/foley/essays/essay_8.html; accessed 11 June 2014.

Foley, G. (1997b) 'Muddy waters: Archie, Mudrooroo and Aboriginality'. www.kooriweb.org/foley/essays/essay_10.html; accessed 5 February 2003.

Foley, G. (1998) 'The power of whiteness'. *Farrago*, 77(7): 18.

Foley, G. (1999) 'Whiteness and blackness in the Koori struggle for self-determination. www.kooriweb.org/foley/essays/essay_9.html; accessed 30 August 2011.

Foley, G. (2000) 'Whiteness and blackness in the Koori struggle for self-determination: Strategic considerations in the struggle for social justice for Indigenous people'. *Just Policy*, 19–20: 74–88.

Foley, G. (2001) 'Black power in Redfern 1968–1972'. www.kooriweb.org/foley/ essays/essay_1.html; accessed 27 March 2010.

Foley, G. (2006) 'Timeline of significant moments in the Indigenous struggle in south east Australia'. www.kooriweb.org/foley/timeline/histimeline.html; accessed 30 October 2011.

Foley, G. (2007) 'Preface'. In J. Maynard (ed.), *Fight for Liberty and Freedom: The Origins of Australian Aboriginal Activism*, pp. v–vi. Aboriginal Studies Press, Canberra.

Foley, G. (2011) *Foley*. Performance at the Melbourne International Arts Festival.

Foley, G. (2012) *An Autobiographical Narrative of the Black Power Movement and the 1972 Aboriginal Embassy*. Ph.D. thesis, University of Melbourne.

Foley, G. (n.d.) '1970 Black Power Conference in Altlanta, Georgia'. www. kooriweb.org/foley/images/history/1970s/ustrip/usdx.html; accessed 11 May 2015.

Foley, G., and Anderson, T. (2006) 'Land rights and Aboriginal voices'. *Australian Journal of Human Rights*, 12(1): 83–108.

Foley, G., and McKinnon, C. (2008) 'Duplicity and deceit: Gary Foley's take on Rudd's apology to the Stolen Generations'. Interview. *Melbourne Historical Journal* 36: 1-6.

Fontana, A., and Frey, J.H. (2000) 'The interview: From structured questions to negotiated text'. In N.K. Denzin and Y.S. Lincoln (eds), *The Handbook of Qualitative Research*, 2nd edn, pp. 645–72. Sage, Thousand Oaks CA.

Frankenberg, R. (1993) *White Women, Race Matters: The Social Construction of Whiteness*. University of Minnesota Press, Minneapolis.

Fraser, N. (1995) 'From redistribution to recognition? Dilemmas of justice in a "post-socialist" age'. *New Left Review*, I(212): 68–93.

Fredericks, B.L. (2010) 'We've had the Redfern Park Speech and The Apology: What's next?', *Outskirts: Feminisms Along the Edge*, 23(1).

Freeman, V. (2010) 'Reconciliation in cyberspace? Lessons from Turning Point: Native peoples and newcomers on-line'. In L. Davis (ed.), *Alliances: Re/envisioning Indigenous-non-Indigenous Relationships*, pp. 149–57. University of Toronto Press, Toronto.

Freire, P. (1985) *Pedagogy of the Oppressed*. Penguin, Harmondsworth.

Gandhi, L. (2006) *Affective Communities: Anticolonial Thought, Fin-de-siècle Radicalism, and the Politics of Friendship*. Duke University Press, Durham NC.

Georgatos, G. (2012) 'Aboriginal passports issued to two asylum seekers incarcerated at Villawood'. 14 May. http://indymedia.org.au/2012/05/14/aboriginal-passports-issued-to-two-asylum-seekers-incarcerated-at-villawood; accessed 20 June 2014.

Giibwanisi (2013) 'Morning coffee thought: Settler ally vs. settler brother/sister'. http://oshkimaadziig.org/2013/12/14/morning-coffee-thought-settler-ally-vs-settler-brothersister; accessed 27 April 2014.

Gillor, G.I. (2011) 'The Program Effectiveness Review as a case study of the relationship between Aboriginal organisations and the state, 1980–1982'. *Journal of Australian Indigenous Issues*, 14(2–3): 151–69.

Goodall, H. (1996) *Invasion to Embassy: Land in Aboriginal Politics in NSW 1770–1972*. Allen & Unwin, Sydney.

Gooder, H., and Jacobs, J. (2000) '"On the border of the unsayable": The apology in postcolonizing Australia'. *Interventions: International Journal of Postcolonial Studies*, 2(2): 229–47.

goori2 (2011,) 'Invasion Day 2003 St Kilda Beach'. 12 April. http://youtu.be/YroyUOwcWgE; accessed 16 June 2014.

Grande, S. (2008) 'Red pedagogy: The un-methodology. In N.K. Denzin, Y.S. Lincoln and L.T. Smith (eds), *Handbook of Critical and Indigenous Methodologies*, pp. 233–54. Sage, Los Angeles.

Green, M.J., Sonn, C.C., and Matsebula, J. (2007) 'Reviewing whiteness: Theory, research and possibilities'. *South African Journal of Psychology*, 37(3): 389–419.

Greer, G. (1972) 'Greer of the land'. *The Review*, 4–10 March: 561.

Gruenewald, D.A. (2003) 'The best of both worlds: A critical pedagogy of place'. *Educational Researcher*, 32(4): 3–12

Haebich, A. (1992) *For Their Own Good: Aborigines and Government in the South West of Western Australia 1900-1940*, 2nd edn. University of Western Australia Press for the Charles and Joy Staples South West Region Publications Fund, Nedlands WA.

Hage, G. (1998) *White Nation: Fantasies of White Supremacy in a Multicultural Society*. Pluto Press, Sydney.

Hardin, R. (1996) 'Trustworthiness'. *Ethics* 107 (October): 26–42.

Hardin, R. (2002) *Trust and Trustworthiness*. Russell Sage Foundation, New York.

Harp, R. (1994) 'Native by nature?' In E.M. Godway and G. Finn (eds), *Who Is This We?: Absence of Community*, pp. 45–55. Black Rose Books, Montreal and New York.

Harris, C. (1993) 'Whiteness as property'. *Harvard Law Review* 106: 1707–91.

Healy, B. (2006) 'Rob Riley, A life lived in the cause of liberation'. Review of Q. Beresford, *Rob Riley, an Aboriginal Leader's Quest for Justice*, *Green Left Weekly*, 7 June 2006. www.kooriweb.org/foley/resources/pdfs/217.pdf; accessed 17 October 2011.

Healy, B., and Riley, R. (n.d.) 'A life lived in the cause of liberation'. www.kooriweb.org/foley/resources/pdfs/217.pdf; accessed 17 October 2011.

Hemingway, M. (2012) *Community Control: Aboriginal Self-determination and Australian Settler Democracy: A History of the Victorian Aboriginal Health Service*. Ph.D. thesis, University of Melbourne.

Hess, M. (1994) 'Black and red: The Pilbara pastoral workers' strike, 1946'. *Aboriginal History*, 18(1): 65–83.

Hesse-Biber, S.N., and Leavy, P. (eds). (2006) *Emergent Methods in Social Research*. Sage, Thousand Oaks CA.

Hinkson, J. (2008) 'Editorial: After the intervention'. *Arena Journal* 29/30: 3–9.

Hinkson, M., and Smith, B. (2005) 'Introduction: Conceptual moves towards an intercultural analysis'. *Oceania*, 75(3): 157–66.

Holt, L. (1999) 'Forum, Thursday 14 October, 1999, 7pm–11pm'. Unpublished manuscript, Box 120/98 item 19, Rowden White Library Archives, University of Melbourne Student Union, Melbourne.

Horner, J.C. (2004) *Seeking Racial Justice: An Insider's Memoir of the Movement for Aboriginal Advancement, 1938–1978*. Aboriginal Studies Press, Canberra.

Horton, D. (1994) *The Encyclopaedia of Aboriginal Australia*. AIATSIS Press, Canberra.

Hoskins, T.K. (2012) 'A fine risk: Ethics in Kaupapa Māori politics'. *New Zealand Journal of Educational Studies*, 47(2): 85–99.

Howard, G.R. (1999) 'White man dancing: A story of personal transformation'. In J. O'Donnell and C. Clark (eds), *Becoming and Unbecoming White: Owning and Disowning a Racial Identity*, pp. 212–23. Bergin & Garvey, Wetsport CT.

Howell, E. (2013) *Tangled up in Black: A Study of the Activist Strategies of the*

Black Power Movement through the Life of Gary Foley. Ph.D. thesis, Monash University, Melbourne.

Huggins, J. (1998) *Sister Girl: The Writings of Aboriginal Activist and Historian Jackie Huggins*. University of Queensland Press, Brisbane.

Hunt, J. (2005) *Capacity Development in the International Development Context: Implications for Indigenous Australia*. Centre for Aboriginal Economic Policy Research, Australian National University, Canberra. http://caepr.anu.edu. au/sites/default/files/Publications/DP/2005_DP278.pdf; accessed 6 April, 2014.

Huygens, I. (1999) 'An Accountability Model for Pakeha Practitioners'. Paper presented at the conference Maori and Psychology: Research and Practice, University of Waikato, Hamilton.

Jensen, R. (2003) 'A moral level of consumption?' *CounterPunch*. www.counter-punch.org/2003/10/30/a-moral-level-of-consumption; accessed 12 December 2011.

Jensen, R. (2005) *The Heart of Whiteness: Confronting Race, Racism, and White Privilege*. City Lights, San Francisco.

Johnstone, D., and Norman, M. (2008) *A Race to Remember: The Peter Norman Story*. JoJo Publishing, Docklands.

Jones, A., and Jenkins, K. (2008) 'Rethinking collaboration: Working the Indigene-colonizer hyphen'. In N.K. Denzin, Y.S. Lincoln and L.T. Smith (eds), *Handbook of Critical and Indigenous Methodologies*, pp. 471–86. Sage, Los Angeles.

Jordan, M.E. (2005) *Balanda: My Year in Arnhem Land*. Allen & Unwin, Crows Nest NSW.

Keefer, T. (2007) 'The politics of solidarity: Six Nations, leadership, and the settler left'. *Upping the Anti*, 4 May.

Kendall, F.E. (2006) *Understanding White Privilege: Creating Pathways to Authentic Relationships across Race*. Routledge, New York.

Kessaris, T.N. (2006) 'About being Mununga (whitefulla): Making covert group racism visible'. *Journal of Community and Applied Psychology* 16: 347–62.

Koutsoukis, J. (2010) 'A tribute to 6 million lost and one man's stand'. *The Age*, 14 December.

Kowal, E. (2006) *The Proximate Advocate: Improving Indigenous Health on the Postcolonial Frontier*. Ph.D. thesis, University of Melbourne, Melbourne.

Kowal, E. (2010) 'The stigma of white privilege: Australian anti-racists and Indigenous improvement'. *Cultural Studies*, 6 October. http://dx.doi.org/10.1080/09502386.2010.491159.

Kowal, E. (2015). *Trapped in the Gap: Doing Good in Indigenous Australia*. Berghahn Books, New York.

Kuokkanen, R. (2003) 'Toward a new relation of hospitality in the academy'. *American Indian Quarterly*, 27(1/2): 267–95.

Kupa Piti Kungka Tjuta. (2003) 'Kulini Kulini: "Are you listening?": Invitation to all – big meeting at 10 mile creek bush camp'. http://lists.indymedia.org.

au/pipermail/imc-sydney/2003-August/001464.html; accessed 11 April 2011.

Ladson-Billings, G. (2000) 'Racialized discourses and ethnic epistemologies'. In N.K. Denzin and Y.S. Lincoln (eds), *The Handbook of Qualitative Research*, 2nd edn, pp. 257–77. Sage, Thousand Island CA.

Lake, M. (1999) *Getting Equal: The History of Australian Feminism*. Allen & Unwin, St Leonards.

Lake, M. (2003) 'Woman, Black, Indigenous: Recognition struggles in dialogue'. In B. Hobson (ed.), *Recognition Struggles and Social Movements: Contested Identities, Agency and Power*, pp. 145–60. Cambridge University Press, New York.

Lake, M. (2007) '"The discovery of personal whiteness is a very modern thing": W.E.B. Du Bois on the global and the personal'. In L. Boucher, J. Carey and K. Ellinghaus (eds), *Historicising Whiteness: Transnational Perspectives on the Construction of an Identity*, pp. 320–27. RMIT Publishing and School of Historical Studies, University of Melbourne, Melbourne.

Lampert, J. (2003) 'The alabaster academy: Being a non-Indigenous academic in Indigenous studies'. *Social Alternatives*, 22(3): 23–6.

La Nauze, J. (2009). 'The History of the Barmah-Millewa Campaign'. *Chain Reaction* 105: 22–25.

Land, C. (2001) 'Covering up colonial violence'. In K. Fielding and E. Vincent (eds), *Cover Your Tracks: Creative Histories by Young Victorians*, pp. 94–9. Express Media, Fitzroy.

Land, C. (2006) 'Law and the construction of "race": Critical race theory and the Aborigines Protection Act, 1886, Victoria, Australia'. In P. Edmonds and S. Furphy (eds), *Rethinking Colonial Histories: New and Alternative Approaches*, pp. 137–56. RMIT Publishing, Melbourne.

Land, C. (2011a) 'Decolonizing activism/deactivating colonialism'. *Action Learning Action Research Journal*, special edition on 'Decolonising Action Research', 17(2): 42–62.

Land, C. (2011b) 'Trust/worthiness and accountability'. *Journal of Australian Indigenous Issues*, 14(2–3): 54–69.

Land, C., and Vincent, E. (2005) 'Thinking for ourselves'. *New Matilda*, 29 June. www.newmatilda.com.au/2005/06/29/thinking-ourselves; accessed 20 December 2011.

Lasky, J. (2011) 'Indigenism, anarchism, feminism: An emerging framework for exploring post-imperial futures'. *Affinities: A Journal of Radical Theory, Culture, and Action*, 5(1) , special edition on 'Anarch@Indigenism: Working across Difference for Post-imperial Futures: Intersections between Anarchism, Indigenism and Feminism'.

Lawrence, B., and Dua, E. (2005) 'Decolonizing antiracism'. *Social Justice: A Journal of Crime, Conflict and World Order*, 32(4): 120–43.

Lea, T. (2008) *Bureaucrats and Bleeding Hearts: Indigenous Health in Northern Australia*. University of New South Wales Press, Sydney.

Lea, T., Kowal, E., and Cowlishaw, G.K. (2006) *Moving Anthropology: Critical Indigenous Studies*. Charles Darwin University Press, Darwin.

Lewis, P. (2010) *Acting in Solidarity? The Church's Journey with the Indigenous Peoples of Australia*. Uniting Academic Press, Parkville.

L'Hirondelle, C., Naytowhow, J., and Yael, b.h. (2011) 'Land project: A conversation between Canada and Israel/Palestine'. In A. Mathur, J. Dewar and M. DeGagné (eds), *Cultivating Canada: Reconciliation through the Lens of Cultural Diversity*, pp. 35–51. Aboriginal Healing Foundation, Ottawa.

Limb, P. (2008). 'The anti-apartheid movements in Australia and Aotearoa/New Zealand'. In South African Democracy Education Trust, *The Road to Democracy in South Africa*, vol. 3, pp. 907–82. Pretoria: University of South Africa.

Lindqvist, S. (1997) *The Skull Measurer's Mistake: And Other Portraits of Men and Women Who Spoke out against Racism*. New Press, New York.

Lugones, M. (1987) 'Playfulness, 'world'-travelling, and loving perception'. *Hypatia*, 2(2): 3–19.

Lynch, K., and Walsh, J. (2009) 'Love, care and solidarity: What is and is not commodifiable'. In K. Lynch, J. Baker and M. Lyons (eds), *Affective Equality: Love, Care and Injustice*, pp. 35–53. Palgrave Macmillan, Basingstoke.

Lyons, J. (2010) 'Israel honours elder for defying Nazis'. *The Australian*, 31 July.

Maddison, S. (2009) *Black Politics: Inside the Complexity of Aboriginal Political Culture*. Allen & Unwin, Crows Nest NSW.

Maddison, S. (2011) *Beyond White Guilt: The Real Challenge for Black–White Relations in Australia*. Allen & Unwin, Sydney.

Maher, L. (2000) *Sexed Work: Gender, Race and Resistance in a Brooklyn Drug Market*. Clarendon Press, Oxford.

Makuwira, J. (2007) 'The politics of community capacity-building: Contestations, contradictions, tensions and ambivalences in the discourse in Indigenous communities in Australia'. *Australian Journal of Indigenous Education* 36: 129–36.

Malcolm X and Haley, A. (1968) *The Autobiography of Malcolm X*. Penguin/Hutchinson, London.

Mallory, G. (2005) *Uncharted Waters: Social Responsibility in Australian Trade Unions*. Greg Mallory, Annerley QLD.

Mansell, M. (2003) 'The decline of the Aboriginal protest movement'. *Green Left Weekly*, 27 August.

Margaret, J. (2009) *Learning in Social Movements: Experiences in the Pakeha Treaty Workers Movement*. Master's thesis, University of Auckland.

Margaret, J. (2010) 'Working as allies'. Winston Churchill Fellowship report. http://awea.org.nz/allies_north_america; accessed 30 August 2010.

Margaret, J. (2013) *Working as Allies: Supporters of Indigenous Justice Reflect*. AWEA, Auckland.

Marks, R. (2009) 'Towards an intellectual history of the Australian new left: Some definitional problems'. *Melbourne Journal of Politics* 34: 82–104.

Martin, K.L. (2008) *Please Knock before You Enter: Aboriginal Regulation of Outsiders and the Implications for Researchers*. Post Pressed, Teneriffe QLD.

Matthew, H. (2003) *The Widow of Wappan: The Story*. MMuDS Project Wappan, Mansfield.

Maynard, J. (2005) '"Light in the darkness": Elizabeth McKenzie Hatton'. In F. Paisley, A. Cole and V. Haskins (eds), *Uncommon Ground: White Women in Aboriginal History*, new edn, pp. 3–27. Aboriginal Studies Press, Canberra.

Maynard, J. (2007) *Fight for Liberty and Freedom: The Origins of Australian Aboriginal Activism*. Aboriginal Studies Press, Canberra.

McGregor, R. (2009) 'Another nation: Aboriginal activism in the late 1960s and early 1970s'. *Australian Historical Studies*, 40 (3): 343–60.

McGuinness, B. (n.d.) 'Aboriginal community initiative, involvement/participation and control of Aboriginal affairs'. www.kooriweb.org/bbm/essay4. html; accessed 6 April 2014.

McIntosh, P. (2006) 'White privilege and male privilege: A personal account of coming to correspondences through work in women's studies'. In M. L. Andersen and P.H. Collins (eds), *Race, Class, Gender: An Anthology*, pp. 70-81. Wadsworth/Thomson Learning, Belmont CA.

Memmi, A. (1965) *The Colonizer and the Colonized*. Orio Press, New York.

Merlan, F. (2005) 'Indigenous movements in Australia'. *Annual Review of Anthropology* 34: 473–94.

Message Stick (2008) 'A will to fight'. ABC Television, www.abc.net.au/tv/ messagestick/stories/s2261799.htm; accessed 13 December 2011.

Miller, E. (2012) 'NGO that wants Palestinian refugees let into Israel is barred from Ramallah for being Israeli'. www.timesofisrael.com/the-irony-of-bds-right-of-return-conference-pushed-out-of-ramallah; accessed 18 May 2014.

Mita, M. (director). (1983) *Patu!* Awatea Films, New Zealand.

Molyneux, M. (1985) 'Mobilization without emancipation? Women's interests, the state, and revolution in Nicaragua'. *Feminist Studies*, 11(2): 227–54

Monsour, A. (2007) 'Becoming white: How early Syrian/Lebanese in Australia recognised the value of whiteness'. In L. Boucher, J. Carey and K. Ellinghaus (eds), *Historicising Whiteness: Transnational Perspectives on the Construction of an Identity*, pp. 124–32. RMIT Publishing and School of Historical Studies, University of Melbourne, Melbourne.

Moore, S.E.H. (2008) *Ribbon Culture: Charity, Compassion, and Public Awareness*. Palgrave Macmillan, Basingstoke.

Moreton-Robinson, A. (2000) *Talkin' up to the White Woman: Aboriginal Women and Feminism*. University of Queensland Press, Brisbane.

Moreton-Robinson, A. (2003) 'I still call Australia home: Indigenous belonging and place in a white postcolonizing society'. In S. Ahmed (ed.), *Uprootings/ Regroundings: Questions of Home and Migration*, pp. 23–40. Berg, New York.

Moreton-Robinson, A. (2006) 'How white possession moves: After the word'. In T. Lea, E. Kowal and G.K. Cowlishaw (eds), *Moving Anthropology: Critical Indigenous Studies*, pp. 219–32. Charles Darwin University Press, Darwin.

Moreton-Robinson, A. (2008) 'Writing off treaties: White possession in the United States critical whiteness studies literature'. In A. Moreton-Robinson,

M. Casey and F.J. Nicoll (eds), *Transnational Whiteness Matters*, pp. 81–96. Lexington Books, Lanham MD.

Moses, A.D. (2010) 'Time, indigeneity, and peoplehood: The postcolony in Australia'. *Postcolonial Studies*, 13(1): 9–32.

Muecke, S. (1998) 'Cultural activism: Indigenous Australia 1972–94'. In K.-H. Chen (ed.), *Trajectories: Inter-Asia Cultural Studies*, pp. 299–313. Routledge, London.

Muldoon, P., and Schaap, A. (2012) 'Aboriginal sovereignty and the politics of reconciliation: The constituent power of the Aboriginal Embassy in Australia'. *Environment And Planning D: Society And Space*, 30(3): 534–50.

Mundey, J. (1998) 'Green bans and urban environmentalism'. In Historic Houses Trust of New South Wales, *Protest! Environmental Activism in NSW 1968–1998*, pp. 28–40. Historic Houses Trust of New South Wales, Glebe NSW.

Nanni, G. (producer) (2010) 'Gary Foley, advice for white Indigenous activists in Australia'. www.youtube.com/watch?v=uEGsBV9VGTQ.

Nathan, P. (1980) *A Home Away from Home: A Study of the Aboriginal Health Service in Fitzroy, Victoria*. Preston Institute of Technology, Bundoora.

National Health and Medical Research Council (1999) 'National statement on ethical conduct in research involving humans'. www7.health.gov.au/nhmrc/publications/humans/front.htm; accessed 6 August 2006.

National Tribal Council (1999) 'Policy manifesto, adopted 13 September 1970'. In B. Attwood and A. Markus (eds), *The Struggle for Aboriginal Rights: A Documentary History*. Allen & Unwin, St Leonards.

Nelson, J.K., Dunn, K.M., and Paradies, Y. (2011) 'Bystander anti-racism: A review of the literature'. *Analyses of Social Issues and Public Policy*, 11(1): 263–84.

Neveu, L.P. (2010) 'Beyond recognition and coexistence: Living together'. In L. Davis (ed.), *Alliances: Re/envisioning Indigenous–non-Indigenous Relationships*, pp. 234–55. University of Toronto Press, Toronto.

Ngũgĩ wa Thiong'o (1986) *Decolonising the Mind: The Politics of Language in African Literature*. Heinemann, London/ J. Currey, Portsmouth NH.

Nicoll, F. (2000) 'Indigenous sovereignty and the violence of perspective: A white woman's coming out story'. *Australian Feminist Studies*, 15(33): 369–86.

Nicoll, F. (2008) 'Consuming pathologies: The Australian against Indigenous sovereignties'. In A. Moreton-Robinson, M. Casey and F.J. Nicoll (eds), *Transnational Whiteness Matters*, pp. 57–79. Lexington Books, Lanham MD.

Noakes, D. (dir.) (1987) *How the West Was Lost*. Friends Film Production and Market Street Films. Perth.

Occupy Melbourne (2011) 'Occupy Melbourne calls for treaty with Indigenous Australia'. *Green Left Weekly*, 27 October.

O'Donnell, P., and Simons, L. (1995) *Australians Against Racism: Testimonies from the Anti-apartheid Movement in Australia*. Pluto Press, Annandale NSW.

Onus v. Alcoa of Australia Ltd (1981) HCA 50; (1981) 149 CLR 27; (High Court of Australia, 18 September 1981).

O'Shea, E. (2014) 'Why we need to speak out on refugees: A response to Liz

Thompson'. http://overland.org.au/2014/03/speaking-out-on-refugees-a-response-to-liz-thompson; accessed 19 March 2014.

Paasonen, K.-E. (2007) *Between Movements of Crisis and Movements of Affluence: An Analysis of the Campaign against the Jabiluka Uranium Mine, 1997–2000*. Ph.D. thesis, University of Queensland.

PACBI (2011) 'Israel's exceptionalism: Normalizing the abnormal'. www.pacbi. org/etemplate.php?id=1749; accessed 23 June 2014.

Paisley, F. (2000) *Loving Protection?: Australian Feminism and Aboriginal Women's Rights 1919–39*. Melbourne University Press, Melbourne.

Paisley, F., Cole, A., and Haskins, V. (2005) *Uncommon Ground: White Women in Aboriginal History*, new edn. Aboriginal Studies Press, Canberra.

Pallotta-Chiarolli, M., and Pease, B. (eds) (2013) *The Politics of Recognition and Social Justice: Transforming Subjectivities and New Forms of Resistance*. Routledge, New York.

Paradies, Y.C. (2006) 'Beyond black and white: Essentialism, hybridity and Indigeneity'. *Journal of Sociology*, 42(4): 355–67.

Pease, B. (1997) *Men and Sexual Politics: Towards a Profeminist Practice*. Dulwich Centre Publications, Adelaide.

Pease, B. (2002) '(Re)Constructing men's interests'. *Men and Masculinities*, 5(2): 165–77.

Pease, B. (2006) 'Encouraging critical reflections on privilege in social work and the human services'. *Practice Reflexions*, 1(1): 15–26.

Pease, B. (2010a) 'Interrogating privileged subjectivities: Tensions and dilemmas in writing reflexive personal accounts of privilege'. Paper presented at the Action Learning, Action Research Association (ALARA) World Congress.

Pease, B. (2010b) *Undoing Privilege: Unearned Advantage in a Divided World*. Zed Books, London.

Pease, B. (2012) 'The politics of gendered emotions: Disrupting men's emotional investment in privilege'. *Australian Journal of Social Issues*, 47(1): 125–42.

Pickerill, J. (2009) 'Finding common ground? Spaces of dialogue and the negotiation of Indigenous interests in environmental campaigns in Australia'. *Geoforum*, 40(1): 66–79.

Povinelli, E.A. (2006) *The Empire of Love: Toward a Theory of Intimacy, Genealogy and Carnality*. Duke University Press, Durham NC.

Probyn, F. (2004) 'Playing chicken at the intersection: The white critic of whiteness'. *Borderlands e-journal*, 3(2).

Raweno:kwas, W.W. (2010) 'Iroquoian condolence practised on a civic scale'. In L. Davis (ed.), *Alliances: Re/envisioning Indigenous–non-Indigenous Relationships*, pp. 25–41. University of Toronto Press, Toronto.

Rawlins, W.K. (1992) *Friendship Matters: Communication, Dialectics, and the Life Course*. Aldine de Gruyter, New York.

Read, P. (1990a) *Charles Perkins, a Biography*. Viking, Melbourne.

Read, P. (1990b) 'Cheeky, insolent and anti-white: The split in the Federal Council for the Advancement of Aboriginal and Torres Strait Islanders:

Easter 1970'. *Australian Journal of Politics and History*, 36(1): 73–83.

Reed, L. (2005) 'Mrs Bon's verandah "full of Aboriginals": Race, class and friendship'. *History Australia*, 2(2): 39.1–39.15.

Regan, P. (2005) 'A transformative framework for decolonizing Canada: A non-Indigenous approach'. Paper presented at Indigenous Governance (IGOV) Doctoral Student Symposium, University of Victoria, Canada. 20 January.

Reynolds, H. (2006) *The Other Side of the Frontier: Aboriginal Resistance to the European Invasion of Australia*. University of New South Wales Press, Sydney.

Rhodes, D. (2014) *Capacity across Cultures: Global Lessons from Pacific Experiences*. Inkshed Press, Fairfield.

Richardson, L. (1995) 'Writing-stories: Co-authoring "The sea monster", a writing-story'. *Qualitative Inquiry*, 1(2): 189–203.

Rieske, T.V. (2008) 'Un/staging white beauty: A glimpse into the diary of Thomas Viola Rieske'. In A. Kuntsman and E. Miyake (eds), *Out of Place: Interrogating Silences in Queerness/Raciality*, pp. 97–111. Raw Nerve Books, York.

Riggs, D., and Augoustinos, M. (2004) 'Projecting threat: Managing subjective investments in whiteness'. *Psychoanalysis, Culture & Society*, 9(2): 216–24.

Rigney, L.-I. (1999) 'Internationalization of an Indigenous anticolonial cultural critique of research methodologies: A guide to Indigenist research methodology and its principles'. *Wicazo Sa Review*, 14(2): 109–21.

Robinson, S. (1994) 'The Aboriginal Embassy: An account of the protests of 1972'. *Aboriginal History* 18: 49–63.

Roediger, David R. (1999) *The Wages of Whiteness: Race and the Making of the American Working Class*, rev. edn. Verso, London and New York.

Roman, L.G. (1997) 'Denying (white) racial privilege: Redemption discourses and the uses of fantasy'. In M. Fine (ed.), *Off White: Readings on Race, Power, and Society*, pp. 270–83. Routledge, New York.

Rugendyke, B. (1991) 'Unity in diversity: The changing face of the Australian NGO community'. In L. Zivetz et al. (eds), *Doing Good: The Australian NGO Community*, pp. 1–19. Allen & Unwin, North Sydney.

Ryan, A. (1991) 'Action for world development'. In L. Zivetz et al. (eds), *Doing Good: The Australian NGO Community*, pp. 124–30. Allen & Unwin, North Sydney.

Ryan, L. (2012) *Tasmanian Aborigines: A History since 1803*. Allen & Unwin, Sydney.

Sacks, M.A., and Lindholm, M. (2002) 'A room without a view: Social distance and the structuring of privileged identity'. In C. Levine-Rasky (ed.), *Working through Whiteness: International Perspectives*, pp. 129–51. State University of New York Press, Albany.

Santos-Granero, F. (2007) 'Of fear and friendship: Amazonian sociality beyond kinship and affinity'. *Journal of the Royal Anthropological Institute*, 13(1): 1–18.

Schaap, A. (2009) 'The absurd proposition of Aboriginal sovereignty'. In A. Schaap (ed.), *Law and Agonistic Politics*, pp. 209–23. Ashgate, Farnham.

Scott, S. (2004) 'Why wasn't genocide a crime in Australia?: Accounting for the half-century delay in Australia implementing the genocide convention'. *Australian Journal of Human Rights*, 10(2).

Segrest, M. (2001) 'The souls of white folks'. In B. Brander Rasmussen (ed.), *The Making and Unmaking of Whiteness*, pp. 43–71. Duke University Press, Durham NC.

Seidman, S. (2004) *Contested Knowledge: Social Theory Today*, 3rd edn. Blackwell, Malden MA.

Sheehan, S.M. (2003) *Anarchism*. Reaktion Books, London.

Sheizaf, N. (2012) 'A conversation on "no normalisation" that we had to have: On anti-normalization, dialogue and activism'. http://972mag.com/on-anti-normalization-dialogue-and-activism/55611; accessed 18 May 2014.

Short, D. (2010) 'Australia: a continuing genocide?' *Journal of Genocide Research*, 12(1/2): 45–68.

Silverman, D., and Seale, C. (2005) *Doing Qualitative Research: A Practical Handbook*, 2nd edn. Sage, London.

Simpson, L. (2010) 'First words'. In L. Davis (ed.), *Alliances: Re/envisioning Indigenous–non-Indigenous Relationships*, pp. xiii–xiv. University of Toronto Press, Toronto.

Smith, L.T. (1999) *Decolonizing Methodologies: Research and Indigenous Peoples*. Zed Books, London/University of Otago Press, Dunedin.

Spindler, S. (2007) 'Justice before reconciliation: a history of ANTaR Victoria'. *Unfinished Business: ANTaR Vic turns 10!*, pp. 4–12. ANTaR Victoria, Melbourne.

Sullivan, B. (2007) 'Feminism and Indigenous rights in Australia in the 1990s'. In M. Haussman and B. Sauer (eds.), *Gendering the State in the Age of Globalization: Women's Movements and State Feminism in Postindustrial Democracies*, pp. 39–58. Rowman & Littlefield, Lanham MD.

Sullivan, S. (2006) *Revealing Whiteness: The Unconscious Habits of Racial Privilege*. Indiana University Press, Bloomington.

Taffe, S. (2005) *Black and White Together: FCAATSI: The Federal Council for the Advancement of Aborigines and Torres Strait Islanders, 1958-1973*. University of Queensland Press, St Lucia.

Taffe, S. (2008) 'Collaborating for Indigenous Rights 1957–1973'. www.indigenousrights.net.au; accessed 30 October 2011.

Tamasese, K., and Waldegrave, C. (1996) 'Cultural and gender accountability in the "Just Therapy" approach'. In C. White, C. McLean and M. Carey (eds), *Men's Ways of Being*, pp. 51–62. Westview Press, Boulder CO.

Tamasese, K., Waldegrave, C., Tuhaka, F., and Campbell, W. (1998) 'Furthering conversation about partnerships of accountability: Talking about issues of leadership, ethics and care'. *Dulwich Centre Journal* 4: 51–62.

Tatz, C. (2004) 'An essay in disappointment: The Aboriginal–Jewish relationship'. *Aboriginal History* 28: 100–121.

Tedlock, B. (2000) 'Ethnography and ethnographic representation'. In N.K.

Denzin and Y.S. Lincoln (eds), *The Handbook of Qualitative Research*, 2nd edn, pp. 455–86. Sage, London.

Thompson, B.W. (2001) *A Promise and a Way of Life: White Antiracist Activism*. University of Minnesota Press, Minneapolis.

Thompson, L. (2014) 'Liz Thompson explains why she is not speaking at the Close Manus rally on Saturday'. http://xborderoperationalmatters.wordpress.com/2014/02/28/thompson-re-rally; accessed 19 March 2014.

Thornton, R. (2002) 'Repatriation as healing the wounds of the trauma of history: Cases of Native Americans in the United States of America'. In C. Fforde, J. Hubert and P. Turnbull (eds), *The Dead and Their Possessions: Repatriation in Principle, Policy and Practice*, pp. 17–24. Routledge, New York.

Thorpe v. The Commonwealth of Australia (No. 3) (1997) HCA 21 (1997) 71 ALJR 767.

Transgender Victoria (2013a) 'Definitions'. www.transgendervictoria.com; accessed 21 June 2014.

Transgender Victoria (2013b) 'What makes an ally?' project. www.transgendervictoria.com; accessed 21 June 2014.

UC Davis LGBTQIA Resource Center (2014) 'Trans ally tips: Some ways to be a good trans ally'. http://lgbtcenter.ucdavis.edu/lgbt-education/trans-ally-tips; accessed 21 June 2014.

Valiente, C. (2003) 'Mobilizing for recognition and redistribution on behalf of others? The case of mothers against drugs in Spain'. In B. Hobson (ed.), *Recognition Struggles and Social Movements: Contested Identities, Agency and Power*, pp. 239–61. Cambridge University Press, New York.

Venkateswar, S., and Hughes, E. (eds) (2011) *The Politics of Indigeneity: Dialogues and Reflections on Indigenous Activism*. Zed Books, London.

Vernon, M. (2005) *The Philosophy of Friendship*. Palgrave Macmillan, New York.

VicHealth Koori Health Research and Community Development Unit (2000) *We Don't Like Research: But in Koori Hands It Could Make a Difference*. VicHealth Koori Health Research and Community Development Unit, Melbourne.

Vickery, Aunty Joan, Thorpe, Aunty Alma, Johnson, Auntie Melva, Robinson, Auntie Kella, Bamblett, Auntie Merle, Williams, Auntie Georgina, Austin, Uncle Graham, Bamblett, Auntie Rose, Peters, Auntie Beverley, Bell, Auntie Laura, McInnes, Auntie Lyn, Bamblett, Esme, Thorpe, Lisa, Kennedy, Helen, Clarke, Angela, Waddell, Nicole, Phillips, Greg, Selam, Jason, Vickery, Annette, Muir, Jan, Smith, Rosie, Atkinson, Neville, Fredericks, Bronwyn L., Rose, Daryl, Morris, Irene, Arbon, Veronica, Rose, Mark, and Brabham, Wendy (2010) 'Indigenous research and broader issues in the academy'. *Journal of the World Indigenous Nations Higher Education Consortium* 1: 1–10.

Victorian Aborigines Advancement League (1985) *Victims or Victors? The Story of the Victorian Aborigines Advancement League*. Hyland House, South Yarra.

Victorian Aboriginal Education Association (n.d.) 'VAEAI timeline'. www.vaeai.org.au; accessed 13 December 2011.

Vincent, D.N., and Nader, C. (2012) *The Boy Who Wouldn't Die*. Fairfax Books, Crows Nest NSW.

Vincent, E., and Land, C. (2003) 'Silenced voices: Absence of Indigenous voices from the "history wars"'. *Arena Magazine* 67: 19–21.

Vorauer, J.D., and Turpie, C.A. (2004) 'Disruptive effects of vigilance on dominant group members' treatment of outgroup members: Choking versus shining under pressure'. *Journal of Personality and Social Psychology*, 87(3): 384–99.

Wallace, R. (2013) *Merging Fires: Grassroots Peacebuilding between Indigenous and Non-Indigenous Peoples in Canada*. MAN Fernwood Publishing, Winnipeg.

Wallace, R., Struthers, M., and Bauman, R.C. (2010) 'Winning fishing rights: The successes and challenges of building grassroots relations between the Chipewas of Nawash and their allies'. In L. Davis (ed.), *Alliances: Re/envisioning Indigenous–Non-Indigenous Relationships*, pp. 91–113. University of Toronto Press, Toronto.

Waples-Crowe, P., and Pyett, P. (2005) *The Making of a Great Relationship: A Review of a Healthy Partnership between Mainstream and Indigenous Organisations*. Victorian Community Controlled Health Organisation, Melbourne.

Warriors of the Aboriginal Resistance (2014) 'Manifesto'. http://issuu.com/brisbaneblacks/docs/war_manifesto_d91595ceee8754; accessed 18 April 2015.

Watson, I. (2000a) 'The Aboriginal Tent Embassy 28 years after it was established: Interview with Isobell Coe'. *Indigenous Law Bulletin*, 5(1).

Watson, I. (2000b) 'Walking the land for our ancient rights: Interview with Kevin Buzzacott'. *Indigenous Law Bulletin*, 5(1).

Watson, I. (2005) 'Settled and unsettled spaces: Are we free to roam?' *Australian Critical Race and Whiteness Studies Association Journal* 1: 40–52.

Watson, S., Abbs, J., Beattie, D., Watson, J., and Watson, R. (2007) 'Personal stories: Indigenous activism'. *Queensland Review*, 14(1): 39–49.

Williams, C. (1998) 'Protest, police and the green world view: The search for a brave new paradigm'. Historic Houses Trust of New South Wales, *Protest! Environmental activism in NSW 1968–1998*, pp. 5–17. Historic Houses Trust of New South Wales, Glebe NSW.

Williams, P. (1998) 'Spirit-murdering the messenger: The discourse of finger-pointing as the law's response to racism'. *University of Miami Law Review* 42: 127–57.

Wolfe, P. (1994) 'Nation and miscegenation: Discursive continuity in the post-Mabo era'. *Social Analysis* [Adelaide] 36: 93–152.

Yancy, G. (2012) *Look, a White!: Philosophical Essays on Whiteness*. Temple University Press, Philadelphia.

Index